"*I ask no one who may read this book to accept my views. I ask him to think for himself.*"

SOCIAL
PROBLEMS

Henry George

SOCIAL PROBLEMS

Henry George

ROBERT SCHALKENBACH FOUNDATION
41 East 72nd Street, New York
1996

THE
ROBERT SCHALKENBACH
FOUNDATION

*incorporated in 1925, to administer a Trust Fund
left by the will of the late Robert Schalkenbach,
former president of the New York Typothetae,
and such other funds as may be donated to it,
for the purpose of spreading among the people
of this and other countries
a wider acquaintance
with the social and economic philosophy
of Henry George.*

First edition published by Belford, Clarke and Company, Chicago,
1883. Subsequent editions published in London in 1931, 1932, and
1938. In the United States, subsequent hardcover editions published
by Henry George and Company, New York, 1886; Robert
Schalkenbach Foundation, New York, 1934, 1963, 1966, and 1981.
This hardcover edition published in 1996.

George, Henry, 1839-1897
Social Problems

Reprint. Originally published: New York : Robert
Schalkenbach Foundation, 1934.
Includes index.
1. Economics—Addresses, essays, lectures. 2. Social
Sciences—Addresses, essays, lectures. I. Title
HB171.G37 1981   302   81.11896
ISBN 0-911312-17-X

Printed in the United States of America by Sherwin Dodge, Printers
Binding by New Hampshire Bindery
Design by A.L. Morris

To the memory

of

Francis George Shaw

"Yea, saith the Spirit, "that they may rest from
their labors; and their works do follow them."

*Then shall they also answer him, saying, "Lord,
when saw we thee an hungered, or athirst, or a
stranger, or naked, or sick, or in prison, and
did not minister unto thee?"*

*Then shall he answer them, saying, "Verily
I say unto you, Inasmuch as ye did it not to
one of the least of these, ye did it not to me."*

—MATTHEW.

CONTENTS

PREFACE
to the
1981 EDITION

SOCIAL PROBLEMS, when written in 1883 by Henry George, was more than a perceptive account of the problems of society which afflicted not only the nation but the world of his time. It was a harbinger of things to come. We in the latter half of the twentieth century know only too well how accurately his predictions have turned out.

He warned that unless our system of land tenure was reformed, and unless the individual's freedom of action was enhanced, even graver ecological, economic, moral and ethical problems would plague us than his generation faced.

He noted the despoiling of nature which today even the dullest can see and warned of "the destructive character of our agriculture which is year by year decreasing the productiveness of our soil, and virtually lessening the area of land available for the support of our increasing millions."

"We have made," he said, "and still are making, enormous advances on material lines." But he added, "it is necessary that we commensurately advance on moral lines. Civilization, as it progresses, *requires* a higher conscience, a keener sense of justice, a warmer brotherhood, a wider, loftier, truer public spirit. Failing these, civilization must pass into destruction."

That ethically we have been retrogressing instead of advancing is obvious from the physical and spiritual degradation so evident in our great cities, and from the moral degeneracy of our permissive society.

ix

George recognized that the solution of our problems can be found in studying the laws of nature. "The domain of law is not confined to physical nature," he said. "It just as certainly embraces the mental and moral universe, and social growth and social life have their laws as fixed as those of matter and motion. Would we make social life healthy and happy, we must discover those laws, and seek our ends in accordance with them."

Though "the social and political problems that confront us are darker than they realize who have not given thought to them; yet their solution is a mere matter of the proper adjustment of social forces."

His advice on how to help spread knowledge about ways to improve society is as valid today as when he gave it. He noted, "the great work of the present for every man, and every organization of men, who would improve social conditions, is the work of education—the propagation of ideas. It is only as it aids this that anything else can avail. And in this work every one who can think may aid—first by forming clear ideas himself, and then by endeavoring to arouse the thought of those with whom he comes in contact."

He was in advance of his times in urging the equality of women with men, for he argued that "we could in no way so increase the attention, the intelligence and the devotion which may be brought to the solution of social problems as by enfranchising our women."

George is best known for his unique program for land reform as set forth in *Progress and Poverty,* one of America's great classics. In the twenty-two essays of *Social Problems* he expounded thought-provoking ideas for dealing with many of the ills which plagued his generation and which still persist in our day. If we would but take to heart the advice of this discerning man and put his ideas into action the probability is great that many of these problems would be satisfactorily solved.

Lancaster M. Greene
President,
Robert Schalkenbach Foundation

May, 1981

NOTE

to the

ORIGINAL EDITION

THIS BOOK was written in New York in 1883, which
will explain references made in its pages to time and
place. My endeavor has been to present the momentous social problems of our time, unencumbered by tech-
nicalities and without that abstract reasoning which some of the
principles of political economy require for thorough explanation. I have spoken in this book of some points not touched
upon, or but lightly touched upon, in "Progress and Poverty,"
but there are other points as to which I think it would be worth
the while of those who may be interested by this book to read
that.

Henry George.

SOCIAL PROBLEMS

SOCIAL PROBLEMS.

CHAPTER I.

THE INCREASING IMPORTANCE OF SOCIAL QUESTIONS.

THERE come moments in our lives that summon all
our powers—when we feel that, casting away illu-
sions, we must decide and act with our utmost intelligence
and energy. So in the lives of peoples come periods
specially calling for earnestness and intelligence.

We seem to have entered one of these periods. Over
and again have nations and civilizations been confronted
with problems which, like the riddle of the Sphinx, not
to answer was to be destroyed; but never before have
problems so vast and intricate been presented. This is not
strange. That the closing years of this century must bring
up momentous social questions follows from the material
and intellectual progress that has marked its course.

Between the development of society and the development
of species there is a close analogy. In the lowest forms of
animal life there is little difference of parts; both wants
and powers are few and simple; movement seems automatic; and instincts are scarcely distinguishable from
those of the vegetable. So homogeneous are some of these
living things, that if cut in pieces, each piece still lives.
But as life rises into higher manifestations, simplicity gives

way to complexity, the parts develop into organs having separate functions and reciprocal relations, new wants and powers arise, and a greater and greater degree of intelligence is needed to secure food and avoid danger. Did fish, bird or beast possess no higher intelligence than the polyp, nature could bring them forth only to die.

This law—that the increasing complexity and delicacy of organization which give higher capacity and increased power are accompanied by increased wants and dangers, and require, therefore, increased intelligence—runs through nature. In the ascending scale of life at last comes man, the most highly and delicately organized of animals. Yet not only do his higher powers require for their use a higher intelligence than exists in other animals, but without higher intelligence he could not live. His skin is too thin; his nails too brittle; he is too poorly adapted for running, climbing, swimming or burrowing. Were he not gifted with intelligence greater than that of any beast, he would perish from cold, starve from inability to get food, or be exterminated by animals better equipped for the struggle in which brute instinct suffices.

In man, however, the intelligence which increases all through nature's rising scale passes at one bound into an intelligence so superior, that the difference seems of kind rather than degree. In him, that narrow and seemingly unconscious intelligence that we call instinct becomes conscious reason, and the godlike power of adaptation and invention makes feeble man nature's king.

But with man the ascending line stops. Animal life assumes no higher form; nor can we affirm that, in all his generations, man, as an animal, has a whit improved. But progression in another line begins. Where the development of species ends, social development commences, and that advance of society that we call civilization so increases human powers, that between savage and civilized man there is a gulf so vast as to suggest the gulf between the highly organized animal and the oyster glued to the rocks. And with every advance upon this line new vistas open. When we try to think what knowledge and power progressive civilization may give to the men of the future, imagination fails.

In this progression which begins with man, as in that which leads up to him, the same law holds. Each advance makes a demand for higher and higher intelligence. With the beginnings of society arises the need for social intelligence—for that consensus of individual intelligence which forms a public opinion, a public conscience, a public will, and is manifested in law, institutions and administration. As society develops, a higher and higher degree of this social intelligence is required, for the relation of individuals to each other becomes more intimate and important, and the increasing complexity of the social organization brings liability to new dangers.

In the rude beginning, each family produces its own food, makes its own clothes, builds its own house, and, when it moves, furnishes its own transportation. Compare with this independence the intricate interdependence of the denizens of a modern city. They may supply themselves with greater certainty, and in much greater variety and abundance, than the savage; but it is by the coöperation of thousands. Even the water they drink, and the artificial light they use, are brought to them by elaborate machinery, requiring the constant labor and watchfulness of many men. They may travel at a speed incredible to the savage; but in doing so resign life and limb to the care of others. A broken rail, a drunken engineer, a careless switchman, may hurl them to eternity. And the power of applying labor to the satisfaction of desire passes, in the same way, beyond the direct control of the individual. The laborer becomes but part of a great machine, which may at any time be paralyzed by causes beyond his power, or even his foresight. Thus does the well-being of each become more and more dependent upon the well-being of all—the individual more and more subordinate to society.

And so come new dangers. The rude society resembles the creatures that though cut into pieces will live; the highly civilized society is like a highly organized animal: a stab in a vital part, the suppression of a single function, is death. A savage village may be burned and its people driven off—but, used to direct recourse to nature, they can maintain themselves. Highly civilized man, however, accustomed to capital, to machinery, to the minute division of labor, becomes helpless when suddenly deprived of these and thrown upon nature. Under the factory system, some sixty persons, with the aid of much costly machinery, coöperate to the making of a pair of shoes. But, of the sixty, not one could make a whole shoe. This is the tendency in all branches of production, even in agriculture. How many farmers of the new generation can use the flail? How many farmers' wives can now make a coat from the wool? Many of our farmers do not even make their own butter or raise their own vegetables! There is an enormous gain in productive power from this division of labor, which assigns to the individual the production of but a few of the things, or even but a small part of one of the things, he needs, and makes each dependent upon others with whom he never comes in contact; but the social organization becomes more sensitive. A primitive village community may pursue the even tenor of its life without feeling disasters which overtake other villages but a few miles off; but in the closely knit civilization to which we have attained, a war, a scarcity, a commercial crisis, in one hemisphere produces powerful effects in the other, while shocks and jars from which a primitive community easily recovers would to a highly civilized community mean wreck.

It is startling to think how destructive in a civilization like ours would be such fierce conflicts as fill the history of the past. The wars of highly civilized countries, since the opening of the era of steam and machinery, have been duels of armies rather than conflicts of peoples or classes. Our only glimpse of what might happen, were passion fully aroused, was in the struggle of the Paris Commune. And, since 1870, to the knowledge of petroleum has been added that of even more destructive agents. The explosion of a little nitro-glycerin under a few water-mains would make a great city uninhabitable; the blowing up of a few railroad bridges and tunnels would bring famine quicker than the wall of circumvallation that Titus drew around Jerusalem; the pumping of atmospheric air into the gas-mains, and the application of a match, would tear up every street and level every house. The Thirty Years' War set back civilization in Germany; so fierce a war now would all but destroy it. Not merely have destructive powers vastly increased, but the whole social organization has become vastly more delicate.

In a simpler state master and man, neighbor and neighbor, know each other, and there is that touch of the elbow which, in times of danger, enables society to rally. But present tendencies are to the loss of this. In London, dwellers in one house do not know those in the next; the tenants of adjoining rooms are utter strangers to each other. Let civil conflict break or paralyze the authority that preserves order and the vast population would become a terror-stricken mob, without point of rally or principle of cohesion, and your London would be sacked and burned by an army of thieves. London is only the greatest of great cities. What is true of London is true of New York, and in the same measure true of the many cities whose hundreds of thousands are steadily growing toward millions. These vast aggregations of humanity, where he who seeks isolation may find it more truly than in the desert; where wealth and poverty touch and jostle; where one revels and another starves within a few feet of each other, yet separated by as great a gulf as that fixed between Dives in Hell and Lazarus in Abraham's bosom—they are centers and types of our civilization. Let jar or shock dislocate the complex and delicate organization, let the policeman's club be thrown down or wrested from him, and the fountains of the great deep are opened, and quicker than ever before chaos comes again. Strong as it may seem, our civilization is evolving destructive forces. Not desert and forest, but city slums and country roadsides are nursing the barbarians who may be to the new what Hun and Vandal were to the old.

Nor should we forget that in civilized man still lurks the savage. The men who, in past times, oppressed or revolted, who fought to the death in petty quarrels and drunk fury with blood, who burned cities and rent empires, were men essentially such as those we daily meet. Social progress has accumulated knowledge, softened manners, refined tastes and extended sympathies, but man is yet capable of as blind a rage as when, clothed in skins, he fought wild beasts with a flint. And present tendencies, in some respects at least, threaten to kindle passions that have so often before flamed in destructive fury.

There is in all the past nothing to compare with the rapid changes now going on in the civilized world. It seems as though in the European race, and in the nineteenth century, man was just beginning to live—just grasping his tools and becoming conscious of his powers. The snail's pace of crawling ages has suddenly become the headlong rush of the locomotive, speeding faster and faster. This rapid progress is primarily in industrial methods and material powers. But industrial changes imply social changes and necessitate political changes. Progressive societies outgrow institutions as children outgrow clothes. Social progress always requires greater intelligence in the management of public affairs; but this the more as progress is rapid and change quicker.

And that the rapid changes now going on are bringing up problems that demand most earnest attention may be seen on every hand. Symptoms of danger, premonitions of violence, are appearing all over the civilized world. Creeds are dying, beliefs are changing; the old forces of conservatism are melting away. Political institutions are failing, as clearly in democratic America as in monarchical Europe. There is growing unrest and bitterness among the masses, whatever be the form of government, a blind groping for escape from conditions becoming intolerable. To attribute all this to the teachings of demagogues is like attributing the fever to the quickened pulse. It is the new wine beginning to ferment in old bottles. To put into a sailing-ship the powerful engines of a first-class ocean steamer would be to tear her to pieces with their play. So the new powers rapidly changing all the relations of society must shatter social and political organizations not adapted to meet their strain.

To adjust our institutions to growing needs and changing conditions is the task which devolves upon us. Prudence, patriotism, human sympathy, and religious sentiment, alike call upon us to undertake it. There is danger in reckless change; but greater danger in blind conservatism. The problems beginning to confront us are grave—so grave that there is fear they may not be solved in time to prevent great catastrophes. But their gravity comes from indisposition to recognize frankly and grapple boldly with them.

These dangers, which menace not one country alone, but modern civilization itself, do but show that a higher civilization is struggling to be born—that the needs and the aspirations of men have outgrown conditions and institutions that before sufficed.

A civilization which tends to concentrate wealth and power in the hands of a fortunate few, and to make of others mere human machines, must inevitably evolve anarchy and bring destruction. But a civilization is possible in which the poorest could have all the comforts and conveniences now enjoyed by the rich; in which prisons and almshouses would be needless, and charitable societies unthought of. Such a civilization waits only for the social intelligence that will adapt means to ends. Powers that might give plenty to all are already in our hands. Though there is poverty and want, there is, yet, seeming embarrassment from the very excess of wealth-producing forces. "Give us but a market," say manufacturers, "and we will supply goods without end!" "Give us but work!" cry idle men.

The evils that begin to appear spring from the fact that the application of intelligence to social affairs has not kept pace with the application of intelligence to individual needs and material ends. Natural science strides forward, but political science lags. With all our progress in the arts which produce wealth, we have made no progress in securing its equitable distribution. Knowledge has vastly increased; industry and commerce have been revolutionized; but whether free trade or protection is best for a nation we are not yet agreed. We have brought machinery to a pitch of perfection that, fifty years ago, could not have been imagined; but, in the presence of political corruption, we seem as helpless as idiots. The East River bridge is a crowning triumph of mechanical skill; but to get it built a leading citizen of Brooklyn had to carry to New York sixty thousand dollars in a carpet-bag to bribe New York aldermen. The human soul that thought out the great bridge is prisoned in a crazed and broken body that lies bedfast, and could watch it grow only by peering through a telescope. Nevertheless, the weight of the immense mass is estimated and adjusted for every inch. But the skill of the engineer could not prevent condemned wire being smuggled into the cable.

The progress of civilization requires that more and more intelligence be devoted to social affairs, and this not the intelligence of the few, but that of the many. We cannot safely leave politics to politicians, or political economy to college professors. The people themselves must think, because the people alone can act.

In a "journal of civilization" a professed teacher declares the saving word for society to be that each shall mind his own business. This is the gospel of selfishness, soothing as soft flutes to those who, having fared well themselves, think everybody should be satisfied. But the salvation of society, the hope for the free, full development of humanity, is in the gospel of brotherhood—the gospel of Christ. Social progress makes the well-being of all more and more the business of each; it binds all closer and closer together in bonds from which none can escape. He who observes the law and the proprieties, and cares for his family, yet takes no interest in the general weal, and gives no thought to those who are trodden under foot, save now and then to bestow alms, is not a true Christian. Nor is he a good citizen. The duty of the citizen is more and harder than this.

The intelligence required for the solving of social problems is not a thing of the mere intellect. It must be animated with the religious sentiment and warm with sympathy for human suffering. It must stretch out beyond self-interest, whether it be the self-interest of the few or of the many. It must seek justice. For at the bottom of every social problem we will find a social wrong.

CHAPTER II.

POLITICAL DANGERS.

THE American Republic is to-day unquestionably foremost of the nations—the van leader of modern civilization. Of all the great peoples of the European family, her people are the most homogeneous, the most active and most assimilative. Their average standard of intelligence and comfort is higher; they have most fully adopted modern industrial improvements, and are the quickest to utilize discovery and invention; their political institutions are most in accordance with modern ideas, their position exempts them from dangers and difficulties besetting the European nations, and a vast area of unoccupied land gives them room to grow.

At the rate of increase so far maintained, the English-speaking people of America will, by the close of the century, number nearly one hundred million—a population as large as owned the sway of Rome in her palmiest days. By the middle of the next century—a time which children now born will live to see—they will, at the same rate, number more than the present population of Europe; and by its close nearly equal the population which, at the beginning of this century, the whole earth was believed to contain.

But the increase of power is more rapid than the increase of population, and goes on in accelerating progression. Discovery and invention stimulate discovery and invention; and it is only when we consider that the industrial progress of the last fifty years bids fair to pale before the achievements of the next that we can vaguely imagine the future that seems opening before the American people. The center of wealth, of art, of luxury and learning, must pass to this side of the Atlantic even before the center of population. It seems as if this continent had been reserved—shrouded for ages from the rest of the world— as the field upon which European civilization might freely bloom. And for the very reason that our growth is so rapid and our progress so swift; for the very reason that all the tendencies of modern civilization assert themselves here more quickly and strongly than anywhere else, the problems which modern civilization must meet, will here first fully present themselves, and will most imperiously demand to be thought out or fought out.

It is difficult for any one to turn from the history of the past to think of the incomparable greatness promised by the rapid growth of the United States without something of awe—something of that feeling which induced Amasis of Egypt to dissolve his alliance with the successful Polycrates, because "the gods do not permit to mortals such prosperity." Of this, at least, we may be certain: the rapidity of our development brings dangers that can be guarded against only by alert intelligence and earnest patriotism.

There is a suggestive fact that must impress any one who thinks over the history of past eras and preceding civilizations. The great, wealthy and powerful nations have always lost their freedom; it is only in small, poor and isolated communities that Liberty has been maintained. So true is this that the poets have always sung that Liberty loves the rocks and the mountains; that she shrinks from wealth and power and splendor, from the crowded city and the busy mart. So true is this that philosophical historians have sought in the richness of material resources the causes of the corruption and enslavement of peoples.

Liberty is natural. Primitive perceptions are of the equal rights of the citizen, and political organization always starts from this base. It is as social development goes on that we find power concentrating, and institutions based upon the equality of rights passing into institutions which make the many the slaves of the few. How this is we may see. In all institutions which involve the lodgment of governing power there is, with social growth, a tendency to the exaltation of their function and the centralization of their power, and in the stronger of these institutions a tendency to the absorption of the powers of the rest. Thus the tendency of social growth is to make government the business of a special class. And as numbers increase and the power and importance of each become less and less as compared with that of all, so, for this reason, does government tend to pass beyond the scrutiny and control of the masses. The leader of a handful of warriors, or head man of a little village, can command or govern only by common consent, and any one aggrieved can readily appeal to his fellows. But when the tribe becomes a nation and the village expands to a populous country, the powers of the chieftain, without formal addition, become practically much greater. For with increase of numbers scrutiny of his acts becomes more difficult, it is harder and harder successfully to appeal from them, and the aggregate power which he directs becomes irresistible as against individuals. And gradually, as power thus concentrates, primitive ideas are lost, and the habit of thought grows up which regards the masses as born but for the service of their rulers.

Thus the mere growth of society involves danger of the gradual conversion of government into something indepen-

dent of and beyond the people, and the gradual seizure of
its powers by a ruling class—though not necessarily a class
marked off by personal titles and a hereditary status, for,
as history shows, personal titles and hereditary status do
not accompany the concentration of power, but follow it.
The same methods which, in a little town where each
knows his neighbor and matters of common interest are
under the common eye, enable the citizens freely to govern
themselves, may, in a great city, as we have in many cases
seen, enable an organized ring of plunderers to gain and
hold the government. So, too, as we see in Congress, and
even in our State legislatures, the growth of the country
and the greater number of interests make the proportion
of the votes of a representative, of which his constituents
know or care to know, less and less. And so, too, the
executive and judicial departments tend constantly to pass
beyond the scrutiny of the people.

But to the changes produced by growth are, with us,
added the changes brought about by improved industrial
methods. The tendency of steam and of machinery is to
the division of labor, to the concentration of wealth and
power. Workmen are becoming massed by hundreds and
thousands in the employ of single individuals and firms;
small storekeepers and merchants are becoming the clerks
and salesmen of great business houses; we have already
corporations whose revenues and pay-rolls belittle those
of the greatest States. And with this concentration grows
the facility of combination among these great business
interests. How readily the railroad companies, the coal
operators, the steel producers, even the match manufacturers, combine, either to regulate prices or to use the
powers of government! The tendency in all branches of
industry is to the formation of rings against which the
individual is helpless, and which exert their power upon
government whenever their interests may thus be served.

It is not merely positively, but negatively, that great aggregations of wealth, whether individual or corporate, tend to corrupt government and take it out of the control of the masses of the people. "Nothing is more timorous than a million dollars—except two million dollars." Great wealth always supports the party in power, no matter how corrupt it may be. It never exerts itself for reform, for it instinctively fears change. It never struggles against misgovernment. When threatened by the holders of political power it does not agitate, nor appeal to the people; it buys them off. It is in this way, no less than by its direct interference. that aggregated wealth corrupts government, and helps to make politics a trade. Our organized lobbies, both legislative and Congressional, rely as much upon the fears as upon the hopes of moneyed interests. When "business" is dull, their resource is to get up a bill which some moneyed interest will pay them to beat. So, too, these large moneyed interests will subscribe to political funds, on the principle of keeping on the right side of those in power, just as the railroad companies deadhead President Arthur when he goes to Florida to fish.

The more corrupt a government the easier wealth can use it. Where legislation is to be bought, the rich make the laws; where justice is to be purchased, the rich have the ear of the courts. And if, for this reason, great wealth does not absolutely prefer corrupt government to pure government, it becomes none the less a corrupting influence. A community composed of very rich and very poor falls an easy prey to whoever can seize power. The very poor have not spirit and intelligence enough to resist; the very rich have too much at stake.

The rise in the United States of monstrous fortunes, the aggregation of enormous wealth in the hands of corporations, necessarily implies the loss by the people of governmental control. Democratic forms may be maintained, but there can be as much tyranny and misgovernment under democratic forms as any other—in fact, they lend themselves most readily to tyranny and misgovernment. Forms count for little. The Romans expelled their kings, and continued to abhor the very name of king. But under the name of Cæsars and Imperators, that at first meant no more than our "Boss," they crouched before tyrants more absolute than kings. We have already, under the popular name of "bosses," developed political Cæsars in municipalities and states. If this development continues, in time there will come a national boss. We are young; but we are growing. The day may arrive when the "Boss of America" will be to the modern world what Cæsar was to the Roman world. This, at least, is certain : Democratic government in more than name can exist only where wealth is distributed with something like equality—where the great mass of citizens are personally free and independent, neither fettered by their poverty nor made subject by their wealth. There is, after all, some sense in a property qualification. The man who is dependent on a master for his living is not a free man. To give the suffrage to slaves is only to give votes to their owners. That universal suffrage may add to, instead of decreasing, the political power of wealth we see when mill-owners and mine operators vote their hands. The freedom to earn, without fear or favor, a comfortable living, ought to go with the freedom to vote. Thus alone can a sound basis for republican institutions be secured. How can a man be said to have a country where he has no right to a square inch of soil; where he has nothing but his hands, and. urged by starvation, must bid against his fellows for the privilege of using them ? When it comes to voting tramps. some principle has been carried to a ridiculous and dangerous extreme. I have known elections to be decided by the carting of paupers from the almshouse to the polls. But such decisions can scarcely be in the interest of good government.

Beneath all political problems lies the social problem of the distribution of wealth. This our people do not generally recognize, and they listen to quacks who propose to cure the symptoms without touching the disease. "Let us elect good men to office," say the quacks. Yes; let us catch little birds by sprinkling salt on their tails!

It behooves us to look facts in the face. The experiment of popular government in the United States is clearly a failure. Not that it is a failure everywhere and in everything. An experiment of this kind does not have to be fully worked out to be proved a failure. But speaking generally of the whole country, from the Atlantic to the Pacific, and from the Lakes to the Gulf, our government by the people has in large degree become, is in larger degree becoming, government by the strong and unscrupulous.

The people, of course, continue to vote; but the people are losing their power. Money and organization tell more and more in elections. In some sections bribery has become chronic, and numbers of voters expect regularly to sell their votes. In some sections large employers regularly bulldoze their hands into voting as *they* wish. In municipal, State and Federal politics the power of the "machine" is increasing. In many places it has become so strong that the ordinary citizen has no more influence in the government under which he lives than he would have in China. He is, in reality, not one of the governing classes, but one of the governed. He occasionally, in disgust, votes for "the other man," or "the other party;" but, generally, to find that he has effected only a change of masters, or secured the same masters under different names. And he is beginning to accept the situation, and to leave politics to politicians, as something with which an honest, self-respecting man cannot afford to meddle.

We are steadily differentiating a governing class, or rather a class of Pretorians, who make a business of gaining political power and then selling it. The type of the rising party leader is not the orator or statesman of an earlier day, but the shrewd manager, who knows how to handle the workers, how to combine pecuniary interests, how to obtain money and to spend it, how to gather to himself followers and to secure their allegiance. One party machine is becoming complementary to the other party machine, the politicians, like the railroad managers, having discovered that combination pays better than competition. So rings are made impregnable and great pecuniary interests secure their ends no matter how elections go. There are sovereign States so completely in the hands of rings and corporations that it seems as if nothing short of a revolutionary uprising of the people could dispossess them. Indeed, whether the General Government has not already passed beyond popular control may be doubted. Certain it is that possession of the General Government has for some time past secured possession. And for one term, at least, the Presidential chair has been occupied by a man not elected to it. This, of course, was largely due to the crookedness of the man who was elected, and to the lack of principle in his supporters. Nevertheless, it occurred.

As for the great railroad managers, they may well say, "The people be d—d!" When they want the power of the people they buy the people's masters. The map of the United States is colored to show States and Territories. A map of real political powers would ignore State lines. Here would be a big patch representing the domains of Vanderbilt; there Jay Gould's dominions would be brightly marked. In another place would be set off the empire of

Stanford and Huntington; in another the newer empire
of Henry Villard. The States and parts of States that own
the sway of the Pennsylvania Central would be distinguished from those ruled by the Baltimore and Ohio; and
so on. In our National Senate, sovereign members of the
Union are supposed to be represented; but what are more
truly represented are railroad kings and great moneyed
interests, though occasionally a mine jobber from Nevada
or Colorado, not inimical to the ruling powers, is suffered
to buy himself a seat for glory. And the Bench as well
as the Senate is being filled with corporation henchmen.
A railroad king makes his attorney a judge of last resort,
as the great lord used to make his chaplain a bishop.

We do not get even cheap government. We might
keep a royal family, house them in palaces like Versailles
or Sans Souci, provide them with courts and guards,
masters of robes and rangers of parks, let them give balls
more costly than Mrs. Vanderbilt's, and build yachts finer
than Jay Gould's, for much less than is wasted and stolen
under our nominal government of the people. What a
noble income would be that of a Duke of New York, a
Marquis of Philadelphia, or a Count of San Francisco, who
would administer the government of these municipalities
for fifty per cent. of present waste and stealage! Unless
we got an esthetic Chinook, where could we get an absolute
ruler who would erect such a monument of extravagant
vulgarity as the new Capitol of the State of New York?
While, as we saw in the Congress just adjourned, the
benevolent gentlemen whose desire it is to protect us
against the pauper labor of Europe quarrel over their
respective shares of the spoil with as little regard for the
taxpayer as a pirate crew would have for the consignees
of a captured vessel.

The people are largely conscious of all this, and there
is among the masses much dissatisfaction. But there is a

lack of that intelligent interest necessary to adapt political organization to changing conditions. The popular idea of reform seems to be merely a change of men or a change of parties, not a change of system. Political children, we attribute to bad men or wicked parties what really springs from deep general causes. Our two great political parties have really nothing more to propose than the keeping or the taking of the offices from the other party. On their outskirts are the Greenbackers, who, with a more or less definite idea of what they want to do with the currency, represent vague social dissatisfaction; civil service reformers, who hope to accomplish a political reform while keeping it out of politics; and anti-monopolists, who propose to tie up locomotives with packthread. Even the labor organizations seem to fear to go further in their platforms than some such propositions as eight-hour laws, bureaus of labor statistics, mechanics' liens, and prohibition of prison contracts.

All this shows want of grasp and timidity of thought. It is not by accident that government grows corrupt and passes out of the hands of the people. If we would really make and continue this a government of the people, for the people and by the people, we must give to our politics earnest attention; we must be prepared to review our opinions, to give up old ideas and to accept new ones. We must abandon prejudice, and make our reckoning with free minds. The sailor, who, no matter how the wind might change, should persist in keeping his vessel under the same sail and on the same tack, would never reach his haven.

CHAPTER III.

COMING INCREASE OF SOCIAL PRESSURE.

THE trees, as I write, have not yet begun to leaf, nor even the blossoms to appear; yet, passing down the lower part of Broadway these early days of spring, one breasts a steady current of uncouthly dressed men and women, carrying bundles and boxes and all manner of baggage. As the season advances, the human current will increase; even in winter it will not wholly cease its flow. It is the great gulf-stream of humanity which sets from Europe upon America—the greatest migration of peoples since the world began. Other minor branches has the stream. Into Boston and Philadelphia, into Portland, Quebec and Montreal, into New Orleans, Galveston, San Francisco and Victoria, come offshoots of the same current; and as it flows it draws increasing volume from wider sources. Emigration to America has, since 1848, reduced the population of Ireland by more than a third; but as Irish ability to feed the stream declines, English emigration increases; the German outpour becomes so vast as to assume the first proportions, and the millions of Italy, pressed by want as severe as that of Ireland, begin to turn to the emigrant ship as did the Irish. In Castle Garden one may see the garb and hear the speech of all European peoples. From the fiords of Norway, from the plains of Russia and Hungary, from the mountains of Wallachia, and from Mediterranean shores and islands, once the center

of classic civilization, the great current is fed.   Every year
increases the facility of its flow.   Year by year improvements in steam navigation are practically reducing the
distance between the two continents; year by year European railroads are making it easier for interior populations
to reach the seaboard, and the telegraph, the newspaper,
the schoolmaster and the cheap post are lessening those
objections of ignorance and sentiment to removal that are
so strong with people long rooted in one place.   Yet, in
spite of this great exodus, the population of Europe, as a
whole, is steadily increasing.

And across the continent, from east to west, from the
older to the newer States, an even greater migration is
going on.   Our people emigrate more readily than those
of Europe, and increasing as European immigration is, it
is yet becoming a less and less important factor of our
growth, as compared with the natural increase of our
population.   At Chicago and St. Paul, Omaha and Kansas
City, the volume of the westward-moving current has
increased, not diminished.   From what, so short a time
ago, was the new West of unbroken prairie and native
forest, goes on, as children grow up, a constant migration
to a newer West.

This westward expansion of population has gone on
steadily since the first settlement of the Eastern shore.   It
has been the great distinguishing feature in the conditions
of our people.   Without its possibility we would have been
in nothing what we are.   Our higher standard of wages
and of comfort and of average intelligence, our superior
self-reliance, energy, inventiveness, adaptability and assimilative power, spring as directly from this possibility
of expansion as does our unprecedented growth.   All that
we are proud of in national life and national character
comes primarily from our background of unused land.
We are but transplanted Europeans, and, for that matter

mostly of the "inferior classes." It is not usually those
whose position is comfortable and whose prospects are
bright who emigrate; it is those who are pinched and
dissatisfied, those to whom no prospect seems open. There
are heralds' colleges in Europe that drive a good business
in providing a certain class of Americans with pedigrees
and coats of arms; but it is probably well for this sort of
self-esteem that the majority of us cannot truly trace our
ancestry very far. We had some Pilgrim Fathers, it is
true; likewise some Quaker fathers, and other sorts of
fathers; yet the majority even of the early settlers did not
come to America for "freedom to worship God," but
because they were poor, dissatisfied, unsuccessful, or
recklessly adventurous—many because they were evicted,
many to escape imprisonment, many because they were
kidnapped, many as self-sold bondsmen, as indentured
apprentices, or mercenary soldiers. It is the virtue of new
soil, the freedom of opportunity given by the possibility
of expansion, that has here transmuted into wholesome
human growth material that, had it remained in Europe,
might have been degraded and dangerous, just as in
Australia the same conditions have made respected and
self-respecting citizens out of the descendants of convicts,
and even out of convicts themselves.

It may be doubted if the relation of the opening of the
New World to the development of modern civilization is
yet fully recognized. In many respects the discovery of
Columbus has proved the most important event in the
history of the European world since the birth of Christ.
How important America has been to Europe as furnishing an outlet for the restless, the dissatisfied, the oppressed
and the downtrodden; how influences emanating from the
freer opportunities and freer life of America have reacted
upon European thought and life—we can begin to realize
only when we try to imagine what would have been the

present condition of Europe had Columbus found only a watery waste between Europe and Asia, or even had he found here a continent populated as India, or China, or Mexico, were populated.

And, correlatively, one of the most momentous events that could happen to the modern world would be the ending of this possibility of westward expansion. That it must sometime end is evident when we remember that the earth is round.

Practically, this event is near at hand. Its shadow is even now stealing over us. Not that there is any danger of this continent being really overpopulated. Not that there will not be for a long time to come, even at our present rate of growth, plenty of unused land or of land only partially used. But to feel the results of what is called pressure of population, to realize here pressure of the same kind that forces European emigration upon our shores, we shall not have to wait for that. Europe to-day is not overpopulated. In Ireland, whence we have received such an immense immigration, not one-sixth of the soil is under cultivation, and grass grows and beasts feed where once were populous villages. In Scotland there is the solitude of the deer forest and the grouse moor where a century ago were homes of men. One may ride on the railways through the richest agricultural districts of England and see scarcely as many houses as in the valley of the Platte, where the buffalo herded a few years back.

Twelve months ago, when the hedges were blooming, I passed along a lovely English road near by the cottage of that "Shepherd of Salisbury Plain" of whom I read, when a boy, in a tract which is a good sample of the husks frequently given to children as religious food, and which is still, I presume, distributed by the American, as it is by the English, Tract Society. On one side of the road was a wide expanse of rich land, in which no plowshare had

that season been struck, because its owner demanded a
higher rent than the farmers would give. On the other,
stretched, for many a broad acre, a lordly park, its velvety
verdure untrodden save by a few light-footed deer. And,
as we passed along, my companion, a native of those parts,
bitterly complained that, since this lord of the manor had
inclosed the little village green and set out his fences to
take in the grass of the roadside, the cottagers could not
keep even a goose, and the children of the village had no
place to play ! Place there was in plenty, but, so far as
the children were concerned, it might as well be in Africa
or in the moon. And so in our Far West, I have seen
emigrants toiling painfully for long distances through
vacant land without finding a spot on which they dared
settle. In a country where the springs and streams are
all inclosed by walls he cannot scale, the wayfarer, but for
charity, might perish of thirst, as in a desert. There is
plenty of vacant land on Manhattan Island. But on
Manhattan Island human beings are packed closer than
anywhere else in the world. There is plenty of fresh air
all around—one man owns forty acres of it, a whiff of
which he never breathes, since his home is on his yacht in
European waters; but, for all that, thousands of children
die in New York every summer for want of it, and thousands more would die did not charitable people subscribe
to fresh-air funds. The social pressure which forces on
our shores this swelling tide of immigration arises not
from the fact that the land of Europe is all in use, but
that it is all appropriated. That will soon be our case as
well. Our land will not all be used; but it will all be
" fenced in."

We still talk of our vast public domain, and figures
showing millions and millions of acres of unappropriated
public land yet swell grandly in the reports of our Land
Office. But already it is so difficult to find public land fit

for settlement, that the great majority of those wishing to settle find it cheaper to buy, and rents in California and the New Northwest run from a quarter to even one-half the crop. It must be remembered that the area which yet figures in the returns of our public domain includes all the great mountain chains, all the vast deserts and dry plains fit only for grazing, or not even for that; it must be remembered that of what is really fertile, millions and millions of acres are covered by railroad grants as yet unpatented, or what amounts to the same thing to the settler, are shadowed by them; that much is held by appropriation of the water, without which it is useless; and that much more is held under claims of various kinds, which, whether legal or illegal, are sufficient to keep the settler off unless he will consent to pay a price, or to mortgage his labor for years.

Nevertheless, land with us is still comparatively cheap. But this cannot long continue. The stream of immigration that comes swelling in, added to our steadily augmenting natural increase, will soon now so occupy the available lands as to raise the price of the poorest land worth settling on to a point we have never known. Nearly twenty years ago Mr. Wade, of Ohio, in a speech in the United States Senate, predicted that by the close of the century every acre of good agricultural land in the Union would be worth at least $50. That his prediction will be even more than verified we may already see. By the close of the century our population, at the normal rate of increase, will be over forty millions more than in 1880. That is to say, within the next seventeen years an additional population greater than that of the whole United States at the close of the civil war will be demanding room. Where will they find cheap land? There is no farther West. Our advance has reached the Pacific, and beyond the Pacific is the East, with its teeming millions. From

San Diego to Puget Sound there is no valley of the coastline that is not settled or preëmpted. To the very farthest corners of the Republic settlers are already going. The pressure is already so great that speculation and settlement are beginning to cross the northern border into Canada and the southern border into Mexico; so great that land is being settled and is becoming valuable that a few years ago would have been rejected—land where winter lasts for six months and the thermometer goes down into the forties below zero; land where, owing to insufficient rainfall, a crop is always a risk; land that cannot be cultivated at all without irrigation. The vast spaces of the western half of the continent do not contain anything like the proportion of arable land that does the eastern. The "great American desert" yet exists, though not now marked upon our maps. There is not to-day remaining in the United States any considerable body of good land unsettled and unclaimed, upon which settlers can go with the prospect of finding a homestead on government terms. Already the tide of settlement presses angrily upon the Indian reservations, and but for the power of the General Government would sweep over them. Already, although her population is as yet but a fraction more than six to the square mile, the last acre of the vast public domain of Texas has passed into private hands, the rush to purchase during the past year having been such that many thousands of acres more than the State had were sold.

We may see what is coming by the avidity with which capitalists, and especially foreign capitalists, who realize what is the value of land where none is left over which population may freely spread, are purchasing land in the United States. This movement has been going on quietly for some years, until now there is scarcely a rich English peer or wealthy English banker who does not, either individually or as the member of some syndicate, own a great tract of our new land, and the purchase of large bodies for foreign account is going on every day. It is with these absentee landlords that our coming millions must make terms.

Nor must it be forgotten that, while our population is increasing, and our "wild lands" are being appropriated, the productive capacity of our soil is being steadily reduced, which, practically, amounts to the same thing as reducing its quantity. Speaking generally, the agriculture of the United States is an exhaustive agriculture. We do not return to the earth what we take from it; each crop that is harvested leaves the soil the poorer. We are cutting down forests which we do not replant; we are shipping abroad, in wheat and cotton and tobacco and meat, or flushing into the sea through the sewers of our great cities, the elements of fertility that have been embedded in the soil by the slow processes of nature, acting for long ages.

The day is near at hand when it will be no longer possible for our increasing population freely to expand over new land; when we shall need for our own millions the immense surplus of food-stuffs now exported; when we shall not only begin to feel that social pressure which comes when natural resources are all monopolized, but when increasing social pressure here will increase social pressure in Europe. How momentous is this fact we begin to realize when we cast about for such another outlet as the United States has furnished. We look in vain. The British possessions to the north of us embrace comparatively little arable land; the valleys of the Saskatchewan and the Red River are being already taken up, and land speculation is already raging there in fever. Mexico offers opportunities for American enterprise and American capital and American trade, but scarcely for American emigration. There is some room for our settlers in that northern zone that has been kept desolate by fierce Indians; but it is very little. The table-land of Mexico and those portions of Central and South America suited to our people are already well filled by a population whom we cannot displace unless, as the Saxons displaced the ancient Britons, by a war of extermination. Anglo-Saxon capital and enterprise and influence will doubtless dominate those regions, and many of our people will go there; but it will be as Englishmen go to India or British Guiana. Where land is already granted and where peon labor can be had for a song, no such emigration can take place as that which has been pushing its way westward over the United States. So of Africa. Our race has made a permanent lodgment on the southern extremity of that vast continent, but its northern advance is met by tropical heats and the presence of races of strong vitality. On the north, the Latin branches of the European family seem to have again become acclimated, and will probably in time revive the ancient populousness and importance of Mediterranean Africa; but it will scarcely furnish an outlet for more than them. As for Equatorial Africa, though we may explore and civilize and develop, we cannot colonize it in the face of the climate and of races that increase rather than disappear in presence of the white man. The arable land of Australia would not merely be soon well populated by anything like the emigration that Europe is pouring on America, but there the forestalling of land goes on as rapidly as here. Thus we come again to that greatest of the continents, from which our race once started on its westward way, Asia—mother of peoples and religions—which yet contains the greater part of the human race—millions who live and die in all but utter unconsciousness of our modern world. In the awakening of those peoples by the impact of Western civilization lies one of the greatest problems of the future.

But it is not my purpose to enter into such speculations. What I want to point out is that we are very soon to lose one of the most important conditions under which our civilization has been developing—that possibility of expansion over virgin soil that has given scope and freedom to American life, and relieved social pressure in the most progressive European nations.   Tendencies, harmless under this condition, may become most dangerous when it is changed.   Gunpowder does not explode until it is confined.   You may rest your hand on the slowly ascending jaw of a hydraulic press.   It will only gently raise it.   But wait a moment till it meets resistance!

CHAPTER IV.

TWO OPPOSING TENDENCIES.

SO much freer, so much higher, so much fuller and wider is the life of our time, that, looking back, we cannot help feeling something like pity, if not contempt, for preceding generations.

Comforts, conveniences, luxuries, that a little while ago wealth could not purchase, are now matters of ordinary use. We travel in an hour, easily and comfortably, what to our fathers was a hard day's journey; we send in minutes messages that, in their time, would have taken weeks. We are better acquainted with remote countries than they with regions little distant; we know as common things what to them were fast-locked secrets of nature; our world is larger, our horizon is wider; in the years of our lives we may see more, do more, learn more.

Consider the diffusion of knowledge, the quickened transmission of intelligence. Compare the school-books used by our children with the school-books used by our fathers; see how cheap printing has brought within the reach of the masses the very treasures of literature; how enormously it has widened the audience of the novelist, the historian, the essayist and the poet; see how superior are even the trashy novels and story-papers in which shop-girls delight, to the rude ballads and "last dying speeches and confessions," which were their prototypes.

Look at the daily newspapers, read even by the poorest, and giving to them glimpses of the doings of all classes of society, news from all parts of the world. Consider the illustrated journals that every week bring to the million pictures of life in all phases and in all countries—bird's-eye views of cities, of grand and beautiful landscapes; the features of noted men and women; the sittings of parliaments, and congresses, and conventions; the splendor of courts, and the wild life of savages; triumphs of art; glories of architecture; processes of industry; achievements of inventive skill. Such a panorama as thus, week after week, passes before the eyes of common men and women, the richest and most powerful could not a generation ago have commanded.

These things, and the many other things that the mention of these will suggest, are necessarily exerting a powerful influence upon thought and feeling. Superstitions are dying out, prejudices are giving way, manners and customs are becoming assimilated, sympathies are widening, new aspirations are quickening the masses.

We come into the world with minds ready to receive any impression. To the eyes of infancy all is new, and one thing is no more wonderful than another. In whatever lies beyond common experience we assume the beliefs of those about us, and it is only the strongest intellects that can in a little raise themselves above the accepted opinions of their times. In a community where that opinion prevailed, the vast majority of us would as unhesitatingly believe that the earth is a plain, supported by a gigantic elephant, as we now believe it a sphere circling round the sun. No theory is too false, no fable too absurd, no superstition too degrading for acceptance when it has become embedded in common belief. Men will submit themselves to tortures and to death, mothers will immolate their children, at the bidding of beliefs they thus accept.

What more unnatural than polygamy? Yet see how long and how widely polygamy has existed!

In this tendency to accept what we find, to believe what we are told, is at once good and evil. It is this which makes social advance possible; it is this which makes it so slow and painful. Each generation thus obtains without effort the hard-won knowledge bequeathed to it; it is thus, also, enslaved by errors and perversions which it in the same way receives.

It is thus that tyranny is maintained and superstition perpetuated. Polygamy is unnatural. Obvious facts of universal experience prove this. The uniform proportion in which the sexes are brought into the world; the exclusiveness of the feeling with which in healthy conditions they attract each other; the necessities imposed by the slow growth and development of children, point to the union of one man with one woman as the intent of Nature. Yet, although it is repugnant to the most obvious facts and to the strongest instincts, polygamy seems a perfectly natural thing to those educated in a society where it has become an accepted institution, and it is only by long effort and much struggling that this idea can be eradicated. So with slavery. Even to such minds as those of Plato and Aristotle, to own a man seemed as natural as to own a horse. Even in this nineteenth century and in this "land of liberty," how long has it been since those who denied the right of property in human flesh and blood were denounced as "communists," as "infidels," as "incendiaries," bent on uprooting social order and destroying all property rights? So with monarchy, so with aristocracy, so with many other things as unnatural that are still unquestioningly accepted. Can anything be more unnatural—that is to say, more repugnant to right reason and to the facts and laws of nature—than that those who work least should get most of the things that work produces?

"He that will not work, neither shall he˙ eat." That is not merely the word of the Apostle; it is the obvious law of Nature. Yet all over the world, hard and poor is the fare of the toiling masses; while those who aid production neither with hand nor with head live luxuriously and fare sumptuously. This we have been used to, and it has therefore seemed to us natural; just as polygamy, slavery, aristocracy and monarchy seem natural to those accustomed to them.

But mental habits which made this state of things seem natural are breaking up; superstitions which prevented its being questioned are melting away. The revelations of physical science, the increased knowledge of other times and other peoples, the extension of education, emigration, travel, the rise of the critical spirit and the changes in old methods everywhere going on, are destroying beliefs which made the masses of men content with the position of hewers of wood and drawers of water, are softening manners and widening sympathies, are extending the idea of human equality and brotherhood.

All over the world the masses of men are becoming more and more dissatisfied with conditions under which their fathers would have been contented. It is in vain that they are told that their situation has been much improved; it is in vain that it is pointed out to them that comforts, amusements, opportunities, are within their reach that their fathers would not have dreamed of. The having got so much, only leads them to ask why they should not have more. Desire grows by what it feeds on. Man is not like the ox. He has no fixed standard of satisfaction. To arouse his ambition, to educate him to new wants, is as certain to make him discontented with his lot as to make that lot harder. We resign ourselves to what we think cannot be bettered; but when we realize that improvement is possible, then we become restive. This is the explanation of the paradox that De Tocqueville thought astonishing : that the masses find their position the more intolerable the more it is improved. The slave codes were wise that prescribed pains and penalties for teaching bondsmen to read, and they reasoned well who opposed popular education on the ground that it would bring revolution.

But there is in the conditions of the civilized world to-day something more portentous than a growing restive- ness under evils long endured. Everything tends to awake the sense of natural equality, to arouse the aspi- rations and ambitions of the masses, to excite a keener and keener perception of the gross injustice of existing inequalities of privilege and wealth. Yet, at the same time, everything tends to the rapid and monstrous increase of these inequalities. Never since great estates were eating out the heart of Rome has the world seen such enormous fortunes as are now arising—and never more utter pro- letarians. In the paper which contained a many-column account of the Vanderbilt ball, with its gorgeous dresses and its wealth of diamonds, with its profusion of roses, costing $2 each, and its precious wines flowing like water, I also read a brief item telling how, at a station-house near by, thirty-nine persons—eighteen of them women—had sought shelter, and how they were all marched into court next morning and sent for six months to prison. "The women," said the item, "shrieked and sobbed bitterly as they were carried to prison." Christ was born of a woman. And to Mary Magdalen he turned in tender blessing. But such vermin have some of these human creatures, made in God's image, become, that we must shovel them off to prison without being too particular.

The railroad is a new thing. It has scarcely begun its work. Yet it has already differentiated the man who counts his income by millions every month, and the thousands of men glad to work for him at from 90 cents to $1.50 a day. Who shall set bounds, under present tendencies, to the great fortunes of the next generation? Or to the correlatives of these great fortunes, the tramps?

The tendency of all the inventions and improvements so wonderfully augmenting productive power is to concentrate enormous wealth in the hands of a few, to make the condition of the many more hopeless; to force into the position of machines for the production of wealth they are not to enjoy, men whose aspirations are being aroused. Without a single exception that I can think of, the effect of all modern industrial improvements is to production upon a large scale, to the minute division of labor, to the giving to the possession of large capital an overpowering advantage. Even such inventions as the telephone and the typewriter tend to the concentration of wealth, by adding to the ease with which large businesses can be managed, and lessening limitations that after a certain point made further extension more difficult.

The tendency of the machine is in everything not merely to place it out of the power of the workman to become his own employer, but to reduce him to the position of a mere attendant or feeder; to dispense with judgment, skill and brains, save in a few overseers; to reduce all others to the monotonous work of automatons, to which there is no future save the same unvarying round.

Under the old system of handicraft, the workman may have toiled hard and long, but in his work he had companionship, variety, the pleasure that comes of the exercise of creative skill, the sense of seeing things growing under his hand to finished form. He worked in his own home or side by side with his employer. Labor was lightened by emulation, by gossip, by laughter, by discussion. As apprentice, he looked forward to becoming a journeyman; as a journeyman, he looked forward to becoming a master and taking an apprentice of his own. With a few tools and a little raw material he was independent. He dealt directly with those who used the finished articles he produced. If he could not find a market for money he could find a market in exchange. That terrible dread—the dread of having the opportunities of livelihood shut off; of finding himself utterly helpless to provide for his family —never cast its shadow over him.

Consider the blacksmith of the industrial era now everywhere passing—or rather the "black and white smith," for the finished workman worked in steel as well. The smithy stood by roadside or street. Through its open doors were caught glimpses of nature; all that was passing could be seen. Wayfarers stopped to inquire, neighbors to tell or hear the news, children to see the hot iron glow and watch the red sparks fly. Now the smith shoed a horse; now he put on a wagon-tire; now he forged and tempered a tool; again he welded a broken andiron, or beat out with graceful art a crane for the deep chimney-place, or, when there was nothing else to do, he wrought iron into nails.

Go now into one of those enormous establishments covering acres and acres, in which workmen by the thousand are massed together, and, by the aid of steam and machinery, iron is converted to its uses at a fraction of the cost of the old system. You cannot enter without permission from the office, for over each door you will find the sign, "Positively no admittance." If you are permitted to go in, you must not talk to the workmen; but that makes little difference, as amid the din and the clatter, and whir of belts and wheels, you could not if you would. Here you find men doing over and over the selfsame thing —passing, all day long, bars of iron through great rollers; presenting plates to steel jaws; turning, amid clangor in which you can scarcely "hear yourself think," bits of iron over and back again, sixty times a minute. for hour after

hour, for day after day, for year after year.   In the whole
great establishment there will be not a man, save here and
there one who got his training under the simpler system
now passing away, who can do more than some minute
part of what goes to the making of a salable article.   The
lad learns in a little while how to attend his particular
machine.   Then his progress stops.   He may become gray-
headed without learning more.   As his children grow, the
only way he has of augmenting his income is by setting
them to work.   As for aspiring to become master of such
an establishment, with its millions of capital in machinery
and stock, he might as well aspire to be King of England
or Pope of Rome.   He has no more control over the conditions that give him employment than has the passenger
in a railroad car over the motion of the train.   Causes
which he can neither prevent nor foresee may at any time
stop his machine and throw him upon the world, an utterly
unskilled laborer, unaccustomed even to swing a pick or
handle a spade.   When times are good, and his employer
is coining money, he can only get an advance by a strike
or a threatened strike.   At the least symptoms of harder
times his wages are scaled down, and he can only resist by a
strike, which means, for a longer or shorter time, no wages.

I have spoken of but one trade; but the tendency is the
same in all others.   This is the form that industrial organization is everywhere assuming, even in agriculture.   Great
corporations are now stocking immense ranges with cattle,
and "bonanza farms" are cultivated by gangs of nomads
destitute of anything that can be called home.   In all
occupations the workman is steadily becoming divorced
from the tools and opportunities of labor; everywhere the
inequalities of fortune are becoming more glaring.   And
this at a time when thought is being quickened; when the
old forces of conservatism are giving way: when the idea
of human equality is growing and spreading.

When between those who work and want and those who
live in idle luxury there is so great a gulf fixed that in
popular imagination they seem to belong to distinct orders
of beings; when, in the name of religion, it is persistently
instilled into the masses that all things in this world are
ordered by Divine Providence, which appoints to each his
place; when children are taught from the earliest infancy
that it is, to use the words of the Episcopal catechism,
their duty toward God and man to "honor and obey the
civil authority," to " order themselves lowly and reverently
to all their betters, and to do their duty in that state of life
unto which it shall please God to call them; " when these
counsels of humility, of contentment and of self-abasement
are enforced by the terrible threat of an eternity of torture,
while on the other hand the poor are taught to believe
that if they patiently bear their lot here God will after
death translate them to a heaven where there is no private
property and no poverty, the most glaring inequalities in
condition may excite neither envy nor indignation.

But the ideas that are stirring in the world to-day are
different from these.

Near nineteen hundred years ago, when another civilization was developing monstrous inequalities, when the
masses everywhere were being ground into hopeless
slavery, there arose in a Jewish village an unlearned
carpenter, who, scorning the orthodoxies and ritualisms of
the time, preached to laborers and fishermen the gospel
of the fatherhood of God, of the equality and brotherhood
of men, who taught his disciples to pray for the coming of
the kingdom of heaven on earth.   The college professors
sneered at him, the orthodox preachers denounced him.
He was reviled as a dreamer, as a disturber, as a " communist," and, finally, organized society took the alarm,
and he was crucified between two thieves.   But the word
went forth, and, spread by fugitives and slaves, made its

way against power and against persecution till it revolutionized the world, and out of the rotting old civilization brought the germ of the new. Then the privileged classes rallied again, carved the effigy of the man of the people in the courts and on the tombs of kings, in his name consecrated inequality, and wrested his gospel to the defense of social injustice. But again the same great ideas of a common fatherhood, of a common brotherhood, of a social state in which none shall be overworked and none shall want, begin to quicken in common thought.

When a mighty wind meets a strong current, it does not portend a smooth sea. And whoever will think of the opposing tendencies beginning to develop will appreciate the gravity of the social problems the civilized world must soon meet. He will also understand the meaning of Christ's words when he said :

" *Think not that I am come to send peace on earth. I came not to send peace, but a sword.*"

CHAPTER V.

IN 1790, at the time of the first census of the United States, the cities contained but 3.3 per cent. of the whole population. In 1880 the cities contained 22.5 per cent. of the population. This tendency of population to concentrate is one of the marked features of our time. All over the civilized world the great cities are growing even faster than the growth of population. The increase in the population of England and Scotland during the present century has been in the cities. In France, where population is nearly stationary, the large cities are year by year becoming larger. In Ireland, where population is steadily declining, Dublin and Belfast are steadily growing.

The same great agencies—steam and machinery—that are thus massing population in cities are operating even more powerfully to concentrate industry and trade. This is to be seen wherever the new forces have had play, and in every branch of industry, from such primary ones as agriculture, stock-raising, mining and fishing, up to those created by recent invention, such as railroading, telegraphing, or the lighting by gas or electricity.

It has been stated on the authority of the United States Census Bureau that the average size of farms is decreasing in the United States. This statement is inconsistent not only with facts obvious all over the United States, and with the tendencies of agriculture in other countries, such as Great Britain, but it is inconsistent with the returns furnished by the Census Bureau itself. According to the "Compendium of the Tenth Census," the increase of the number of farms in the United States during the decade between 1870 and 1880 was about 50 per cent., and the returns in the eight classes of farms enumerated show a steady diminution in the smaller-sized farms and a steady increase in the larger. In the class under three acres, the decrease during the decade was about 37 per cent.; between three and ten acres, about 21 per cent.; between ten and twenty acres, about 14 per cent.; between twenty and fifty acres, something less than 8 per cent. With the class between 50 and 100 acres, the increase begins, amounting in this class to about 37 per cent. In the next class, between 100 and 500 acres, the increase is nearly 200 per cent. In the class between 500 and 1000 acres, it is nearly 400 per cent. In the class over 1000 acres, the largest given, it amounts to almost 700 per cent.

How, in the face of these figures, the Census Bureau can report a decline in the average size of farms in the United States from 153 acres in 1870 to 134 acres in 1880 I cannot understand. Nor is it worth while here to inquire. The incontestable fact is that, like everything else, the ownership of land is concentrating, and farming is assuming a larger scale. This is due to the improvements in agricultural machinery, which make farming a business requiring more capital, to the enhanced value of land, to the changes produced by railroads, and the advantage which special rates give the large over the small producer. That it is an accelerating tendency there is no question. The new era in farming is only beginning. And whatever be its gains, it involves the reduction

of the great body of American farmers to the ranks of
tenants or laborers. There are no means of discovering
the increase of tenant farming in the United States during
the last decade, as no returns as to tenantry were made
prior to the last census; but that shows that there were
in the United States in 1880 no less than 1,024,601 tenant
farmers. If, in addition to this, we could get at the
number of farmers nominally owning their own land, but
who are in reality paying rent in the shape of interest on
mortgages, the result would be astounding.

How in all other branches of industry the same process
is going on, it is scarcely necessary to speak. It is
everywhere obvious that the independent mechanic is
becoming an operative, the little storekeeper a salesman
in a big store, the small merchant a clerk or bookkeeper,
and that men, under the old system independent, are being
massed in the employ of great firms and corporations.
But the effect of this is scarcely realized. A large class
of people, including many professed public teachers, are
constantly talking as though energy, industry and economy
were alone necessary to business success—are constantly
pointing to the fact that men who began with nothing are
now rich, as proof that any one can begin with nothing
and get rich.

That most of our rich men did begin with nothing is
true. But that the same success could be as easily won
now is not true. Times of change always afford opportunities for the rise of individuals, which disappear when
social relations are again adjusted. We have been not
only overrunning a new continent, but the introduction of
steam and the application of machinery have brought
about industrial changes such as the world never before
saw.

When William the Conqueror parceled out England
among his followers, a feudal aristocracy was created out

of an army of adventurers. But when society had hardened again, an hereditary nobility had formed into which no common man could hope to win his way, and the descendants of William's adventurers looked down upon men of their fathers' class as upon beings formed of inferior clay. So when a new country is rapidly settling, those who come while land is cheap and industry and trade are in process of organization have opportunities that those who start from the same plane when land has become valuable and society has formed cannot have.

The rich men of the first generation in a new country are always men who started with nothing, but the rich men of subsequent generations are generally those who inherited their start. In the United States, when we hear of a wealthy man, we naturally ask, "How did he make his money?" for the presumption, over the greater part of the country, is that he acquired it himself. In England they do not ordinarily ask that question—there the presumption is that he inherited it. But, though the soil of England was parceled out long ago, the great changes consequent upon the introduction of steam and machinery have there, as here, opened opportunities to rise from the ranks of labor to great wealth. Those opportunities are now closed or closing. When a railroad train is slowly moving off, a single step may put one on it. But in a few minutes those who have not taken that step may run themselves out of breath in the hopeless endeavor to overtake the train. It is absurd to think that it is easy to step aboard a train at full speed because those who got on board at starting did so easily. So is it absurd to think that opportunities open when steam and machinery were beginning their concentrating work will remain open.

An English friend, a wealthy retired Manchester manufacturer, once told me the story of his life. How he went to work at eight years of age helping make twine, when

twine was made entirely by hand. How, when a young
man, he walked to Manchester, and having got credit for
a bale of flax, made it into twine and sold it. How,
building up a little trade, he got others to work for him.
How, when machinery began to be invented and steam
was introduced, he took advantage of them, until he had
a big factory and made a fortune, when he withdrew to
spend the rest of his days at ease, leaving his business to
his son.

"Supposing you were a young man now," said I, "could
you walk into Manchester and do that again?"

"No," replied he; "no one could. I couldn't with fifty
thousand pounds in place of my five shillings."

So in every branch of business in which the new
agencies have begun to reach anything like development.
Leland Stanford drove an ox-team to California; Henry
Villard came here from Germany a poor boy, became a
newspaper reporter, and rode a mule from Kansas City to
Denver when the plains were swarming with Indians—a
thing no one with a bank-account would do. Stanford
and his associates got hold of the Central Pacific enterprise, with its government endowments, and are now
masters of something like twelve thousand miles of rail,
millions of acres of land, steamship lines, express companies, banks and newspapers, to say nothing of legislatures, congressmen, judges, etc. So Henry Villard, by a
series of fortunate accidents, which he had energy and
tact to improve, got hold of the Oregon Steam Navigation
combination, and of the Northern Pacific endowment, and
has become the railroad king of the immense domain north
of the Stanford dominions, having likewise his thousands
of miles of road, millions of acres of land, his newspapers,
political servitors, and literary brushers off of flies, and
being able to bring over a shipload of lords and barons
to see him drive a golden spike.

Now, it is not merely that such opportunities as these which have made the Stanfords and Villards so great, come only with the opening of new countries and the development of new industrial agents; but that the rise of the Stanfords and Villards makes impossible the rise of others such as they. Whoever now starts a railroad within the domains of either must become subordinate and tributary to them. The great railroad king alone can fight the great railroad king, and control of the railroad system not only gives the railroad kings control of branch roads, of express companies, stage lines, steamship lines, etc., not only enables them to make or unmake the smaller towns, but it enables them to " size the pile " of any one who develops a business requiring transportation, and to transfer to their own pockets any surplus beyond what, after careful consideration, they think he ought to make. The rise of these great powers is like the growth of a great tree, which draws the moisture from the surrounding soil, and stunts all other vegetation by its shade.

So, too, does concentration operate in all businesses. The big mill crushes out the little mill. The big store undersells the little store till it gets rid of its competition. On the top of the building of the American News Company, on Chambers Street, New York, stands a newsboy carved in marble. It was in this way that the managing man of that great combination began. But what was at first the union of a few sellers of newspapers for mutual convenience has become such a powerful concern, that combination after combination, backed with capital and managed with skill, have gone down in the attempt to break or share its monopoly. The newsboy may look upon the statue that crowns the building as the young Englishman who goes to India to take a clerical position may look upon the statue of Lord Clive. It is a lesson and an incentive, to be sure: but just as Clive's victories, by establishing the English dominion in India, made such a career as his impossible again, so does the success of such a concern as the American News Company make it impossible for men of small capital to establish another such business.

So may the printer look upon the *Tribune* building, or the newspaper writer upon that of the *Herald*. A Greeley or a Bennett could no longer hope to establish a first-class paper in New York, or to get control of one already established, unless he got a Jay Gould to back him. Even in our newest cities the day has gone by when a few printers and a few writers could combine and start a daily paper. To say nothing of the close corporation of the Associated Press, the newspaper has become an immense machine, requiring large capital, and for the most part it is written by literary operatives, who must write to suit the capitalist that controls it.

In the last generation a full-rigged Indiaman would be considered a very large vessel if she registered 500 tons. Now we are building coasting schooners of 1000 tons. It is not long since our first-class ocean steamers were of 1200 or 1500 tons. Now the crack steamers of the trans-Atlantic route are rising to 10,000 tons. Not merely are there relatively fewer captains, but the chances of modern captains are not as good. The captain of a great trans-Atlantic steamer recently told me that he got no more pay now than when as a young man he commanded a small sailing-ship. Nor is there now any "primage," any "venture," any chance of becoming owner as well as captain of one of these great steamers.

Under any condition of things short of a rigid system of hereditary caste, there will, of course, always be men who, by force of great abilities and happy accidents, win their way from poverty to wealth, and from low to high position; but the strong tendencies of the time are to make this more and more difficult. Jay Gould is probably an abler man than the present Vanderbilt. Had they started even, Vanderbilt might now have been peddling mouse-traps or working for a paltry salary as some one's clerk, while Gould counted his scores of millions. But with all his money-making ability Gould cannot overcome the start given by the enormous acquisitions of the first Vanderbilt. And when the sons of the present great money-makers take their places, the chances of rivalry on the part of anybody else's sons will be much less.

All the tendencies of the present are not merely to the concentration, but to the perpetuation, of great fortunes. There are no crusades; the habits of the very rich are not to that mad extravagance that could dissipate such fortunes; high play has gone out of fashion, and the gambling of the Stock Exchange is more dangerous to short than to long purses. Stocks, bonds, mortgages, safe-deposit and trust companies aid the retention of large wealth, and all modern agencies enlarge the sphere of its successful employment.

On the other hand, the mere laborer is becoming more helpless, and small capitals find it more and more difficult to compete with larger capitals. The greater railroad companies are swallowing up the lesser railroad companies; one great telegraph company already controls the telegraph wires of the continent, and, to save the cost of buying up more patents, pays inventors not to invent. As in England, nearly all the public houses have passed into the hands of the great brewers, so here, large firms start young men, taking chattel mortgages on their stock. As in Great Britain, the supplying of railway passengers with eatables and drinkables has passed into the hands of a single great company, and in Paris one large restaurateur, with numerous branches, is taking the trade of the smaller ones. so here, the boys who sell papers and peanuts on the trains are employees of companies, and bundles are carried and errands run by corporations.

I am not denying that this tendency is largely to subserve public convenience. I am merely pointing out that it exists. A great change is going on all over the civilized world similar to that infeudation which, in Europe, during the rise of the feudal system, converted free proprietors into vassals, and brought all society into subordination to a hierarchy of wealth and privilege. Whether the new aristocracy is hereditary or not makes little difference. Chance alone may determine who will get the few prizes of a lottery. But it is not the less certain that the vast majority of all who take part in it must draw blanks. The forces of the new era have not yet had time to make status hereditary, but we may clearly see that when the industrial organization compels a thousand workmen to take service under one master, the proportion of masters to men will be but as one to a thousand, though the one may come from the ranks of the thousand. "Master"! We don't like the word. It is not American! But what is the use of objecting to the word when we have the thing? The man who gives me employment, which I must have or suffer, that man is my master, let me call him what I will.

CHAPTER VI.

THE WRONG IN EXISTING SOCIAL CONDITIONS.

THE comfortable theory that it is in the nature of things that some should be poor and some should be rich, and that the gross and constantly increasing inequalities in the distribution of wealth imply no fault in our institutions, pervades our literature, and is taught in the press, in the church, in school and in college.

This is a free country, we are told—every man has a vote and every man has a chance. The laborer's son may become President; poor boys of to-day will be millionaires thirty or forty years from now, and the millionaire's grandchildren will probably be poor. What more can be asked? If a man has energy, industry, prudence and foresight, he may win his way to great wealth. If he has not the ability to do this he must not complain of those who have. If some enjoy much and do little, it is because they, or their parents, possessed superior qualities which enabled them to "acquire property" or "make money." If others must work hard and get little, it is because they have not yet got their start, because they are ignorant, shiftless, unwilling to practise that economy necessary for the first accumulation of capital; or because their fathers were wanting in these respects. The inequalities in condition result from the inequalities of human nature, from the difference in the powers and capacities of different men. If one has to toil ten or twelve hours a day for a

few hundred dollars a year, while another, doing little or
no hard work, gets an income of many thousands, it is
because all that the former contributes to the augmentation
of the common stock of wealth is little more than the mere
force of his muscles. He can expect little more than the
animal, because he brings into play little more than animal
powers. He is but a private in the ranks of the great
army of industry, who has but to stand still or march, as
he is bid. The other is the organizer, the general, who
guides and wields the whole great machine, who must
think, plan and provide; and his larger income is only
commensurate with the far higher and rarer powers which
he exercises, and the far greater importance of the function he fulfils. Shall not education have its reward, and
skill its payment? What incentive would there be to the
toil needed to learn to do anything well were great prizes
not to be gained by those who learn to excel? It would
not merely be gross injustice to refuse a Raphael or a
Rubens more than a house-painter, but it would prevent
the development of great painters. To destroy inequalities
in condition would be to destroy the incentive to progress.
To quarrel with them is to quarrel with the laws of nature.
We might as well rail against the length of the days or
the phases of the moon; complain that there are valleys
and mountains; zones of tropical heat and regions of eternal ice. And were we by violent measures to divide wealth
equally, we should accomplish nothing but harm; in a
little while there would be inequalities as great as before.

This, in substance, is the teaching which we constantly
hear. It is accepted by some because it is flattering to
their vanity, in accordance with their interests or pleasing
to their hope; by others, because it is dinned into their
ears. Like all false theories that obtain wide acceptance,
it contains much truth. But it is truth isolated from
other truth or alloyed with falsehood.

To try to pump out a ship with a hole in her hull would be hopeless; but that is not to say that leaks may not be stopped and ships pumped dry. It is undeniable that, under present conditions, inequalities in fortune would tend to reassert themselves even if arbitrarily leveled for a moment; but that does not prove that the conditions from which this tendency to inequality springs may not be altered. Nor because there are differences in human qualities and powers does it follow that existing inequalities of fortune are thus accounted for. I have seen very fast compositors and very slow compositors, but the fastest I ever saw could not set twice as much type as the slowest, and I doubt if in other trades the variations are greater. Between normal men the difference of a sixth or seventh is a great difference in height—the tallest giant ever known was scarcely more than four times as tall as the smallest dwarf ever known, and I doubt if any good observer will say that the mental differences of men are greater than the physical differences. Yet we already have men hundreds of millions of times richer than other men.

That he who produces should have, that he who saves should enjoy, is consistent with human reason and with the natural order. But existing inequalities of wealth cannot be justified on this ground. As a matter of fact, how many great fortunes can be truthfully said to have been fairly earned? How many of them represent wealth produced by their possessors or those from whom their present possessors derived them? Did there not go to the formation of all of them something more than superior industry and skill? Such qualities may give the first start, but when fortunes begin to roll up into millions there will always be found some element of monopoly, some appropriation of wealth produced by others. Often there is a total absence of superior industry, skill or self-denial, and merely better luck or greater unscrupulousness.

An acquaintance of mine died in San Francisco recently, leaving $4,000,000, which will go to heirs to be looked up in England. I have known many men more industrious, more skilful, more temperate than he—men who did not or who will not leave a cent. This man did not get his wealth by his industry, skill or temperance. He no more produced it than did those lucky relations in England who may now do nothing for the rest of their lives. He became rich by getting hold of a piece of land in the early days, which, as San Francisco grew, became very valuable. His wealth represented not what he had earned, but what the monopoly of this bit of the earth's surface enabled him to appropriate of the earnings of others.

A man died in Pittsburgh, the other day, leaving $3,000,000. He may or may not have been particularly industrious, skilful and economical, but it was not by virtue of these qualities that he got so rich. It was because he went to Washington and helped lobby through a bill which, by way of "protecting American workmen against the pauper labor of Europe," gave him the advantage of a sixty-per-cent. tariff. To the day of his death he was a stanch protectionist, and said free trade would ruin our "infant industries." Evidently the $3,000,000 which he was enabled to lay by from his own little cherub of an "infant industry" did not represent what he had added to production. It was the advantage given him by the tariff that enabled him to scoop it up from other people's earnings.

This element of monopoly, of appropriation and spoliation will, when we come to analyze them, be found largely to account for all great fortunes.

There are two classes of men who are always talking as though great fortunes resulted from the power of increase belonging to capital—those who declare that present social adjustments are all right; and those who denounce capital

and insist that interest should be abolished. The typical
rich man of the one set is he who, saving his earnings,
devotes the surplus to aiding production, and becomes rich
by the natural growth of his capital. The other set make
calculations of the enormous sum a dollar put out at six
per cent. compound interest will amount to in a hundred
years, and say we must abolish interest if we would
prevent the growth of great fortunes.

But I think it difficult to instance any great fortune
really due to the legitimate growth of capital obtained by
industry.

The great fortune of the Rothschilds springs from the
treasure secured by the Landgrave of Hesse-Cassel by
selling his people to England to fight against our forefathers in their struggle for independence. It began in
the blood-money received by this petty tyrant from greater
tyrants as the price of the lives of his subjects. It has
grown to its present enormous dimensions by the jobbing
of loans raised by European kings for holding in subjection the people and waging destructive wars upon each
other. It no more represents the earnings of industry or
of capital than do the sums now being wrung by England
from the poverty-stricken fellahs of Egypt to pay for the
enormous profits on loans to the Khedive, which he wasted
on palaces, yachts, harems, ballet-dancers, and cart-loads
of diamonds, such as he gave to the Shermans.

The great fortune of the Duke of Westminster, the
richest of the rich men of England, is purely the result of
appropriation. It no more springs from the earnings of
the present Duke of Westminster or any of his ancestors
than did the great fortunes bestowed by Russian monarchs
on their favorites when they gave them thousands of the
Russian people as their serfs. An English king, long
since dead, gave to an ancestor of the present Duke of
Westminster a piece of land over which the city of London

has now extended—that is to say, he gave him the privi·
lege, still recognized by the stupid English people, which
enables the present duke to appropriate so much of the
earnings of so many thousands of the present generation
of Englishmen.

So, too, the great fortunes of the English brewers and
distillers have been largely built up by the operation of
the excise in fostering monopoly and concentrating the
business.

Or, turning again to the United States, take the great
fortune of the Astors. It represents for the most part a
similar appropriation of the earnings of others, as does the
income of the Duke of Westminster and other English
landlords. The first Astor made an arrangement with
certain people living in his time by virtue of which his
children are now allowed to tax other people's children—
to demand a very large part of their earnings from many
thousands of the present population of New York. Its
main element is not production or saving. No human
being can produce land or lay up land. If the Astors had
all remained in Germany, or if there had never been any
Astors, the land of Manhattan Island would have been
here all the same.

Take the great Vanderbilt fortune. The first Vanderbilt
was a boatman who earned money by hard work and saved
it. But it was not working and saving that enabled him
to leave such an enormous fortune. It was spoliation and
monopoly. As soon as he got money enough he used it
as a club to extort from others their earnings. He ran
off opposition lines and monopolized routes of steamboat
travel. Then he went into railroads, pursuing the same
tactics. The Vanderbilt fortune no more comes from
working and saving than did the fortune that Captain
Kidd buried.

Or take the great Gould fortune. Mr. Gould might have
got his first little start by superior industry and superior

self-denial. But it is not that which has made him the
master of a hundred millions. It was by wrecking railroads, buying judges, corrupting legislatures, getting up
rings and pools and combinations to raise or depress stock
values and transportation rates.

So, likewise, of the great fortunes which the Pacific
railroads have created. They have been made by lobbying
through profligate donations of lands, bonds and subsidies,
by the operations of Crédit Mobilier and Contract and
Finance Companies, by monopolizing and gouging. And
so of fortunes made by such combinations as the Standard
Oil Company, the Bessemer Steel Ring, the Whisky Tax
Ring, the Lucifer Match Ring, and the various rings for
the " protection of the American workman from the pauper
labor of Europe."

Or take the fortunes made out of successful patents.
Like that element in so many fortunes that comes from
the increased value of land, these result from monopoly,
pure and simple. And though I am not now discussing
the expediency of patent laws, it may be observed, in
passing, that in the vast majority of cases the men who
make fortunes out of patents are not the men who make
the inventions.

Through all great fortunes, and, in fact, through nearly
all acquisitions that in these days can fairly be termed
fortunes, these elements of monopoly, of spoliation, of
gambling run. The head of one of the largest manufacturing firms in the United States said to me recently, " It
is not on our ordinary business that we make our money ;
it is where we can get a monopoly." And this, I think, is
generally true.

Consider the important part in building up fortunes
which the increase of land values has had, and is having,
in the United States. This is, of course, monopoly, pure
and simple. When land increases in value it does not
mean that its owner has added to the general wealth. The

owner may never have seen the land or done aught to improve it. He may, and often does, live in a distant city or in another country. Increase of land values simply means that the owners, by virtue of their appropriation of something that existed before man was, have the power of taking a larger share of the wealth produced by other people's labor. Consider how much the monopolies created and the advantages given to the unscrupulous by the tariff and by our system of internal taxation—how much the railroad (a business in its nature a monopoly), telegraph, gas, water and other similar monopolies, have done to concentrate wealth; how special rates, pools, combinations, corners, stock-watering and stock-gambling, the destructive use of wealth in driving off or buying off opposition which the public must finally pay for, and many other things which these will suggest, have operated to build up large fortunes, and it will at least appear that the unequal distribution of wealth is due in great measure to sheer spoliation; that the reason why those who work hard get so little, while so many who work little get so much, is, in very large measure, that the earnings of the one class are, in one way or another, filched away from them to swell the incomes of the other.

That individuals are constantly making their way from the ranks of those who get less than their earnings to the ranks of those who get more than their earnings, no more proves this state of things right than the fact that merchant sailors were constantly becoming pirates and participating in the profits of piracy, would prove that piracy was right and that no effort should be made to suppress it.

I am not denouncing the rich, nor seeking, by speaking of these things, to excite envy and hatred; but if we would get a clear understanding of social problems, we must recognize the fact that it is due to monopolies which we permit and create, to advantages which we give one man over another, to methods of extortion sanctioned by law and by public opinion, that some men are enabled to get so enormously rich while others remain so miserably poor. If we look around us and note the elements of monopoly, extortion and spoliation which go to the building up of all, or nearly all, fortunes, we see on the one hand how disingenuous are those who preach to us that there is nothing wrong in social relations and that the inequalities in the distribution of wealth spring from the inequalities of human nature ; and on the other hand, we see how wild are those who talk as though capital were a public enemy, and propose plans for arbitrarily restricting the acquisition of wealth.   Capital is a good ; the capitalist is a helper, if he is not also a monopolist.   We can safely let any one get as rich as he can if he will not despoil others in doing so.

There are deep wrongs in the present constitution of society, but they are not wrongs inherent in the constitution of man nor in those social laws which are as truly the laws of the Creator as are the laws of the physical universe. They are wrongs resulting from bad adjustments which it is within our power to amend.   The ideal social state is not that in which each gets an equal amount of wealth, but in which each gets in proportion to his contribution to the general stock.   And in such a social state there would not be less incentive to exertion than now ; there would be far more incentive.   Men will be more industrious and more moral, better workmen and better citizens, if each takes his earnings and carries them home to his family, than where they put their earnings in a "pot" and gamble for them until some have far more than they could have earned, and others have little or nothing.

CHAPTER VII.

IS IT THE BEST OF ALL POSSIBLE WORLDS?

THERE are worlds and worlds—even within the bounds
of the same horizon. The man who comes into New
York with plenty of money, who puts up at the Windsor
or Brunswick, and is received by hospitable hosts in Fifth
Avenue mansions, sees one New York. The man who
comes with a dollar and a half, and goes to a twenty-five-
cent lodging-house, sees another. There are also fifteen
cent lodging-houses, and people too poor to go even to
them.

Into the pleasant avenues of the Park, in the bright May
sunshine, dashes the railroad-wrecker's daughter, her tasty
riding-habit floating free from the side of her glistening
bay, and her belted groom, in fresh top-boots and smart
new livery, clattering after, at a respectful distance, on
another blooded horse, that chafes at the bit. The stock-
gambler's son, rising from his trotter at every stride, in
English fashion, his English riding-stick grasped by the
middle, raises his hat to her nod. And as he whirls past
in his London-made dog-cart, a liveried servant sitting
with folded arms behind him, she exchanges salutations
with the high-born descendant of the Dutch gardener,
whose cabbage-patch, now covered with brick and mortar,
has become an "estate" of lordly income. While in the
soft, warm air rings a musical note, and drawn by mettled
steeds, the four-in-hands of the coaching club rush by,

with liveried guards and coach-tops filled with chattering
people, to whom life, with its round of balls, parties,
theaters, flirtations and excursions, is a holiday, in which,
but for the invention of new pleasures, satiety would make
time drag.

How different this bright world from that of the old
woman who, in the dingy lower street, sits from morning
to night beside her little stock of apples and candy; from
that of the girls who stand all day behind counters and
before looms, who bend over sewing-machines for weary,
weary hours, or who come out at night to prowl the
streets!

One railroad king puts the great provinces of his realm
in charge of satraps and goes to Europe; the new steel
yacht of another is being fitted, regardless of expense, for
a voyage around the world, if it pleases him to take it; a
third will not go abroad—he is too busy buying in his
"little old railroad" every day. Other human beings are
gathered into line every Sunday afternoon by the Rev.
Coffee-and-rolls-man, and listen to his preaching for the
dole they are to get. And upon the benches in the squares
sit men from whose sullen, deadened faces the fire of
energy and the light of hope have gone—"tramps" and
"bums," the broken, rotted, human driftwood, the pariahs
of our society.

I stroll along Broadway in the evening, and by the
magnificent saloon of the man who killed Jim Fisk, I meet
a good fellow whom I knew years ago in California, when
he could not jingle more than one dollar on another. It
is different now, and he takes a wad of bills from his
pocket to pay for the thirty-five-cent cigars we light. He
has rooms in the most costly of Broadway hotels, his
clothes are cut by Blissert, and he thinks Delmonico's
about the only place to get a decent meal. He tells me
about some "big things" he has got into, and talks about

millions as though they were marbles. If a man has any speed in him at all, he says, it is just as easy to deal in big things as in little things, and the men who play such large hands in the great game are no smarter than other men, when you get alongside of them and take their measure. As to politics, he says, it is only a question who hold the offices. The corporations rule the country, and are going to rule it, and the man is a fool who doesn't get on their side. As for the people, what do they know or care! The press rules the people, and capital rules the press. Better hunt with the dogs than be hunted with the hare.

We part, and as I turn down the street another acquaintance greets me, and, as his conversation grows interesting, I go out of my way, for to delay him were sin, as he must be at work by two in the morning. He has been trying to read " Progress and Poverty," he says: but he has to take it in such little snatches, and the children make such a noise in his two small rooms—for his wife is afraid to let them out on the street to learn so much bad—that it is hard work to understand some parts of it. He is a journeyman baker, but he has a good situation as journeyman bakers go. He works in a restaurant, and only twelve hours a day. Most bakers, he tells me, have to work fourteen and sixteen hours. Some of the places they work in would sicken a man not used to it, and even those used to it are forced to lie off every now and again, and to drink, or they could not stand it. In some bakeries they use good stock, he says, but they have to charge high prices, which only the richer people will pay. In most of them you often have to sift the maggots out of the flour, and the butter is always rancid. He belongs to a Union, and they are trying to get in all the journeyman bakers; but those that work longest, and have most need of it, are the hardest to get. Their long hours make them stupid, and take all the spirit out of them. He has tried to get into business for himself, and he and his wife once pinched and saved till they got a few hundred dollars, and then set up a little shop. But he had not money enough to buy a share in the Flour Association—a coöperative association of boss bakers, by which the members get stock at lowest rates—and he could not compete, lost his money, and had to go to work again as a journeyman. He can see no chance at all of getting out of it, he says; he sometimes thinks he might as well be a slave. His family grows larger and it costs more to keep them. His rent was raised two dollars on the 1st of May. His wife remonstrated with the agent, said they were making no more, and it cost them more to live. The agent said he could not help that; the property had increased in value, and the rents must be raised. The reason people complained of rents was that they lived too extravagantly, and thought they must have everything anybody else had. People could live, and keep strong and fat, on nothing but oatmeal. If they would do that they would find it easy enough to pay their rent.

There is such a rush across the Atlantic that it is difficult to engage a passage for months ahead. The doors of the fine, roomy houses in the fashionable streets will soon be boarded up, as their owners leave for Europe, for the sea-shore, or the mountains. "Everybody is out of town," they will say. Not quite everybody, though. Some twelve or thirteen hundred thousand people, without counting Brooklyn, will be left to swelter through the hot summer. The swarming tenement-houses will not be boarded up; every window and door will be open to catch the least breath of air. The dirty streets will be crawling with squalid life, and noisy with the play of unkempt children, who never saw a green field or watched the curl of a breaker, save perhaps, when charity gave them a treat.

Dragged women will be striving to quiet pining babies, sobbing and wailing away their little lives for the want of wholesome nourishment and fresh air; and degradation and misery that hide during the winter will be seen on every hand.

In such a city as this, the world of some is as different from the world in which others live as Jupiter may be from Mars. There are worlds we shut our eyes to, and do not bear to think of, still less to look at, but in which human beings yet live—worlds in which vice takes the place of virtue, and from which hope here and hope hereafter seem utterly banished—brutal, discordant, torturing hells of wickedness and suffering.

"Why do they cry for bread?" asked the innocent French princess, as the roar of the fierce, hungry mob resounded through the courtyard of Versailles. "If they have no bread, why don't they eat cake?"

Yet, not a fool above other fools was the pretty princess, who never in her whole life had known that cake was not to be had for the asking. "Why are not the poor thrifty and virtuous and wise and temperate?" one hears whenever in luxurious parlors such subjects are mentioned. What is this but the question of the French princess? Thrift and virtue and wisdom and temperance are not the fruits of poverty.

But it is not this of which I intended here to speak so much as of that complacent assumption which runs through current thought and speech, that this world in which we, nineteenth-century, Christian, American men and women live, is, in its social adjustments, at least, about such a world as the Almighty intended it to be.

Some say this in terms, others say it by implication, but in one form or another it is constantly taught. Even the wonders of modern invention have, with a most influential part of society, scarcely shaken the belief that social

improvement is impossible. Men of the sort who, a little
while ago, derided the idea that steam-carriages might be
driven over the land and steam-vessels across the sea,
would not now refuse to believe in the most startling
mechanical invention. But he who thinks society may be
improved, he who thinks that poverty and greed may be
driven from the world, is still looked upon in circles that
pride themselves on their culture and rationalism as a
dreamer, if not as a dangerous lunatic.

The old idea that everything in the social world is
ordered by the Divine Will—that it is the mysterious
dispensations of Providence that give wealth to the few
and order poverty as the lot of the many, make some
rulers and the others serfs—is losing power; but another
idea that serves the same purpose is taking its place, and
we are told, in the name of science, that the only social
improvement that is possible is by a slow race-evolution,
of which the fierce struggle for existence is the impelling
force; that, as I have recently read in "a journal of civilization" from the pen of a man who has turned from the
preaching of what he called Christianity to the teaching of what he calls political economy, "only the *élite* of
the race has been raised to the point where reason and
conscience can even curb the lower motive forces," and
'that for all but a few of us the limit of attainment in
life, in the best case, is to live out our term, to pay our
debts, to place three or four children in a position as good
as the father's was, and there make the account balance."
As for "friends of humanity," and those who would "help
the poor," they get from him the same scorn which the
Scribes and Pharisees eighteen hundred years ago visited
on a pestilent social reformer whom they finally crucified.

Lying beneath all such theories is the selfishness that
would resist any inquiry into the titles to the wealth which
greed has gathered, and the difficulty and indisposition on

the part of the comfortable classes of realizing the existence of any other world than that seen through their own
eyes.

That "one-half of the world does not know how the
other half live," is much more true of the upper than of
the lower half. We look upon that which is pleasant
rather than that which is disagreeable. The shop-girl
delights in the loves of the Lord de Maltravers and the
Lady Blanche, just as children without a penny will gaze
in confectioners' windows, as hungry men dream of feasts,
and poor men relish tales of sudden wealth. And social
suffering is for the most part mute. The well-dressed take
the main street, but the ragged slink into the byways.
The man in a good coat will be listened to where the same
man in tatters would be hustled off. It is that part of
society that has the best reason to be satisfied with things
as they are that is heard in the press, in the church, and
in the school, and that forms the conventional opinion
that this world in which we American Christians, in the
latter half of the nineteenth century, live is about as good
a world as the Creator (if there is a Creator) intended it
should be.

But look around. All over the world the beauty and
the glory and the grace of civilization rest on human lives
crushed into misery and distortion.

I will not speak of Germany, of France, of England.
Look even here, where European civilization flowers in
the free field of a new continent; where there are no kings,
no great standing armies, no relics of feudal servitude;
where national existence began with the solemn declaration
of the equal and inalienable rights of men. I clip, almost
at random, from a daily paper, for I am not seeking the
blackest shadows:

Margaret Hickey, aged 30 years, came to this city a few days ago
from Boston with a seven-weeks-old baby. She tried to get work, but

was not successful. Saturday night she placed the child in a cellar at No. 226 West Forty-second Street. At midnight she called at Police Headquarters and said she had lost her baby in Forty-third Street. In the meantime an officer found the child. The mother was held until yesterday morning, when she was taken to Yorkville Court and sent to the Island for six months.

Morning and evening, day after day, in these times of peace and prosperity, one may read in our daily papers such items as this, and worse than this. We are so used to them that they excite no attention and no comment. We know what the fate of Margaret Hickey, aged thirty years, and of her baby, aged seven weeks, sent to the Island for six months, will be. Better for them and better for society were they drowned outright, as we would drown a useless cat and mangy kitten; but so common are such items that we glance at them as we glance at the number of birds wounded at a pigeon-match, and turn to read "what is going on in society;" of the last new opera or play; of the cottages taken for the season at Newport or Long Branch; of the millionaire's divorce or the latest great defalcation; how Heber Newton is to be driven out of the Episcopal Church for declaring the Song of Solomon a love-drama, and the story of Jonah and the whale a poetical embellishment; or how the great issue which the American people are to convulse them-selves about next year is the turning of the Republican party out of power.

I read the other day in a Brooklyn paper of a coroner's jury summoned to inquire, as the law directs, into the cause of death of a two days' infant. The unwholesome room was destitute of everything save a broken chair, a miserable bed and an empty whisky-bottle. On the bed lay, uncared for, a young girl, mother of the dead infant; over the chair, in drunken stupor, sprawled a man—her father. "The horror-stricken jury," said the report "rendered a verdict in accordance with the facts, and left the place as fast as they could." So do we turn from these horrors. Are there not policemen and station-houses, almshouses and charitable societies?

Nevertheless, we send missionaries to the heathen; and I read the other day how the missionaries, sent to preach to the Hindus the Baptist version of Christ's gospel, had been financed out of the difference between American currency and Indian rupees by the godly men who stay at home and boss the job. Yet, from Arctic to Antarctic Circle, where are the heathen among whom such degraded and distorted human beings are to be found as in our centers of so-called Christian civilization, where we have such a respect for the all-seeing eye of God that if you want a drink on Sunday you must go into the saloon by the back door? Among what tribe of savages, who never saw a missionary, can the cold-blooded horrors testified to in the Tewksbury Almshouse investigation be matched? "Babies don't generally live long here," they told the farmer's wife who brought them a little waif. And neither did they—seventy-three out of seventy-four dying in a few weeks, their little bodies sold off at a round rate per dozen to the dissecting-table, and a six months' infant left there two days losing three pounds in weight. Nor did adults—the broken men and women who there sought shelter—fare better. They were robbed, starved, beaten, turned into marketable corpses as fast as possible, while the highly respectable managers waxed fat and rich, and set before legislative committees the best of dinners and the choicest of wines. It were slander to dumb brutes to speak of the bestial cruelty disclosed by the opening of this whited sepulcher. Yet, not only do the representatives of the wealth and culture and "high moral ideas" of Massachusetts receive coldly these revelations, they fight bitterly the man who has made them, as though the dragging of such horrors to light, not the doing of them, were the unpardonable sin. They were only paupers! And I read in the journal founded by Horace Greeley, that "the woes of the Tewksbury paupers are no worse than the common lot of all inmates of pauper refuges the country over."

Or take the revelations made this winter before a legislative committee of the barbarities practised in New York state prisons. The system remains unaltered; not an official has been even dismissed. The belief that dominates our society is evidently that which I find expressed in "a journal of civilization" by a reverend professor at Yale, that "the criminal has no claims against society at all. What shall be done with him is a question of expediency"! I wonder if our missionaries to the heathen ever read the American papers? I am certain they don't read them to the heathen.

Behind all this is social disease. Criminals, paupers, prostitutes, women who abandon their children, men who kill themselves in despair of making a living, the existence of great armies of beggars and thieves, prove that there are large classes who find it difficult with the hardest toil to make an honest and sufficient livelihood. So it is. "There is," incidentally said to me, recently, a New York Supreme Judge, "a large class—I was about to say a majority—of the population of New York and Brooklyn, who just live, and to whom the rearing of two more children means inevitably a boy for the penitentiary and a girl for the brothel." A partial report of charitable work in New York city, not embracing the operations of a number of important societies, shows 36,000 families obtaining relief, while it is estimated that were the houses in New York city containing criminals and the recipients of charity set side by side they would make a street twenty-two miles long. One charitable society in New

York city extended aid this winter to the families of three hundred tailors. Their wages are so small when they do work that when work gives out they must beg, steal or starve.

Nor is this state of things confined to the metropolis. In Massachusetts the statistician of the Labor Bureau declares that among wage laborers the earnings (exclusive of the earnings of minors) are less than the cost of living ; that in the majority of cases working-men do not support their families on their individual earnings alone, and that fathers are forced to depend upon their children for from one-quarter to one-third of the family earnings, children under fifteen supplying from one-eighth to one-sixth of the total earnings. Miss Emma E. Brown has shown how parents are forced to evade the law prohibiting the employ- ment of young children, and in Pennsylvania, where a similar law has been passed, I read how, forced by the same necessity, the operatives of a mill have resolved to boycott a storekeeper whose relative had informed that children under thirteen were employed. While in Canada last winter it was shown that children under thirteen were kept at work in the mills from six in the evening to six in the morning, a man on duty with a strap to keep them awake.

Illinois is one of the richest States of the Union. It is scarcely yet fairly settled, for the last census shows the male population in excess of the female, and wages are considerably higher than in more eastern States. In their last report the Illinois Commissioners of Labor Statistics say that their tables of wages and cost of living are repre- sentative only of intelligent working-men who make the most of their advantages, and do not reach " the confines of that world of helpless ignorance and destitution in which multitudes in all large cities continually live, and whose only statistics are those of epidemics, pauperism and

crime." Nevertheless, they go on to say, an examination
of these tables will demonstrate that one-half of these
intelligent working-men of Illinois "are not even able to
earn enough for their daily bread, and have to depend
upon the labor of women and children to eke out their
miserable existence."

It is the fool who saith in his heart there is no God.
But what shall we call the man who tells us that with this
sort of a world God bids us be content?

CHAPTER VIII.

THAT WE ALL MIGHT BE RICH.

THE terms rich and poor are of course frequently used in a relative sense. Among Irish peasants, kept on the verge of starvation by the tribute wrung from them to maintain the luxury of absentee landlords in London or Paris, "the woman of three cows" will be looked on as rich, while in the society of millionaires a man with only $500,000 will be regarded as poor. Now, we cannot, of course, all be rich in the sense of having more than others; but when people say, as they so often do, that we cannot all be rich, or when they say that we must always have the poor with us, they do not use the words in this comparative sense. They mean by the rich those who have enough, or more than enough, wealth to gratify al reasonable wants, and by the poor those who have not.

Now, using the words in this sense, I join issue with those who say that we cannot all be rich; with those who declare that in human society the poor must always exist. I do not, of course, mean that we all might have an array of servants; that we all might outshine each other in dress, in equipage, in the lavishness of our balls or dinners, in the magnificence of our houses. That would be a contradiction in terms. What I mean is, that we all might have leisure, comfort and abundance, not merely of the necessaries, but even of what are now esteemed the elegancies and luxuries of life. I do not mean to say that absolute equality could be had, or would be desirable. I do not mean to say that we could all have, or would want, the same quantity of all the different forms of wealth. But I do mean to say that we might all have enough wealth to satisfy reasonable desires; that we might all have so much of the material things we now struggle for, that no one would want to rob or swindle his neighbor; that no one would worry all day, or lie awake at nights, fearing he might be brought to poverty, or thinking how he might acquire wealth.

Does this seem an utopian dream? What would people of fifty years ago have thought of one who would have told them that it was possible to sew by steam-power; to cross the Atlantic in six days, or the continent in three; to have a message sent from London at noon delivered in Boston three hours before noon; to hear in New York the voice of a man talking in Chicago?

Did you ever see a pail of swill given to a pen of hungry hogs? That is human society as it is.

Did you ever see a company of well-bred men and women sitting down to a good dinner, without scrambling, or jostling, or gluttony, each, knowing that his own appetite will be satisfied, deferring to and helping the others? That is human society as it might be.

"Devil catch the hindmost" is the motto of our so-called civilized society to-day. We learn early to "take care of No. 1," lest No. 1 should suffer; we learn early to grasp from others that we may not want ourselves. The fear of poverty makes us admire great wealth; and so habits of greed are formed, and we behold the pitiable spectacle of men who have already more than they can by any possibility use, toiling, striving, grasping to add to their store up to the very verge of the grave—that grave which, whatever else it may mean, does certainly mean the parting with all earthly possessions however great they be.

In vain, in gorgeous churches, on the appointed Sunday, is the parable of Dives and Lazarus read. What can it mean in churches where Dives would be welcomed and Lazarus shown the door? In vain may the preacher preach of the vanity of riches, while poverty engulfs the hindmost. But the mad struggle would cease when the fear of poverty had vanished. Then, and not till then, will a truly Christian civilization become possible.

And may not this be?

We are so accustomed to poverty that even in the most advanced countries we regard it as the natural lot of the great masses of the people; that we take it as a matter of course that even in our highest civilization large classes should want the necessaries of healthful life, and the vast majority should only get a poor and pinched living by the hardest toil. There are professors of political economy who teach that this condition of things is the result of social laws of which it is idle to complain! There are ministers of religion who preach that this is the condition which an all-wise, all-powerful Creator intended for his children! If an architect were to build a theater so that not more than one-tenth of the audience could see and hear, we would call him a bungler and a botch. If a man were to give a feast and provide so little food that nine-tenths of his guests must go away hungry, we would call him a fool, or worse. Yet so accustomed are we to poverty, that even the preachers of what passes for Christianity tell us that the great Architect of the Universe, to whose infinite skill all nature testifies, has made such a botch job of this world that the vast majority of the human creatures whom he has called into it are condemned by the conditions he has imposed to want, suffering, and brutalizing toil that gives no opportunity for the development of mental powers—must pass their lives in a hard struggle to merely live!

Yet who can look about him without seeing that to whatever cause poverty may be due, it is not due to the niggardliness of nature ; without seeing that it is blindness or blasphemy to assume that the Creator has condemned the masses of men to hard toil for a bare living ?

If some men have not enough to live decently, do not others have far more than they really need ? If there is not wealth sufficient to go around, giving every one abundance, is it because we have reached the limit of the production of wealth ? Is our land all in use ? is our labor all employed ? is our capital all utilized ? On the contrary, in whatever direction we look we see the most stupendous waste of productive forces—of productive forces so potent that were they permitted to play freely the production of wealth would be so enormous that there would be more than a sufficiency for all. What branch of production is there in which the limit of production has been reached ? What single article of wealth is there of which we might not produce enormously more ?

If the mass of the population of New York are jammed into the fever-breeding rooms of tenement-houses, it is not because there are not vacant lots enough in and around New York to give each family space for a separate home. If settlers are going into Montana and Dakota and Manitoba, it is not because there are not vast areas of untilled land much nearer the centers of population. If farmers are paying one-fourth, one-third, or even one-half their crops for the privilege of getting land to cultivate, it is not because there are not, even in our oldest States, great quantities of land which no one is cultivating.

So true is it that poverty does not come from the inability to produce more wealth that from every side we hear that the power to produce is in excess of the ability to find a market ; that the constant fear seems to be not that too little, but that too much, will be produced ! Do we not maintain a high tariff, and keep at every port a horde of Custom-House officers, for fear the people of other countries will overwhelm us with their goods? Is not a great part of our machinery constantly idle? Are there not, even in what we call good times, an immense number of unemployed men who would gladly be at work producing wealth if they could only get the opportunity? Do we not, even now, hear, from every side, of embarrassment from the very excess of productive power, and of combinations to reduce production? Coal operators band together to limit their output; iron-works have shut down, or are running on half-time; distillers have agreed to limit their production to one-half their capacity, and sugar-refiners to sixty per cent.; paper-mills are suspending for one, two or three days a week; the gunny-cloth manufacturers, at a recent meeting, agreed to close their mills until the present overstock on the market is greatly reduced; many other manufacturers have done the same thing. The shoemaking machinery of New England can, in six months' full running, it is said, supply the whole demand of the United States for twelve months; the machinery for making rubber goods can turn out twice as much as the market will take.

This seeming glut of production, this seeming excess of productive power, runs through all branches of industry, and is evident all over the civilized world. From black-berries, bananas or apples, to ocean steamships or plate-glass mirrors, there is scarcely an article of human comfort or convenience that could not be produced in very much greater quantities than now without lessening the production of anything else.

So evident is this that many people think and talk and write as though the trouble is that there is not *work* enough to go around. We are in constant fear that other nations may do for us some of the work we might do for ourselves, and, to prevent them, guard ourselves with a tariff. We laud as public benefactors those who, as we say, "furnish employment." We are constantly talking as though this "furnishing of employment," this "giving of work," were the greatest boon that could be conferred upon society. To listen to much that is talked and much that is written, one would think that the cause of poverty is that there is not work enough for so many people, and that if the Creator had made the rock harder, the soil less fertile, iron as scarce as gold, and gold as diamonds; or if ships would sink and cities burn down oftener, there would be less poverty, because there would be more work to do.

The Lord Mayor of London tells a deputation of unemployed working-men that there is no demand for their labor, and that the only resource for them is to go to the poorhouse or emigrate. The English government is shipping from Ireland able-bodied men and women to avoid maintaining them as paupers. Even in our own land there are at all times large numbers, and in hard times vast numbers, earnestly seeking work—the opportunity to give labor for the things produced by labor.

Perhaps nothing shows more clearly the enormous forces of production constantly going to waste than the fact that the most prosperous time in all branches of business that this country has known was during the civil war, when we were maintaining great fleets and armies, and millions of our industrial population were engaged in supplying them with wealth for unproductive consumption, or for reckless destruction. It is idle to talk about the fictitious prosperity of those "flush" times. The masses of the people lived better, dressed better, found it easier to get a living, and had more luxuries and amusements than in normal times. There was more real, tangible wealth in the North at the close than at the beginning of the war. Nor was it the great issue of paper money, nor the creation of the debt, which caused this prosperity. The government presses struck off promises to pay; they could not print ships, cannon, arms, tools, food and clothing. Nor did we borrow these things from other countries or "from posterity." Our bonds did not begin to go to Europe until the close of the war, and the people of one generation can no more borrow from the people of a subsequent generation than we who live on this planet can borrow from the inhabitants of another planet or another solar system. The wealth consumed and destroyed by our fleets and armies came from the then existing stock of wealth. We could have carried on the war without the issue of a single bond, if, when we did not shrink from taking from wife and children their only bread-winner, we had not shrunk from taking the wealth of the rich.

Our armies and fleets were maintained, the enormous unproductive and destructive use of wealth was kept up, by the labor and capital then and there engaged in production. And it was that the demand caused by the war stimulated productive forces into activity that the enormous drain of the war was not only supplied, but that the North grew richer. The waste of labor in marching and countermarching, in digging trenches, throwing up earthworks, and fighting battles, the waste of wealth consumed or destroyed by our armies and fleets, did not amount to as much as the waste constantly going on from unemployed labor and idle or partially used machinery.

It is evident that this enormous waste of productive power is due, not to defects in the laws of nature, but to social maladjustments which deny to labor access to the natural opportunities of labor and rob the laborer of his just reward. Evidently the glut of markets does not really come from over-production when there are so many who want the things which are said to be over-produced, and would gladly exchange their labor for them did they have opportunity. Every day passed in enforced idleness by a laborer who would gladly be at work could he find opportunity, means so much less in the fund which creates the effective demand for other labor; every time wages are screwed down means so much reduction in the purchasing power of the workmen whose incomes are thus reduced. The paralysis which at all times wastes productive power, and which in times of industrial depression causes more loss than a great war, springs from the difficulty which those who would gladly satisfy their wants by their labor find in doing so. It cannot come from any natural limitation, so long as human desires remain unsatisfied, and nature yet offers to man the raw material of wealth. It must come from social maladjustments which permit the monopolization of these natural opportunities, and which rob labor of its fair reward.

What these maladjustments are I shall in subsequent chapters endeavor to show. In this I wish simply to call attention to the fact that productive power in such a state of civilization as ours is sufficient, did we give it play, to so enormously increase the production of wealth as to give abundance to all—to point out that the cause of poverty is not in natural limitations, which we cannot alter, but in inequalities and injustices of distribution entirely within our control.

The passenger who leaves New York on a trans-Atlantic steamer does not fear that the provisions will give out. The men who run these steamers do not send them to sea without provisions enough for all they carry. Did He who made this whirling planet for our sojourn lack the forethought of man? Not so. In soil and sunshine, in vegetable and animal life, in veins of minerals, and in pulsing forces which we are only beginning to use, are capabilities which we cannot exhaust—materials and powers from which human effort, guided by intelligence, may gratify every material want of every human creature. There is in nature no reason for poverty—not even for the poverty of the crippled or the decrepit. For man is by nature a social animal, and the family affections and the social sympathies would, where chronic poverty did not distort and embrute, amply provide for those who could not provide for themselves.

But if we will not use the intelligence with which we have been gifted to adapt social organization to natural laws—if we allow dogs in the manger to monopolize what they cannot use; if we allow strength and cunning to rob honest labor, we must have chronic poverty, and all the social evils it inevitably brings. Under such conditions there would be poverty in paradise.

"The poor ye have always with you." If ever a scripture has been wrested to the devil's service, this is that scripture. How often have these words been distorted from their obvious meaning to soothe conscience into acquiescence in human misery and degradation—to bolster that blasphemy, the very negation and denial of Christ's teachings, that the All-Wise and Most Merciful, the Infinite Father, has decreed that so many of his creatures must be poor in order that others of his creatures to whom he wills the good things of life should enjoy the pleasure and virtue of doling out alms! "The poor ye have always with you," said Christ; but all his teachings supply the limitation, "until the coming of the Kingdom." In that kingdom of God *on earth*, that kingdom of justice and love for which he taught his followers to strive and pray, there will be no poor. But though the faith and the hope and the striving for this kingdom are of the very essence of Christ's teaching, the stanchest disbelievers and revilers of its possibility are found among those who call themselves Christians. Queer ideas of the Divinity have some of these

Christians who hold themselves orthodox and contribute to the conversion of the heathen. A very rich orthodox Christian said to a newspaper reporter, awhile ago, on the completion of a large work out of which he is said to have made millions: "We have been peculiarly favored by Divine Providence; iron never was so cheap before, and labor has been a drug in the market."

That in spite of all our great advances we have yet with us the poor, those who, without fault of their own, cannot get healthful and wholesome conditions of life, is *our* fault and *our* shame. Who that looks about him can fail to see that it is only the injustice that denies natural opportunities to labor, and robs the producer of the fruits of his toil, that prevents us all from being rich? Consider the enormous powers of production now going to waste; consider the great number of unproductive consumers maintained at the expense of producers—the rich men and dudes, the worse than useless government officials, the pickpockets, burglars and confidence men; the highly respectable thieves who carry on their operations inside the law; the great army of lawyers; the beggars and paupers, and inmates of prisons; the monopolists and cornerers and gamblers of every kind and grade. Consider how much brains and energy and capital are devoted, not to the production of wealth, but to the grabbing of wealth. Consider the waste caused by competition which does not increase wealth; by laws which restrict production and exchange. Consider how human power is lessened by insufficient food, by unwholesome lodgings, by work done under conditions that produce disease and shorten life. Consider how intemperance and unthrift follow poverty. Consider how the ignorance bred of poverty lessens production, and how the vice bred of poverty causes destruction, and who can doubt that under conditions of social justice all might be rich?

The wealth-producing powers that would be evoked in
a social state based on justice, where wealth went to the
producers of wealth, and the banishment of poverty had
banished the fear and greed and lusts that spring from it,
we now can only faintly imagine. Wonderful as have
been the discoveries and inventions of this century, it is
evident that we have only begun to grasp that dominion
which it is given to mind to obtain over matter. Discovery and invention are born of leisure, of material
comfort, of freedom. These secured to all, and who shall
say to what command over nature man may not attain?

It is not necessary that any one should be condemned
to monotonous toil; it is not necessary that any one
should lack the wealth and the leisure which permit the
development of the faculties that raise man above the
animal. Mind, not muscle, is the motor of progress, the
force which compels nature and produces wealth. In
turning men into machines we are wasting the highest
powers. Already in our society there is a favored class
who need take no thought for the morrow—what they
shall eat, or what they shall drink, or wherewithal they
shall be clothed. And may it not be that Christ was more
than a dreamer when he told his disciples that in that
kingdom of justice for which he taught them to work and
pray this might be the condition of all?

CHAPTER IX.

FIRST PRINCIPLES.

WHOEVER considers the political and social problems that confront us, must see that they center in the problem of the distribution of wealth, and he must also see that, though their solution may be simple, it must be radical.

For every social wrong there must be a remedy. But the remedy can be nothing less than the abolition of the wrong. Half-way measures, mere ameliorations and secondary reforms, can at any time accomplish little, and can in the long run avail nothing. Our charities, our penal laws, our restrictions and prohibitions, by which, with so little avail, we endeavor to assuage poverty and check crime, what are they, at the very best, but the device of the clown who, having put the whole burden of his ass into one pannier, sought to enable the poor animal to walk straight by loading up the other pannier with stones?

In New York, as I write, the newspapers and the churches are calling for subscriptions to their "fresh-air funds," that little children may be taken for a day or for a week from the deadly heat of stifling tenement rooms and given a breath of the fresh breeze of sea-shore or mountain; but how little does it avail, when we take such children only to return them to their previous conditions —conditions which to many mean even worse than death of the body; conditions which make it certain that of the lives that may thus be saved, some are saved for the brothel and the almshouse, and some for the penitentiary We may go on forever merely raising fresh-air funds, and how great soever be the funds we raise, the need will only grow, and children—just such children as those of whom Christ said, "Take heed that ye despise not one of these little ones; for I say unto you, that in heaven their angels do always behold the face of my Father"—will die like flies, so long as poverty compels fathers and mothers to the life of the squalid tenement room.   We may open "midnight missions" and support "Christian homes for destitute young girls," but what will they avail in the face of general conditions which render so many men unable to support a wife; which make young girls think it a privilege to be permitted to earn three dollars by eighty-one hours' work, and which can drive a mother to such despair that she will throw her babies from a wharf of our Christian city and then leap into the river herself!   How vainly shall we endeavor to repress crime by our barbarous punishment of the poorer class of criminals so long as children are reared in the brutalizing influences of poverty, so long as the bite of want drives men to crime!   How little better than idle is it for us to prohibit infant labor in factories when the scale of wages is so low that it will not enable fathers to support their families without the earnings of their little children!   How shall we try to prevent political corruption by framing new checks and setting one official to watch another official, when the fear of want stimulates the lust for wealth, and the rich thief is honored while honest poverty is despised?

Nor yet could we accomplish any permanent equalization in the distribution of wealth were we forcibly to take from those who have and give to those who have not.   We would do great injustice; we would work great harm; but, from the very moment of such a forced equalization. the tendencies which show themselves in the present unjust inequalities would begin to assert themselves again, and we would in a little while have as gross inequalities as before.

What we must do if we would cure social disease and avert social danger is to remove the causes which prevent the just distribution of wealth.

This work is only one of removal. It is not necessary for us to frame elaborate and skilful plans for securing the just distribution of wealth. For the just distribution of wealth is manifestly the natural distribution of wealth, and injustice in the distribution of wealth must, therefore, result from artificial obstructions to this natural distribution.

As to what is the just distribution of wealth there can be no dispute. It is that which gives wealth to him who makes it, and secures wealth to him who saves it. So clearly is this the only just distribution of wealth that even those shallow writers who attempt to defend the existing order of things are driven, by a logical necessity, falsely to assume that those who now possess the larger share of wealth made it and saved it, or got it by gift or by inheritance, from those who did make it and save it; whereas the fact is, as I have in a previous chapter shown, that all these great fortunes, whose corollaries are paupers and tramps, really come from the sheer appropriation of the makings and savings of other people.

And that this just distribution of wealth is the natural distribution of wealth can be plainly seen. Nature gives wealth to labor, and to nothing but labor. There is, and there can be, no article of wealth but such as labor has got by making it, or searching for it, out of the raw material which the Creator has given us to draw from. If there were but one man in the world it is manifest that he could have no more wealth than he was able to make and to save. This is the natural order. And, no matter how great be the population, or how elaborate the society, no one can have more wealth than he produces and saves, unless he gets it as a free gift from some one else, or by appropriating the earnings of some one else.

An English writer has divided all men into three classes —workers, beggars and thieves. The classification is not complimentary to the "upper classes" and the "better classes," as they are accustomed to esteem themselves, yet it is economically true. There are only three ways by which any individual can get wealth—by work, by gift or by theft. And, clearly, the reason why the workers get so little is that the beggars and thieves get so much. When a man gets wealth that he does not produce, he necessarily gets it at the expense of those who produce it.

All we need do to secure a just distribution of wealth, is to do that which all theories agree to be the primary function of government—to secure to each the free use of his own powers, limited only by the equal freedom of all others; to secure to each the full enjoyment of his own earnings, limited only by such contributions as he may be fairly called upon to make for purposes of common benefit. When we have done this we shall have done all that we can do to make social institutions conform to the sense of justice and to the natural order.

I wish to emphasize this point, for there are those who constantly talk and write as though whoever finds fault with the present distribution of wealth were demanding that the rich should be spoiled for the benefit of the poor; that the idle should be taken care of at the expense of the industrious, and that a false and impossible equality should be created, which, by reducing every one to the same dead level, would destroy all incentive to excel and bring progress to a halt.

In the reaction from the glaring injustice of present social conditions, such wild schemes have been proposed, and still find advocates. But to my way of thinking they are as impracticable and repugnant as they can seem to those who are loudest in their denunciations of "communism." I am not willing to say that in the progress of humanity a state of society may not be possible which shall realize the formula of Louis Blanc, "From each according to his abilities; to each according to his wants," for there exist to-day in the religious Orders of the Catholic Church, associations which maintain the communism of early Christianity. But it seems to me that the only power by which such a state of society can be attained and preserved is that which the framers of the schemes I speak of generally ignore, even when they do not directly antagonize—a deep, definite, intense, religious faith, so clear, so burning as utterly to melt away the thought of self—a general moral condition such as that which the Methodists declare, under the name of "sanctification," to be individually possible, in which the dream of pristine innocence should become reality, and man, so to speak, should again walk with God.

But the possibility of such a state of society seems to me in the present stage of human development a speculation which comes within the higher domain of religious faith rather than that with which the economist or prac· tical statesman can concern himself. That nature, as it is apparent to us here, in this infinitesimal point in space and time that we call the world, is the highest expression of the power and purpose that called the universe into being, what thoughtful man dare affirm? Yet it is manifest that the only way by which man may attain higher things is by conforming his conduct to those commandments which are as obvious in his relations with his fellows and with external nature as though they were graved by the finger of Omnipotence upon tablets of imperishable stone. In the order of moral development.

Moses comes before Christ—"Thou shalt not kill;"
"Thou shalt not commit adultery;" "Thou shalt not
steal;" before "Thou shalt love thy neighbor as thyself."
The command, "Thou shalt not muzzle the ox that treadeth
out the corn," precedes the entrancing vision of universal
peace, in which even nature's rapine shall cease, when the
lion shall lie down with the lamb, and a little child shall
lead them.

That justice is the highest quality in the moral hierarchy I do not say; but that it is the first. That which is
above justice must be based on justice, and include justice,
and be reached through justice. It is not by accident
that, in the Hebraic religious development which through
Christianity we have inherited, the declaration, "The Lord
thy God is a just God," precedes the sweeter revelation of
a God of Love. Until the eternal justice is perceived, the
eternal love must be hidden. As the individual must be
just before he can be truly generous, so must human
society be based upon justice before it can be based on
benevolence.

This, and this alone, is what I contend for—that our
social institutions be conformed to justice; to those
natural and eternal principles of right that are so obvious
that no one can deny or dispute them—so obvious that
by a law of the human mind even those who try to defend
social injustice must invoke them. This, and this alone,
I contend for—that he who makes should have; that he
who saves should enjoy. I ask in behalf of the poor
nothing whatever that properly belongs to the rich.
Instead of weakening and confusing the idea of property,
I would surround it with stronger sanctions. Instead of
lessening the incentive to the production of wealth, I
would make it more powerful by making the reward more
certain. Whatever any man has added to the general
stock of wealth, or has received of the free will of him who

did produce it, let that be his as against all the world—
his to use or to give, to do with it whatever he may please,
so long as such use does not interfere with the equal
freedom of others.   For my part, I would put no limit on
acquisition.   No matter how many millions any man can
get by methods which do not involve the robbery of others
—they are his: let him have them.   I would not even ask
him for charity, or have it dinned into his ears that it is
his duty to help the poor.   That is his own affair.   Let
him do as he pleases with his own, without restriction and
without suggestion.   If he gets without taking from others,
and uses without hurting others, what he does with his
wealth is his own business and his own responsibility.

I reverence the spirit that, in such cities as London and
New York, organizes such great charities and gives to
them such magnificent endowments, but that there is need
for such charities proves to me that it is a slander upon
Christ to call such cities Christian cities.   I honor the
Astors for having provided for New York the Astor
Library, and Peter Cooper for having given it the Cooper
Institute; but it is a shame and a disgrace to the people
of New York that such things should be left to private
beneficence.   And he who struggles for that recognition
of justice which, by securing to each his own, will make
it needless to beg for alms from one for another, is doing
a greater and a higher work than he who builds churches,
or endows hospitals, or founds colleges and libraries.
This justice, which would first secure to each his own
earnings, is, it seems to me, of that higher than almsgiving,
which the Apostle had in mind, when he said, " *Though I
bestow all my goods to feed the poor, and though I give my body
to be burned, and have not charity, it profiteth me nothing.*"

Let us first ask what are the natural rights of men, and
endeavor to secure them, before we propose either to beg
or to pillage.

In what succeeds I shall consider what are the natural rights of men, and how, under present social adjustments, they are ignored and denied. This is made necessary by the nature of this inquiry. But I do not wish to call upon those my voice may reach to demand their own rights, so much as to call upon them to secure the rights of others more helpless. I believe that the idea of duty is more potent for social improvement than the idea of interest; that in sympathy is a stronger social force than in selfishness. I believe that any great social improvement must spring from, and be animated by, that spirit which seeks to make life better, nobler, happier for others, rather than by that spirit which only seeks more enjoyment for itself. For the Mammon of Injustice can always buy the selfish whenever it may think it worth while to pay enough; but unselfishness it cannot buy.

In the idea of the incarnation—of the God voluntarily descending to the help of men, which is embodied not merely in Christianity, but in other great religions—lies, I sometimes think, a deeper truth than perhaps even the churches teach. This is certain, that the deliverers, the liberators, the advancers of humanity, have always been those who were moved by the sight of injustice and misery rather than those spurred by their own suffering. As it was a Moses, learned in all the lore of the Egyptians, and free to the Court of Pharaoh, and not a tasked slave, forced to make bricks without straw, who led the Children of Israel from the House of Bondage; as it was the Gracchi, of patrician blood and fortune, who struggled to the death against the land-grabbing system which finally destroyed Rome, as it must, should it go on, in time destroy this republic, so has it always been that the oppressed, the degraded, the downtrodden have been freed and elevated rather by the efforts and the sacrifices of those to whom fortune had been more kind than by their own strength

For the more fully men have been deprived of their natural rights, the less their power to regain them. The more men need help, the less can they help themselves.

The sentiment to which I would appeal is not envy, nor yet self-interest, but that nobler sentiment which found strong, though rude, expression in that battle-hymn which rang through the land when a great wrong was going down in blood:

In the beauty of the lilies, Christ was born across the sea,
With a glory in his bosom to transfigure you and me;
As he died to make men holy, let us die to make men free! *

And what is there for which life gives us opportunity that can be compared with the effort to do what we may, be it ever so little, to improve social conditions and enable other lives to reach fuller, nobler development? Old John Brown, dying the death of the felon, launched into eternity with pinioned arms and the kiss of the slave child on his lips—was not his a greater life and a grander death than though his years had been given to self-seeking? Did he not take with him more than the man who grabs for wealth and *leaves* his millions? Envy the rich! Who that realizes that he must some day wake up in the beyond can envy those who spend their strength to gather what they cannot use here and cannot take away? The only thing certain to any of us is death. "Like the swallow darting through thy hall, such, O King, is the life of man!" We come from where we know not; we go—who shall say? Impenetrable darkness behind, and gathering shades before. What, when our time comes, does it matter whether we have fared daintily or not, whether we have worn soft raiment or not, whether we leave a great fortune or nothing at all, whether we shall have reaped honors or been

---

* "Battle-Hymn of the Republic," by Julia Ward Howe.

despised, have been counted learned or ignorant—as compared with how we may have used that talent which has been intrusted to us for the Master's service? What shall it matter, when eyeballs glaze and ears grow dull, if out of the darkness may stretch a hand, and into the silence may come a voice:

" *Well done, thou good and faithful servant: thou hast been faithful over a few things, I will make thee ruler over many things: enter thou into the joy of thy Lord!*"

I shall speak of rights, I shall speak of utility, I shall speak of interest; I shall meet on their chosen ground those who say that the largest production of wealth is the greatest good, and material progress the highest aim. Nevertheless, I appreciate the truth embodied in these words of Mazzini to the working-classes of Italy, and would echo them:

Working-men, brothers! When Christ came and changed the face of the world, he spoke not of rights to the rich, who needed not to achieve them; nor to the poor, who would doubtless have abused them, in imitation of the rich; he spoke not of utility, nor of interest, to a people whom interest and utility had corrupted; he spoke of duty, he spoke of love, of sacrifice and of faith; and he said that they should be first among all who had contributed most by their labor to the good of all.

And the word of Christ breathed in the ear of a society in which all true life was extinct, recalled it to existence, conquered the millions, conquered the world, and caused the education of the human race to ascend one degree on the scale of progress.

Working-men! We live in an epoch similar to that of Christ. We live in the midst of a society as corrupt as that of the Roman Empire, feeling in our inmost souls the need of reanimating and transforming it, and of uniting all its various members in one sole faith, beneath one sole law, in one sole aim—the free and progressive development of all the faculties of which God has given the germ to his creatures. We seek the kingdom of God *on earth as it is in heaven*, or, rather, that earth may become a preparation for heaven, and society an endeavor after the progressive realization of the divine idea.

But Christ's every act was the visible representation of the faith ʌe preached ; and around him stood apostles who incarnated in their actions the faith they had accepted. Be you such and you will conquer. Preach duty to the classes about you, and fulfil, as far as in you lies, your own. Preach virtue, sacrifice and love ; and be yourselves virtuous, loving and ready for self-sacrifice. Speak your thoughts boldly, and make known your wants courageously ; but without anger, without reaction, and without threats. The strongest menace, if indeed there be those for whom threats are necessary, will be the firmness, not the irritation, of your speech.

CHAPTER X.

THERE are those who, when it suits their purpose, say that there are no natural rights, but that all rights spring from the grant of the sovereign political power. It were waste of time to argue with such persons. There are some facts so obvious as to be beyond the necessity of argument. And one of these facts, attested by universal consciousness, is that there are rights as between man and man which existed before the formation of government, and which continue to exist in spite of the abuse of government; that there is a higher law than any human law—to wit, the law of the Creator, impressed upon and revealed through nature, which is before and above human laws, and upon conformity to which all human laws must depend for their validity. To deny this is to assert that there is no standard whatever by which the rightfulness or wrongfulness of laws and institutions can be measured; to assert that there can be no actions in themselves right and none in themselves wrong; to assert that an edict which commanded mothers to kill their children should receive the same respect as a law prohibiting infanticide.

These natural rights, this higher law, form the only true and sure basis for social organization. Just as, if we would construct a successful machine, we must conform to physical laws, such as the law of gravitation, the law of combustion, the law of expansion, etc.; just as, if we would maintain bodily health, we must conform to the laws of physiology; so, if we would have a peaceful and healthful social state, we must conform our institutions to the great moral laws—laws to which we are absolutely subject, and which are as much above our control as are the laws of matter and of motion. And as, when we find that a machine will not work, we infer that in its construction some law of physics has been ignored or defied, so when we find social disease and political evils may we infer that in the organization of society moral law has been defied and the natural rights of man have been ignored.

These natural rights of man are thus set forth in the American Declaration of Independence as the basis upon which alone legitimate government can rest:

We hold these truths to be self-evident—that all men are created equal; that they are endowed by their Creator with certain unalienable rights; that among these are life, liberty, and the pursuit of happiness; that, to secure these rights, governments are instituted among men, deriving their just powers from the consent of the governed; that, whenever any form of government becomes destructive of these ends, it is the right of the people to alter or to abolish it, and to institute a new government, laying its foundations on such principles, and organizing its powers in such form, as shall seem to them most likely to effect their safety and happiness.

So does the preamble to the Constitution of the United States appeal to the same principles:

We, the people of the United States, in order to form a more perfect union, *establish justice*, insure domestic tranquillity, provide for the common defense, promote the general welfare, and *secure the blessings of liberty to ourselves and our posterity*, do ordain and establish this Constitution for the United States of America.

And so, too, is the same fundamental and self-evident truth set forth in that grand Declaration of the Rights of Man and of Citizens, issued by the National Assembly of France in 1789:

The representatives of the people of France, formed into a National Assembly, *considering that ignorance, neglect, or contempt of human rights are the sole causes of public misfortunes and corruptions of government,* have resolved to set forth, in a solemn declaration, those natural, imprescriptible and inalienable rights, [and do] recognize and declare, in the presence of the Supreme Being, and with the hope of His blessing and favor, the following *sacred* rights of men and of citizens :

I. Men are born and always continue free and equal in respect of their rights. Civil distinctions, therefore, can only be founded on public utility.

II. The end of all political associations is the preservation of the natural and imprescriptible rights of man, and these rights are liberty, property, security, and resistance of oppression.

It is one thing to assert the eternal principles, as they are asserted in times of upheaval, when men of convictions and of the courage of their convictions come to the front, and another thing for a people just emerging from the night of ignorance and superstition, and enslaved by habits of thought formed by injustice and oppression, to adhere to and carry them out. The French people have not been true to these principles, nor yet, with far greater advantages, have we. And so, though the ancient *régime*, with its blasphemy of "right divine," its Bastille and its *lettres-de-cachet*, has been abolished in France ; there have come red terror and white terror, Anarchy masquerading as Freedom, and Imperialism deriving its sanction from universal suffrage, culminating in such a poor thing as the French Republic of to-day. And here, with our virgin soil, with our exemption from foreign complications, and our freedom from powerful and hostile neighbors, all we can show is another poor thing of a Republic, with its rings and its bosses, its railroad kings controlling sovereign states, its gangrene of corruption eating steadily toward the political heart, its tramps and its strikes, its ostentation of ill-gotten wealth its children toiling in factories, and its women working out their lives for bread !

It is possible for men to see the truth, and assert the truth, and to hear and repeat, again and again, formulas embodying the truth, without realizing all that that truth involves. Men who signed the Declaration of Independence, or applauded the Declaration of Independence, men who year after year read it, and heard it, and honored it, did so without thinking that the eternal principles of right which it invoked condemned the existence of negro slavery as well as the tyranny of George III. And many who, awakening to the fuller truth, asserted the unalienable rights of man against chattel slavery, did not see that these rights involved far more than the denial of property in human flesh and blood; and as vainly imagined that they had fully asserted them when chattel slaves had been emancipated and given the suffrage, as their fathers vainly imagined they had fully asserted them, when they threw off allegiance to the English king and established here a democratic republic.

The common belief of Americans of to-day is that among us the equal and unalienable rights of man are now all acknowledged, while as for poverty, crime, low wages, "over-production," political corruption, and so on, they are to be referred to the nature of things—that is to say, if any one presses for a more definite answer, they exist because it is the will of God, the Creator, that they should exist. Yet I believe that these evils are demonstrably due to our failure fully to acknowledge the equal and unalienable rights with which, as asserted as a self-evident truth by the Declaration of Independence, all men have been endowed by God, their Creator. I believe the National Assembly of France were right when, a century ago, inspired by the same spirit that gave us political freedom, they declared that the great cause of public misfortunes and corruptions of government is ignorance, neglect or contempt of human rights. And just as the famine which

was then decimating France, the bankruptcy and corruption of her government, the brutish degradation of her
working-classes, and the demoralization of ner aristocracy,
were directly traceable to the denial of the equal, natural
and imprescriptible rights of men, so now the social and
political problems which menace the American Republic,
in common with the whole civilized world, spring from the
same cause.

Let us consider the matter. The equal, natural and
unalienable right to life, liberty and the pursuit of happiness, does it not involve the right of each to the free use
of his powers in making a living for himself and his
family, limited only by the equal right of all others? Does
it not require that each shall be free to make, to save and
to enjoy what wealth he may, without interference with
the equal rights of others; that no one shall be compelled
to give forced labor to another, or to yield up his earnings
to another; that no one shall be permitted to extort from
another labor or earnings? All this goes without the say.
ing. Any recognition of the equal right to life and liberty
which would deny the right to property—the right of a
man to his labor and to the full fruits of his labor—
would be mockery.

But that is just what we do. Our so-called recognition
of the equal and natural rights of man is to large classes
of our people nothing but a mockery, and as social pressure increases, is becoming a more bitter mockery to larger
classes, because our institutions fail to secure the rights
of men to their labor and the fruits of their labor.

That this denial of a primary human right is the cause
of poverty on the one side and of overgrown fortunes on
the other, and of all the waste and demoralization and
corruption that flow from the grossly unequal distribution
of wealth, may be easily seen.

As I am speaking of conditions general over the whole
civilized world, let us first take the case of another coun-

try, for we can sometimes see the faults of our neighbors more clearly than our own. England, the country from which we derive our language and institutions, is behind us in the formal recognition of political liberty; but there is as much industrial liberty there as here—and in some respects more, for England, though she has not yet reached free trade, has got rid of the "protective" swindle, which we still hug. And the English people—poor things—are, as a whole, satisfied with their freedom, and boast of it. They think, for it has been so long preached to them that most of them honestly believe it, that Englishmen are the freest people in the world, and they sing "Britons never shall be slaves," as though it were indeed true that slaves could not breathe British air.

Let us take a man of the masses of this people—a "free-born Englishman," coming of long generations of "free-born Englishmen," in Wiltshire or Devonshire or Somersetshire, on soil which, if you could trace his gene. alogy, you would find his fathers have been tilling from early Saxon times. He grows to manhood, we will not stop to inquire how, and, as is the natural order, he takes himself a wife. Here he stands, a man among his fellows, in a world in which the Creator has ordained that he should get a living by his labor. He has wants, and as, in the natural order, children come to him, he will have more; but he has in brain and muscle the natural power to satisfy these wants from the storehouse of nature. He knows how to dig and plow, to sow and to reap, and there is the rich soil, ready now, as it was thousands of years ago, to give back wealth to labor. The rain falls and the sun shines, and as the planet circles around her orbit, spring follows winter, and summer succeeds spring. It is this man's first and clearest right to earn his living, to trans. mute his labor into wealth, and to possess and enjoy that wealth for his own sustenance and benefit, and for the sustenance and benefit of those whom nature places in

dependence on him. He has no right to demand any one
else's earnings, nor has any one else a right to demand
any portion of his earnings. He has no right to compel
any one else to work for his benefit; nor have others a
right to demand that he shall work for their benefit. This
right to himself, to the use of his own powers and the
results of his own exertions, is a natural, self-evident right,
which, as a matter of principle, no one can dispute, save
upon the blasphemous contention that some men were
created to work for other men. And this primary, natural
right to his own labor, and to the fruits of his own labor,
accorded, this man can abundantly provide for his own
needs and for the needs of his family. His labor will, in
the natural order, produce wealth, which, exchanged in
accordance with mutual desires for wealth which others
have produced, will supply his family with all the material
comforts of life, and in the absence of serious accident,
enable him to bring up his children, and lay by such a
surplus that he and his wife may take their rest, and
enjoy their sunset hour in the declining years when strength
shall fail, without asking any one's alms or being beholden
to any bounty save that of " Our Father which art in
heaven."

But what is the fact ? The fact is, that the right of this
" free-born Englishman " to his own labor and the fruits
of his labor is denied as fully and completely as though
he were made by law a slave ; that he is compelled to work
for the enrichment of others as truly as though English
law had made him the property of an owner. The law of
the land does not declare that he is a slave : on the contrary, it formally declares that he is a free man—free to
work for himself, and free to enjoy the fruits of his labor.
But a man cannot labor without something to labor on,
any more than he can eat without having something to
eat. It is not in human powers to make something out

of nothing. This is not contemplated in the creative
scheme. Nature tells us that if we will not work we must
starve ; but at the same time supplies us with everything
necessary to work. Food, clothing, shelter, all the articles
that minister to desire and that we call wealth, can be
produced by labor, but only when the raw material of
which they must be composed is drawn from the land.

To drop a man in the middle of the Atlantic Ocean and
tell him he is at liberty to walk ashore, would not be more
bitter irony than to place a man where all the land is
appropriated as the property of other people and to tell
him that he is a free man, at liberty to work for himself
and to enjoy his own earnings. That is the situation in
which our Englishman finds himself. He is just as free
as he would be were he suspended over a precipice while
somebody else held a sharp knife to the rope ; just as free
as if thirsting in a desert he found the only spring for
miles walled and guarded by armed men who told him he
could not drink unless he *freely contracted* with them on
their terms. Had this Englishman lived generations ago,
in the time of his Saxon ancestors, he would, when he
became of age, and had taken a wife, have been allotted
his house-plot and his seed-plot ; he would have had an
equal share in the great fields which the villagers cultivated
together, he would have been free to gather his fagots or
take game in the common wood, or to graze his beasts on
the common pasturage. Even a few generations ago, after
the land-grabbing that began with the Tudors had gone
on for some centuries, he would have found in yet existing
commons some faint survival of the ancient principle that
this planet was intended for all men, not for some men.
But now he finds every foot of land inclosed against him.
The fields which his forefathers tilled, share and share
alike, are the private property of " my lord," who rents it
out to large farmers on terms so high that, to get ordinary

interest on their capital, they must grind the faces of their laborers; the ancient woodland is inclosed by a high wall, topped with broken glass, and is patroled by gamekeepers with loaded guns and the authority to take any intruder before the magistrate, who will send him to prison; the old-time common has become "my lord's" great park, on which *his* fat cattle graze, and *his* supple-limbed deer daintily browse. Even the old foot-paths that gave short cuts from road to road, through hazel thicket and by tinkling brook, are now walled in.

Yet this "free-born Englishman," this Briton who never shall be a slave, cannot live without land. He must find some bit of the earth's surface on which he and his wife can rest, which they may call "home." But, save the highroads, there is not as much of their native land as they may cover with the soles of their feet, that they can use without some other human creature's permission; and on the highroad they would not be suffered to lie down, still less to make them a bower of leaves. So, to get living space in his native land, our "free-born Englishman" must consent to work so many days in the month for one of the "owners" of England, or, what amounts to the same thing, he must sell his labor, or the fruits of his labor, to some third party and pay the "owner" of some particular part of the planet for the privilege of living on the planet. Having thus sacrificed a part of his labor to get permission from another fellow-creature to live, if he can, our "free-born Englishman" must next go to work to procure food, clothing, etc. But as he cannot get to work without land to work on, he is compelled, instead of going to work for himself, to sell his labor to those who have land, on such terms as they please, and those terms are only enough just to support life in the most miserable fashion—that is to say, all the produce of his labor is taken from him, and he is given back out of it just what the hardest owner would

be forced to give the slave—enough to support life on.
He lives in a miserable hovel, with its broken floor on the
bare ground, and an ill-kept thatch, through which the
rain comes. He works from morning to night, and his
wife must do the same; and their children, as soon almost
as they can walk, must also go to work, pulling weeds, or
scaring away crows, or doing such like jobs for the landowner, who graciously lets them live and work on his land.
Illness often comes, and death too often. Then there is
no recourse but the parish or "My Lady Bountiful," the
wife or daughter or almoner of "the God Almighty of the
countyside," as Tennyson calls him—the owner (if not
the maker) of the world in these parts—who doles out in
insulting and degrading charity some little stint of the
wealth appropriated from the labor of this family and of
other such families. If he does not "order himself lowly
and reverently to all his betters;" if he does not pull his
poor hat off his sheepish head whenever "my lord" or
"my lady," or "his honor," or any of their understrappers,
go by; if he does not bring up his children in the humility
which these people think proper and becoming in the
"lower classes;" if there is suspicion that he may have
helped himself to an apple or snared a hare, or slyly
hooked a fish from the stream, this "free-born Englishman" loses charity and loses work. He must go on the
parish or starve. He becomes bent and stiff before his
time. His wife is old and worn, when she ought to be in
her prime of strength and beauty. His girls—such as live
—marry such as he, to lead such lives as their mother's,
or, perhaps, are seduced by their "betters," and sent, with
a few pounds, to a great town, to die in a few years in
brothel, or hospital, or prison. His boys grow up ignorant
and brutish; they cannot support him when he grows old,
even if they would, for they do not get back enough of the
proceeds of their labor. The only refuge for the pair in

their old age is the almshouse, where, for shame to let them starve on the roadside, these worked-out slaves are kept to die,—where the man is separated from the wife, and the old couple, over whom the parson of the church, by law established, has said, "Whom God hath joined together let no man put asunder," lead, apart from each other, a prison-like existence until death comes to their relief.

In what is the condition of such a "free-born Englishman" as this, better than that of a slave? Yet if this is not a fair picture of the condition of the English agricultural laborers, it is only because I have not dwelt upon the darkest shades—the sodden ignorance and brutality, the low morality of these degraded and debased classes. In quantity and quality of food, in clothing and housing, in ease and recreation, and in morality, there can be no doubt that the average Southern slave was better off than the average agricultural laborer is in England to-day— that his life was healthier and happier and fuller. So long as a plump, well-kept, hearty negro was worth $1000, no slave-owner, selfish or cold-blooded as he might be, would keep his negroes as great classes of "free-born Englishmen" must live. But these white slaves have no money value. It is not the labor, it is the land that commands the labor, that has a capitalized value. You can get the labor of men for from nine to twelve shillings a week— less than it would cost to keep a slave in good marketable condition; and of children for sixpence a week, and when they are worked out they can be left to die or "go on the parish."

The negroes, some say, are an inferior race. But these white slaves of England are of the stock that has given England her scholars and her poets, her philosophers and statesmen, her merchants and inventors, who have formed the bulwark of the sea-girt isle, and have carried the meteor flag around the world. They are ignorant, and degraded.

and debased; they live the life of slaves and die the death
of paupers, simply because they are robbed of their natural
rights.

In the same neighborhood in which you may find such
people as these, in which you may see squalid laborers'
cottages where human beings huddle together like swine,
you may also see grand mansions set in great, velvety,
oak-graced parks, the habitations of local "God Almight-
ies," as the Laureate styles them, and as these brutalized
English people seem almost to take them to be. They
never do any work—they pride themselves upon the fact
that for hundreds of years their ancestors have never done
any work; they look with the utmost contempt not merely
upon the man who works, but even upon the man whose
grandfather had to work. Yet they live in the utmost
luxury. They have town houses and country houses,
horses, carriages, liveried servants, yachts, packs of
hounds; they have all that wealth can command in the
way of literature and education and the culture of travel.
And they have wealth to spare, which they can invest in
railway shares, or public debts, or in buying up land in
the United States. But not an iota of this wealth do they
produce. They get it because, it being conceded that they
own the land, the people who do produce wealth must
hand their earnings over to them.

Here, clear and plain, is the beginning and primary
cause of that inequality in the distribution of wealth
which, in England, produces such dire, soul-destroying
poverty, side by side with such wantonness of luxury,
and which is to be seen in the cities even more glaringly
than in the country. Here, clear and plain, is the reason
why labor seems a drug, and why, in all occupations in
which mere laborers can engage, wages tend to the merest
pittance on which life can be maintained. Deprived of
their natural rights to land, treated as intruders upon

God's earth, men are compelled to an unnatural competi.
tion for the privilege of mere animal existence, that in
manufacturing towns and city slums reduces humanity to
a depth of misery and debasement in which beings, created
in the image of God, sink below the level of the brutes.

And the same inequality of conditions which we see
beginning here, is it not due to the same primary cause?
American citizenship confers no right to American soil.
The first and most essential rights of man—the rights to
life, liberty and the pursuit of happiness—are denied here
as completely as in England.   And the same results must
follow.

CHAPTER XI.

DUMPING GARBAGE.

THIS gulf-stream of humanity that is setting on our shores with increasing volume is in all respects worthy of more attention than we give it. In many ways one of the most important phenomena of our time, it is one which forcibly brings to the mind the fact that we are living under conditions which must soon begin to change rapidly. But there is one part of the immigration coming to us this year which is specially suggestive. A number of large steamers of the trans-Atlantic lines are calling, under contract with the British government, at small ports on the west coast of Ireland, filling up with men, women and children, whose passages are paid by their government, and then, ferrying them across the ocean, are dumping them on the wharves of New York and Boston with a few dollars apiece in their pockets to begin life in the New World.

The strength of a nation is in its men. It is its people that make a country great and strong, produce its wealth, and give it rank among other countries. Yet, here is a civilized and Christian government, or one that passes for such, shipping off its people, to be dumped upon another continent, as garbage is shipped off from New York to be dumped into the Atlantic Ocean. Nor are these people undesirable material for the making of a nation. Whatever they may sometimes become here, when cooped up in tenement-houses and exposed to the corruption of our politics, and to the temptation of a life greatly differing from that to which they have been accustomed, they are in their own country, as any one who has been among them there can testify, a peaceable, industrious, and, in some important respects, a peculiarly moral people, who lack intellectual and political education, and the robust virtues that personal independence alone can give, simply because of the poverty to which they are condemned. Mr. Trevelyan, the Chief Secretary for Ireland, has declared in the House of Commons that they are physically and morally healthy, well capable of making a living, and yet the government of which he is a member is shipping them away at public expense as New York ships its garbage!

These people are well capable of making a living, Mr. Trevelyan says, yet if they remain at home they will be able to make only the poorest of poor livings in the best of times, and when seasons are not of the best, taxes must be raised and alms begged to keep them alive; and so as the cheapest way of getting rid of them, they are shipped away at public expense.

What is the reason of this? Why is it that people, in themselves well capable of making a living, cannot make a living for themselves in their own country? Simply that the natural, equal, and unalienable rights of man, with which, as asserted by our Declaration of Independence, these human beings have been endowed by their Creator, are denied them. The famine, the pauperism, the misgovernment and turbulence of Ireland, the bitter wrongs which keep aglow the fire of Irish "sedition," and the difficulties with regard to Ireland which perplex English statesmen, all spring from what the National Assembly of France, in 1789, declared to be the cause of all public misfortunes and corruptions of government—the contempt of human rights. The Irish peasant is

forced to starve, to beg, or to emigrate; he becomes in the
eyes of those who rule him mere human garbage, to be
shipped off and dumped anywhere, because, like the English peasant, who, after a slave's life, dies a pauper's death,
his natural rights in his native soil are denied him; because
his unalienable right to procure wealth by his own exertions and to retain it for his own uses is refused him.

The country from which these people are shipped—and
the government-aided emigration is as nothing compared
to the voluntary emigration—is abundantly capable of
maintaining in comfort a very much larger population
than it has ever had. There is no natural reason why in
it people themselves capable of making a living should
suffer want and starvation. The reason that they do is
simply that they are denied natural opportunities for the
employment of their labor, and that the laws permit others
to extort from them the proceeds of such labor as they
are permitted to do. Of these people who are now being
sent across the Atlantic by the English government, and
dumped on our wharves with a few dollars in their
pockets, there are probably none of mature years who have
not by their labor produced wealth enough not only to
have supported them hitherto in a much higher degree of
comfort than that in which they have lived, but to have
enabled them to pay their own passage across the Atlantic,
if they wanted to come, and to have given them on landing
here a capital sufficient for a comfortable start. They are
penniless only because they have been systematically
robbed from the day of their birth to the day they left
their native shores.

A year ago I traveled through that part of Ireland from
which these government-aided emigrants come. What
surprises an American at first, even in Connaught, is the
apparent sparseness of population, and he wonders if this
can indeed be that overpopulated Ireland of which he has

heard so much. There is plenty of good land, but on it
are only fat beasts, and sheep so clean and white that you
at first think that they must be washed and combed every
morning. Once this soil was tilled and was populous, but
now you will find only traces of ruined hamlets, and here
and there the miserable hut of a herd, who lives in a way
no Tierra del Fuegan could envy. For the "owners" of
this land, who live in London and Paris, many of them
never having seen their estates, find cattle more profitable
than men, and so the men have been driven off. It is only
when you reach the bog and the rocks, in the mountains
and by the sea-shore, that you find a dense population.
Here they are crowded together on land on which Nature
never intended men to live. It is too poor for grazing, so
the people who have been driven from the better land are
allowed to live upon it—as long as they pay their rent.
If it were not too pathetic, the patches they call fields
would make you laugh. Originally the surface of the
ground must have been about as susceptible of cultivation
as the surface of Broadway. But at the cost of enormous
labor the small stones have been picked off and piled up,
though the great boulders remain, so that it is impossible
to use a plow; and the surface of the bog has been cut
away, and manured by seaweed brought from the shore
on the backs of men and women, till it can be made to
grow something.

     For such patches of rock and bog—soil it could not be
called, save by courtesy—which have been made to produce anything only by their unremitting toil—these
people are compelled to pay their absentee landlords rents
varying from £1 to £4 per acre, and then they must
pay another rent for the seaweed, which the surf of the
wild Atlantic throws upon the shore, before they are permitted to take it for manure, and another rent still for
the bog from which they cut their turf. As a matter of

fact, these people have to pay more for the land than they can get out of the land. They are really forced to pay not merely for the use of the land and for the use of the ocean, but for the use of the air. Their rents are made up, and they manage to live in good times, by the few shillings earned by the women, who knit socks as they carry their creels to and from the market or sea-shore; by the earnings of the men, who go over to England every year to work as harvesters; or by remittances sent home by husbands or children who have managed to get to America. In spite of their painful industry the poverty of these people is appalling. In good times they just manage to keep above the starvation line. In bad times, when a blight strikes their potatoes, they must eat seaweed, or beg relief from the poor-rates, or from the charitable contributions of the world. When so rich as to have a few chickens or a pig, they no more think of eating them than Vanderbilt thinks of eating his $50,000 trotters. They are sold to help pay the rent. In the loughs you may see fat salmon swimming in from the sea; but, if every one of them were marked by nature with the inscription, "Lord So-and-So, London, with the compliments of God Almighty," they could not be more out of the reach of these people. The best shops to be found in the villages will have for stock a few pounds of sugar and tea weighed out into ounce and half-ounce papers, a little flour, two or three red petticoats, a little coarse cloth, a few yards of flannel, and a few of cotton, some buttons and thread, a little pigtail tobacco, and, perhaps, a bottle or two of "the native" hid away in the ground some distance from the cabin, so that if the police do capture it the shopkeeper cannot be put in jail. For the Queen must live and the army must be supported, and the great distillers of Dublin and Belfast and Cork, who find such a comfortable monopoly in the excise, have churches to build and cathedrals to renovate. So poor are these people, so little is there in their miserable cabins, that a sub-sheriff who, last year, superintended the eviction of near one hundred families in one place, declared that the effects of the whole lot were not worth £3.

But the landlords—ah! the landlords!—they live differently. Every now and again in traveling through this country you come across some landlord's palatial home mansion, its magnificent grounds inclosed with high walls. Pass inside these walls and it is almost like entering another world—wide stretches of rich velvety lawn, beds of bright flowers, noble avenues of arching trees, and a spacious mansion rich with every appointment of luxury, with its great stables, kennels, and appurtenances of every kind. But though they may have these luxurious home places, the large landlords, with few exceptions, live in London or Paris, or pass part of the year in the great cities and the rest in Switzerland or Italy or along the shores of the Mediterranean; and occasionally one of them takes a trip over here to see our new country, with its magnificent opportunities for investing in wild lands which will soon be as valuable as English or Irish estates. They do not have to work; their incomes come without work on their part—all they have to do is to spend. Some collect galleries of the most valuable paintings; some are fanciers of old books, and give fabulous prices for rare editions. Some of them gamble, some keep studs of racers and costly yachts, and some get rid of their money in ways worse than these. Even their agents, whose business it is to extort the rent from the Irishmen who do work, live luxuriously. But it all comes out of the earnings of just such people as are now being dumped on our wharves—out of their earnings, or out of what is sent them by relatives in America, or by charitable contributions.

It is to maintain such a system of robbery as this that Ireland is filled with policemen and troops and spies and

informers, and a people who might be an integral part of
the British nation are made to that nation a difficulty, a
weakness and a danger. Economically, the Irish landlords
are of no more use than so many great, ravenous, destructive beasts—packs of wolves, herds of wild elephants, or
such dragons as St. George is reported to have killed. They
produce nothing; they only consume and destroy. And
what they destroy is more even than what they consume.
For, not merely is Ireland turned into a camp of military
police and red-coated soldiery to hold down the people
while they are robbed; but the wealth producers, stripped
of capital by this robbery of their earnings, and condemned
by it to poverty and ignorance, are unable to produce the
wealth which they could and would produce did labor get
its full earnings, and were wealth left to those who make
it. Surely true statesmanship would suggest that if any
one is to be shoveled out of a country it should be those
who merely consume and destroy; not those who produce
wealth.

But English statesmen think otherwise, and these surplus Irish men and women; these garbage Irish men and
women and little children—surplus and garbage because
the landlords of Ireland have no use for them, are shoveled
out of their own country and dumped on our wharves.
They have reached "the land of the free and the home of
the brave" just in time for the Fourth of July, when they
may hear the Declaration of Independence, with its ringing
assertion of unalienable rights, read again in our annual
national celebration.

Have they, then, escaped from the system which in their
own country made them serfs and human garbage? Not
at all. They have not even escaped the power of their old
landlords to take from them the proceeds of their toil.

For we are not merely getting these surplus tenants of
English, Scotch and Irish landlords—we are getting the
landlords, too. Simultaneously with this emigration is

going on a movement which is making the landlords and monopolists of Great Britain owners of vast tracts of American soil. There is even now scarcely a large landowning family in Great Britain that does not own even larger American estates, and American land is becoming with them a more and more favorite investment. These American estates of "their graces" and "my lords" are not as yet as valuable as their home estates, but the natural increase in our population, augmented by emigration, will soon make them so.

Every "surplus" Irishman, Englishman or Scotsman sent over here assists directly in sending up the value of land and the rent of land. The stimulation of emigration from the Old Country to this is a bright idea on the part of these landlords of two continents. They get rid of people whom, at home, in hard times, they might have to support in some sort of fashion, and lessen, as they think, the forces of disaffection, while at the same time they augment the value of their American estates.

It is not improbable that some of these evicted tenants may find themselves over here paying rent to the very same landlords to swell whose incomes they have so long toiled in their old country; but whether this be so or not, their mere coming here, by its effect in increasing the demand for land, helps to enable those landlords to compel some others of the people of the United States to give up to them a portion of their earnings in return for the privilege of living upon American soil. It is merely with this view, and for this purpose, that the landlords of the Old World are buying so much land in the New. They do not want it to live upon; they prefer to live in London or Paris, as many of the privileged classes of America are now learning to prefer to live. They do not want to work it; they do not propose to work at all. All they want with it is the power, which, as soon as our population increases a little, its ownership will give, of demanding the earnings of other people. And under present conditions it is a matter, not of a generation or two, but of only a few years, before they will be able to draw from their American estates sums even greater than from their Irish estates. That is to say, they will virtually own more Americans than they now own Irishmen.

So far from these Irish immigrants having escaped from the system that has impoverished and pauperized the masses of the Irish people for the benefit of a few of their number, that system has really more unrestricted sway here than in Ireland. In spite of the fact that we read the Declaration of Independence every Fourth of July, make a great noise and have a great jubilation, that first of the unalienable rights with which every man is endowed by his Creator—the equal right to the use of the natural elements without which wealth cannot be produced, nor even life maintained—is no better acknowledged with us than it is in Ireland.

There is much said of "Irish landlordism," as though it were a peculiar kind of landlordism, or a peculiarly bad kind of landlordism. This is not so. Irish landlordism is in nothing worse than English landlordism, or Scotch landlordism, or American landlordism, nor are the Irish landlords harder than any similar class. Being generally men of education and culture, accustomed to an easy life, they are, as a whole, less grasping toward their tenants than the farmers who rent of them are to the laborers to whom they sub-let. They regard the land as their own, that is all, and expect to get an income from it; and the agent who sends them the best income they naturally regard as the best agent.

Such popular Irish leaders as Mr. Parnell and Mr. Sullivan, when they come over here and make speeches, have a good deal to say about the "feudal landlordism" of

Ireland. This is all humbug—an attempt to convey the impression that Irish landlordism is something different from American landlordism, so that American landowners will not take offense, while Irish landowners are denounced. There is in Ireland nothing that can be called feudal landlordism. All the power which the Irish landlord has, all the tyranny which he exercises, springs from his ownership of the soil, from the legal recognition that it is *his* property. If landlordism in Ireland seems more hateful than in England, it is only because the industrial organization is more primitive, and there are fewer intermediaries between the man who is robbed and the man who gets the plunder. And if either Irish or English landlordism seems more hateful than the same system in America, it is only because this is a new country, not yet quite fenced in. But, as a matter of law, these "my lords" and "your graces," who are now getting themselves far greater estates in the United States than they have in their own country, have more power as landlords here than there.

In Ireland, especially, the tendency of legislation for a series of years has been to restrain the power of the landlord in dealing with the tenant. In the United States he has in all its fullness the unrestricted power of doing as he pleases with his own. Rack-renting is with us the common, almost the exclusive, form of renting. There is no long process to be gone through with to secure an eviction, no serving notice upon the relieving officer of the district. The tenant whom the landlord wants to get rid of can be evicted with the minimum of cost and expense.

Says the *Tribune's* "Broadway Lounger" incidentally in his chatter:

Judge Gedney tells me that on the first of this month he signed no less than two hundred and fifty warrants of dispossession against poor tenants. His district includes many blocks of the most squalid variety of tenement-houses, and he has fully as much unpleasant work of this kind as any of his judicial brethren. The first of May is, of course, the heaviest field-day of the year for such business, but there are generally at the beginning of every month at least one hundred warrants granted. And to those who fret about the minor miseries of life, no more wholesome cure could be administered than an enforced attendance in a district court on such occasions. The lowest depths of misery are sounded. Judge Gedney says, too, that in the worst cases the suffering is more generally caused by misfortune than by idleness or dissipation. A man gets a felon on his hand, which keeps him at home until his savings are gone and all his effects are in the pawnshop, and then his children fall sick or his wife dies, and the agent of the house, under instructions from the owner, who is perhaps in Europe enjoying himself, won't wait for the rent, and serves him with a summons.

Awhile ago, when it was bitter cold, I read in the papers an item telling how, in the city of Wilkesbarre, Pa., a woman and her three children were found one night huddled in a hogshead on a vacant lot, famished and almost frozen. The story was a simple one. The man, out of work, had tried to steal, and been sent to prison. Their rent unpaid, their landlord had evicted them, and as the only shelter they knew of, they had gone to the hogshead. In Ireland, bad as it is, the relieving officer would have had to be by to have offered them at least the shelter of the almshouse.

These Irish men and women who are being dumped on our wharves with two or three dollars in their pockets, do they find access to nature any freer here than there? Far out in the West, if they know where to go, and can get there, they may, for a little while yet; but though they may see even around New York plenty of unused land, they will find that it all belongs to somebody. Let them go to work at what they will, they must, here as there, give up some of their earnings for the privilege of working, and pay some other human creature for the privilege of living. On the whole their chances will be better here

than there, for this is yet a new country, and a century
ago our settlements only fringed the eastern seaboard of
a vast continent.   But from the Atlantic to the Pacific we
already have our human garbage, the volume of which
some of this Irish human garbage will certainly go to swell.
Wherever you go throughout the country the "tramp" is
known; and in this metropolitan city there are already, it
is stated by the Charity Organization Society, a quarter
of a million people who live on alms!   What, in a few
years more, are we to do for a dumping-ground?   Will it
make our difficulty the less that our human garbage can
vote?

CHAPTER XII.

OVER-PRODUCTION.

THAT, as declared by the French Assembly, public misfortunes and corruptions of government spring from ignorance, neglect or contempt of human rights, may be seen from whatever point we look.

Consider this matter of "over-production" of which we hear so much—to which is so commonly attributed dullness of trade and the difficulty of finding employment. What, when we come to think of it, can be more preposterous than to speak in any general sense of over-production? Over-production of wealth when there is everywhere a passionate struggle for more wealth; when so many must stint and strain and contrive, to get a living; when there is poverty and actual want among large classes! Manifestly there cannot be over-production, in any general and absolute sense, until desires for wealth are all satisfied; until no one wants more wealth.

Relative over-production, of course, there may be. The production of certain commodities may be so far in excess of the proper proportion to the production of other commodities that the whole quantity produced cannot be exchanged for enough of those other commodities to give the usual returns to the labor and capital engaged in bringing them to market. But this relative over-production is merely disproportionate production. It may proceed from increased production of things of one kind, or from decreased production of things of other kinds.

Thus, what we would call an over-production of watches —meaning not that more watches had been produced than were wanted, but that more had been produced than could be sold at a remunerative price—would be purely relative. It might arise from an increase in the production of watches, outrunning the ability to purchase watches; or from a decrease in the production of other things, lessening the ability to purchase watches. No matter how much the production of watches were to increase, within the limits of the desire for watches, it would not be over-production, if at the same time the production of other things increased sufficiently to allow a proportionally increased quantity of other things to be given for the increased quantity of watches. And no matter how much the production of watches might be decreased, there would be relative over-production, if at the same time the production of other things were decreased in such proportion as to diminish in greater degree the ability to give other things for watches.

In short, desire continuing, the over-production of particular commodities can be only relative to the production of other commodities, and may result from unduly increased production in some branches of industry, or from the checking of production in other branches. But while the phenomena of over-production may thus arise from causes directly operating to increase production, or from causes directly operating to check production, just as the equipoise of a pair of scales may be disturbed by the addition or the removal of a weight, there are certain symptoms by which we may determine from which of these two kinds of causes any disturbance proceeds. For while to a limited extent, and in a limited field, these diverse causes may produce similar effects, their general effects will be

widely different. The increase of production in any branch
of industry tends to the general increase of production;
the checking of production in any branch of industry
tends to the general checking of production.

This may be seen from the different general effects
which follow increase or diminution of production in the
same branch of industry. Let us suppose that from the
discovery of new mines, the improvement of machinery,
the breaking up of combinations that control it, or any
other cause, there is a great and rapid increase in the
production of coal, out of proportion to the increase of
other production. In a free market the price of coal
therefore falls. The effect is to enable all consumers of
coal somewhat to increase their consumption of coal, and
somewhat to increase their consumption of other things,
and to stimulate production, by reducing cost, in all those
branches of industry into which the use of coal directly or
indirectly enters. Thus the general effect is to increase
production, and to beget a tendency to reëstablish the
equilibrium between the production of coal and the produc
tion of other things, by raising the aggregate production

But let the coal operators and syndicates, as they fre
quently do, determine to stop or reduce the production of
coal in order to raise prices. At once a large body of men
engaged in producing coal find their power of purchasing
cut off or decreased. Their demand for commodities they
habitually use thus falls off; demand and production in
other branches of industry are lessened, and other consumers, in turn, are obliged to decrease their demands.
At the same time the enhancement in the price of coal
tends to increase the cost of production in all branches of
industry in which coal is used, and to diminish the amount
both of coal and of other things which the users of coal
can call for. Thus the check to production is perpetuated
through all branches of industry, and when the reëstablish-

ment of equilibrium between the production of coal and the production of other things is effected, it is on a diminished scale of aggregate production.

All trade, it is to be remembered, is the exchange of commodities for commodities—money being merely the measure of values and the instrument for conveniently and economically effecting exchanges. Demand (which is a different thing from desire, as it involves purchasing power) is the asking for things in exchange for an equivalent value of other things. Supply is the offering of things in exchange for an equivalent value of other things. These terms are therefore relative; demand involves supply, and supply involves demand. Whatever increases the quantity of things offered in exchange for other things at once increases supply and augments demand. And, reversely, whatever checks the bringing of things to market at once reduces supply and decreases demand.

Thus, while the same primary effect upon the relative supply of and demand for any particular commodity or group of commodities may be caused either by augmentation of the supply of such commodities, or by reduction in the supply of other commodities—in the one case, the general effect will be to stimulate trade, by calling out greater supplies of other commodities, and increasing aggregate demand; and in the other case, to depress trade, by lessening aggregate demand and diminishing supply. The equation of supply and demand between agricultural productions and manufactured goods might thus be altered in the same direction and to the same extent by such prosperous seasons or improvements in agriculture as would reduce the price of agricultural productions as compared with manufactured goods, or by such restrictions upon the production or exchange of manufactured goods as would raise their price as compared with agricultural productions. But in the one case, the aggregate produce

of the community would be increased. There would be
not only an increase of agricultural products, but the
increased demand thus caused would stimulate the production of manufactured goods; while this prosperity in
manufacturing industries, by enabling those engaged in
them to increase their demand for agricultural productions,
would react upon agriculture. In the other case, the
aggregate produce would be decreased. The increase in
the price of manufactured goods would compel farmers to
reduce their demands, and this would in turn reduce the
ability of those engaged in manufacturing to demand farm
products. Thus trade would slacken, and production be
checked in all directions. That this is so, we may see from
the different general effects which result from good crops
and poor crops, though to an individual farmer high prices
may compensate for a poor yield.

To recapitulate: Relative over-production may proceed
from causes which increase, or from causes which diminish,
production. But increased production in any branch of
industry tends to increase production in all; to stimulate
trade and augment the general prosperity; and any disturbance of equilibrium thus caused must be speedily
readjusted. Diminished production in any branch of
industry, on the other hand, tends to decrease production
in all; to depress trade and lessen the general prosperity;
and depression thus produced tends to perpetuate itself
through larger circles, as in one branch of industry after
another the check to production reduces the power to
demand the products of other branches of industry.

Whoever will consider the wide-spread phenomena
which are currently attributed to over-production can have
no doubt from which of these two classes of causes they
spring. He will see that they are symptoms, not of the
excess of production, but of the restriction and strangula-
tion of production.

There are with us many restrictions of production, direct
and indirect; for production, it must be remembered,
involves the transportation and exchange as well as the
making of things. And restrictions imposed upon commerce or any of its instruments may operate to discourage
production as fully as restrictions imposed upon agriculture or manufactures. The tariff which we maintain for
the express purpose of hampering our foreign commerce,
and restricting the free exchange of our own productions
for the productions of other nations, is in effect a restric
tion upon production. The monopolies which we have
created or permitted to grow up, and which levy their toll
upon internal commerce, or by conspiracy and combination
diminish supply and artificially enhance prices, restrict
production in the same way; while the taxes levied upon
certain manufactures by our internal revenue system
directly restrict production.*

So, too, is production discouraged by the direct taxes

---

* Whether taxes upon liquor and tobacco can be defended upon
other grounds is not here in question. What Adam Smith says upon
this point may, however, be worth quoting:

"If we consult experience, the cheapness of wine seems to be a
cause, not of drunkenness, but of sobriety. The inhabitants of the
wine countries are in general the soberest people in Europe; witness
the Spaniards, the Italians, and the inhabitants of the southern provinces of France. People are seldom guilty of excess in what is their
daily fare. Nobody affects the character of liberality and good fel-
lowship, by being profuse of a liquor which is as cheap as small beer
On the contrary, in the countries which, either from excessive heat
or cold, produce no grapes, and where wine consequently is dear, and
a rarity, drunkenness is a common vice, as among the northern nations, and all those who live between the tropics—the negroes, for
example, on the coast of Guinea. When a French regiment comes
from some of the northern provinces of France, where wine is somewhat dear, to be quartered in the southern, where it is very cheap,
the soldiers, I have frequently heard it observed, are at first debauched by the cheapness and novelty of good wine; but after a few

levied by our States, counties and municipalities, which in the aggregate exceed the taxation of the Federal government. These taxes are generally levied upon all property, real and personal, at the same rate, and fall partly on land, which is not the result of production, and partly on things which are the result of production ; but insomuch as buildings and improvements are not only thus taxed, but the land so built upon and improved is universally rated at a much higher assessment, and generally at a very much higher assessment, than unused land of the same quality,* even the taxation that falls upon land values largely operates as a deterrent to production.

To produce, to improve, is thus fraught with a penalty. We, in fact, treat the man who produces wealth, or accumulates wealth, as though he had done something which public policy calls upon us to discourage. If a house is erected, or a steamship or a factory is built, down comes the tax-gatherer to fine the men who have done such things. If a farmer go upon vacant land, which is adding nothing

months' residence, the greater part of them become as sober as the rest of the inhabitants. Were the duties upon foreign wines, and the excises upon malt, beer, and ale, to be taken away all at once, it might, in the same manner, occasion in Great Britain a pretty general and temporary drunkenness among the middling and inferior ranks of people, which would probably be soon followed by a permanent and almost universal sobriety. At present, drunkenness is by no means the vice of people of fashion, or of those who can easily afford the most expensive liquors. A gentleman drunk with ale has scarce ever been seen among us. The restraints upon the wine trade in Great Britain, besides, do not so much seem calculated to hinder the people from going, if I may say so, to the ale-house, as from going where they can buy the best and cheapest liquor."— *Wealth of Nations*, Book IV., Chapter III.

* This arises from the widely spread but utterly false notion that property should pay taxes only in proportion to the income it yields. In Great Britain, this is carried to such a pitch of absurdity that unused land pays no taxes. no matter how valuable it may be.

to the wealth of the community, reclaim it, cultivate it, cover it with crops, or stock it with cattle, we not only make him pay for having thus increased wealth, but, as an additional discouragement to the doing of such things, we tax him very much more on the value of his land than we do the man who holds an equal piece idle. So, too, if a man saves, our taxes operate to punish him for his thrift. Thus is production checked in every direction.

But this is not all. There is with us a yet greater check to production.

If there be in this universe superior intelligences engaged, with higher powers, in the study of its infinite marvels, who sometimes examine the speck we tenant with such studious curiosity as our microscopists watch the denizens of a drop of water, the manner in which, in such a country as this, population is distributed, must greatly puzzle them. In our cities they find people packed together so closely that they live over one another in tiers; in the country they see people separated so widely that they lose all the advantages of neighborhood. They see buildings going up in the outskirts of our towns, while much more available lots remain vacant. They see men going great distances to cultivate land while there is yet plenty of land to cultivate in the localities from which they come and through which they pass. And as these higher intelligences watch this process of settlement through whatever sort of microscopes they may require to observe such creatures as we, they must notice that, for the most part, these settlers, instead of being attracted by each other, leave between each other large patches of unused land. If there be in the universe any societies which have the same relation to us as our learned societies have to ants and animalculæ, these phenomena must lead to no end of curious theories.

Take in imagination such a bird's-eye view of the city

of New York as might be had from a balloon. The houses are climbing heavenward—ten, twelve, even fifteen stories, tier on tier of people, living, one family above another, without sufficient water, without sufficient light or air, without playground or breathing-space. So close is the building that the streets look like narrow rifts in the brick and mortar, and from street to street the solid blocks stretch until they almost meet; in the newer districts only a space of twenty feet, a mere crack in the masonry through which at high noon a sunbeam can scarcely struggle down, being left to separate the backs of the tenements fronting on one street from the backs of those fronting on another street. Yet, around this city, and within easy access of its center, there is plenty of vacant land; within the city limits, in fact, not one-half the land is built upon; and many blocks of tall tenement-houses are surrounded by vacant lots. If the improvement of our telescopes were to show us on another planet, lakes where the water, instead of presenting a level surface, ruffled only by the action of the wind, stood up here and there in huge columns, it could hardly perplex us more than these phenomena must perplex such extramundane intelligences as I have supposed. How is it, they may well speculate, that the pressure of population which piles families, tier on tier, above each other, and raises such towering ware-houses and workshops, does not cover this vacant land with buildings and with homes? Some restraining cause there must be; but what, it might well puzzle them to tell.

A South Sea Islander, however—one of the old heathen sort, whom, in civilizing, we have well-nigh exterminated, might make a guess. If one of their High Chiefs tabooed a place or object, no one of the common sort of these superstitious savages dare use or touch it. He must go around for miles rather than set his feet on a tabooed path; must parch or die with thirst rather than drink of a tabooed spring; must go hungry though the fruit of a tabooed grove rotted on the ground before his eyes. A South Sea Islander would say that this vacant land must be "taboo." And he would be not far from the truth. This land is vacant, simply because it is cursed by that form of the taboo which we superstitiously venerate under the names of "private property" and "vested rights."

The invisible barrier but for which buildings would rise and the city would spread, is the high price of land, a price that increases the more certainly it is seen that a growing population needs the land. Thus the stronger the incentive to the use of land, the higher the barrier that arises against its use. Tenement-houses are built among vacant lots because the price that must be paid for land is so great that people who have not large means must economize their use of land by living one family above another.

While in all of our cities the value of land, which increases not merely with their growth, but with the expectation of growth, thus operates to check building and improvement, its effect is manifested through the country in a somewhat different way. Instead of unduly crowding people together it unduly separates them. The expectation of profit from the rise in the value of land leads those who take up new land, not to content themselves with what they may most profitably use, but to get all the land they can, even though they must let a great part of it lie idle; and large tracts are seized upon by those who make no pretense of using any part of it, but merely calculate to make a profit out of others who in time will be driven to use it. Thus population is scattered, not only to loss of all the comforts, refinements, pleasures and stimulations that come from neighborhood, but to the great loss of productive power. The extra cost of constructing and maintaining roads and railways, the greater distances over which produce and goods must be transported, the difficulties which separation interposes to that commerce between men which is necessary even to the ruder forms of modern production, all retard and lessen production. While just as the high value of land in and about a great city makes more difficult the erection of buildings, so does increase in the value of agricultural land make improvement difficult. The higher the value of land the more capital does the farmer require if he buys outright; or, if he buys on instalments, or rents, the more of his earnings must he give up every year. Men who would eagerly improve and cultivate land could it be had for the using are thus turned away—to wander long distances and waste their means in looking for better opportunities; to swell the ranks of those seeking for employment as wage-workers; to go back to the cities or manufacturing villages in the endeavor to make a living; or to remain idle, frequently for long periods, and sometimes until they become utterly demoralized and worse than useless tramps.

Thus is production checked in those vocations which form the foundation for all o hers. This check to the production of some forms of wealth lessens demand for other forms of wealth, and so the effect is propagated from one branch of industry to another, begetting the phenomena that are spoken of as over-production, but which are primarily due to restricted production.

And as land values tend to rise, not merely with the growth of population and wealth, but with the expectation of that growth, thus enlisting in pushing on the upward movement, the powerful and illusive sentiment of hope, there is a constant tendency, especially strong in rapidly growing countries, to carry up the price of land beyond the point at which labor and capital can profitably engage in production, and the only check to this is the refusal of labor and capital so to engage. This tendency becomes peculiarly strong in recurring periods, when the fever of speculation runs high, and leads at length to a correspondingly general and sudden check to production, which propagating itself (by checking demand) through all branches of industry, is the main cause of those paroxysms known as commercial or industrial depressions, and which are marked by wasting capital, idle labor, stocks of goods that cannot be sold without loss, and wide-spread want and suffering. It is true that other restrictions upon the free play of productive forces operate to promote, intensify and continue these dislocations of the industrial system, but that here is the main and primary cause I think there can be no doubt.

And this, perhaps, is even more clear : That from whatever cause disturbance of industrial and commercial relations may originally come, these periodical depressions in which demand and supply seem unable to meet and satisfy each other could not become wide-spread and persistent did productive forces have free access to land. Nothing like general and protracted congestion of capital and labor could take place were this natural vent open. The moment symptoms of relative over-production manifested themselves in any derivative branch of industry, the turning of capital and labor toward those occupations which extract wealth from the soil would give relief.

Thus may we see that those public misfortunes which we speak of as "business stagnation" and "hard times," those public misfortunes that in periods of intensity cause more loss and suffering than great wars, spring truly from our ignorance and contempt of human rights; from our disregard of the equal and unalienable right of all men freely to apply to nature for the satisfaction of their needs, and to retain for their own uses the full fruits of their labor.

CHAPTER XIII.

HOW contempt of human rights is the essential element in building up the great fortunes whose growth is such a marked feature of our development, we have already seen. And just as clearly may we see that from the same cause spring poverty and pauperism. The tramp is the complement of the millionaire.

Consider this terrible phenomenon, the tramp—an appearance more menacing to the Republic than that of hostile armies and fleets bent on destruction. What is the tramp? In the beginning, he is a man able to work, and willing to work, for the satisfaction of his needs; but who, not finding opportunity to work where he is, starts out in quest of it; who, failing in this search, is, in a later stage, driven by those imperative needs to beg or to steal, and so, losing self-respect, loses all that animates and elevates and stimulates a man to struggle and to labor; becomes a vagabond and an outcast—a poisonous pariah, avenging on society the wrong that he keenly, but vaguely, feels has been done him by society.

Yet the tramp, known as he is now from the Atlantic to the Pacific, is only a part of the phenomenon. Behind him, though not obtrusive, save in what we call "hard times," there is, even in what we now consider normal times, a great mass of unemployed labor which is unable, unwilling, or not yet forced to tramp, but which bears to the tramp the same relation that the submerged part of an iceberg does to that much smaller part which shows above the surface.

The difficulty which so many men who would gladly work to satisfy their needs find in obtaining opportunity of doing so, is so common as to occasion no surprise, nor, save when it becomes particularly intensified, to arouse any inquiry. We are so used to it, that although we all know that work is in itself distasteful, and that there never yet was a human being who wanted work for the sake of work, we have got into the habit of thinking and talking as though work were in itself a boon. So deeply is this idea implanted in the common mind that we maintain a policy based on the notion that the more work we do for foreign nations and the less we allow them to do for us, the better off we shall be; and in public and in private we hear men lauded and enterprises advocated because they "furnish employment;" while there are many who. with more or less definiteness, hold the idea that labor-saving inventions have operated injuriously by lessening the amount of work to be done.

Manifestly, work is not an end, but a means; manifestly, there can be no real scarcity of work, which is but the means of satisfying material wants, until human wants are all satisfied. How, then, shall we explain the obvious facts which lead men to think and speak as though work were in itself desirable?

When we consider that labor is the producer of all wealth, the creator of all values, is it not strange that labor should experience difficulty in finding employment? The exchange for commodities of that which gives value to all commodities, ought to be the most certain and easy of exchanges. One wishing to exchange labor for food or clothing, or any of the manifold things which labor produces, is like one wishing to exchange gold-dust for coin,

cotton for cloth, or wheat for flour.   Nay, this is hardly
a parallel; for, as the terms upon which the exchange of
labor for commodities takes place are usually that the labor
is first rendered, the man who offers labor in exchange
generally proposes to produce and render value before
value is returned to him.

This being the case, why is not the competition of
employers to obtain workmen as great as the competition
of workmen to find employment?   Why is it that we
do not consider the man who does work as the obliging
party, rather than the man who, as we say, furnishes
work?

So it necessarily would be, if in saying that labor is the
producer of wealth, we stated the whole case.   But labor
is only the producer of wealth in the sense of being the
active factor of production.   For the production of wealth,
labor must have access to preëxisting substance and natural
forces.   Man has no power to bring something out of
nothing.   He cannot create an atom of matter or initiate
the slightest motion.   Vast as are his powers of modify-
ing matter and utilizing force, they are merely powers of
adapting, changing, recombining, what previously exists.
The substance of the hand with which I write these lines,
as of the paper on which I write, has previously formed
the substance of other men and other animals, of plants,
soils, rocks, atmospheres, probably of other worlds and
other systems.   And so of the force which impels my pen.
All we know of it is that it has acted and reacted through
what seem to us eternal circlings, and appears to reach
this planet from the sun.   The destruction of matter and
motion, as the creation of matter and motion, are to us
unthinkable.

In the human being, in some mysterious way which
neither the researches of physiologists nor the speculations of philosophers enable us to comprehend, conscious,

planning intelligence comes into control, for a limited
time and to a limited extent, of the matter and motion
contained in the human frame. The power of contracting
and expanding human muscles is the initial force with
which the human mind acts upon the material world.
By the use of this power other powers are utilized, and
the forms and relations of matter are changed in accordance with human desire. But how great soever be the
power of affecting and using external nature which human
intelligence thus obtains,—and how great this may be we
are only beginning now to realize,—it is still only the
power of affecting and using what previously exists.
Without access to external nature, without the power of
availing himself of her substance and forces, man is not
merely powerless to produce anything, he ceases to exist
in the material world.   He himself, in physical body at
least, is but a changing form of matter, a passing mode
of motion, that must be continually drawn from the
reservoirs of external nature.

Without either of the three elements, land, air and
water, man could not exist; but he is peculiarly a land
animal, living on its surface, and drawing from it his
supplies.   Though he is able to navigate the ocean, and
may some day be able to navigate the air, he can only do
so by availing himself of materials drawn from land.
Land is to him the great storehouse of materials and
reservoir of forces upon which he must draw for his
needs.   And as wealth consists of materials and products
of nature which have been secured, or modified by human
exertion so as to fit them for the satisfaction of human
desires,* labor is the active factor in the production of

---

* However great be its utility, nothing can be counted as wealth
unless it requires labor for its production ; nor however much labor
has been required for its production, can anything retain the character of wealth longer than it can gratify desire.

wealth, but land is the passive factor, without which labor
can neither produce nor exist.

All this is so obvious that it may seem like wasting space
to state it. Yet, in this obvious fact lies the explanation
of that enigma that to so many seems a hopeless puzzle—
the labor question. What is inexplicable, if we lose sight
of man's absolute and constant dependence upon land, is
clear when we recognize it.

Let us suppose, as well as we can, human society in a
world as near as possible like our own, with one essential
difference. Let us suppose this imaginary world and its
inhabitants so constructed that men could support themselves in air, and could from the material of the air produce by their labor what they needed for nourishment
and use. I do not mean to suppose a state of things in
which men might float around like birds in the air or
fishes in the ocean, supplying the prime necessities of
animal life from what they could pick up. I am merely
trying to suppose a state of things in which men as they
are, were relieved of absolute dependence upon land for a
standing-place and reservoir of material and forces. We
will suppose labor to be as necessary as with us, human
desires to be as boundless as with us, the cumulative power
of labor to give to capital as much advantage as with us,
and the division of labor to have gone as far as with us
—the only difference being (the idea of claiming the air
as private property not having been thought of) that no
human creature would be compelled to make terms with
another in order to get a resting-place, and to obtain
access to the material and forces without which labor
cannot produce. In such a state of things, no matter how
minute had become the division of labor, no matter how
great had become the accumulation of capital, or how far
labor-saving inventions had been carried,—there could
never be anything that seemed like an excess of the

supply of labor over the demand for labor; there could never be any difficulty in finding employment; and the spectacle of willing men, having in their own brains and muscles the power of supplying the needs of themselves and their families, yet compelled to beg for work or for alms, could never be witnessed. It being in the power of every one able to labor to apply his labor directly to the satisfaction of his needs without asking leave of any one else, that cutthroat competition, in which men who must find employment or starve are forced to bid against each other, could never arise.

Variations there might be in the demand for particular commodities or services, which would produce variations in the demand for labor in different occupations, and cause wages in those occupations somewhat to rise above or fall below the general level, but the ability of labor to employ itself, the freedom of indefinite expansion in the primary employments, would allow labor to accommodate itself to these variations, not merely without loss or suffering, but so easily that they would be scarcely noticed. For occupations shade into one another by imperceptible degrees, no matter how minute the division of labor—or, rather, the more minute the division of labor the more insensible the gradation—so that there are in each occupation enough who could easily pass to other occupations, readily to allow of such contractions and expansions as might in a state of freedom occur. The possibility of indefinite expansion in the primary occupations, the ability of every one to make a living by resort to them, would produce elasticity throughout the whole industrial system.

Under such conditions capital could not oppress labor. At present, in any dispute between capital and labor, capital enjoys the enormous advantage of being better able to wait. Capital wastes when not employed; but labor starves. Where, however, labor could always employ itself, the disadvantage in any conflict would be on the side of capital, while that surplus of unemployed labor which enables capital to make such advantageous bargains with labor would not exist. The man who wanted to get others to work for him would not find men crowding for employment, but, finding all labor already employed, would have to offer higher wages, in order to tempt them into his employment, than the men he wanted could make for themselves. The competition would be that of employers to obtain workmen, rather than that of workmen to get employment, and thus the advan, tages which the accumulation of capital gives in the production of wealth would (save enough to secure the accumulation and employment of capital) go ultimately to labor. In such a state of things, instead of thinking that the man who employed another was doing him a favor, we would rather look upon the man who went to work for another as the obliging party.

To suppose that under such conditions there could be such inequality in the distribution of wealth as we now see, would require a more violent presumption than we have made in supposing air, instead of land, to be the element from which wealth is chiefly derived. But sup- posing existing inequalities to be translated into such a state, it is evident that large fortunes could avail little, and continue but a short time. Where there is always labor seeking employment on any terms ; where the masses earn only a bare living, and dismissal from employment means anxiety and privation, and even beggary or starva- tion, these large fortunes have monstrous power. But in a condition of things where there was no unemployed labor, where every one could make a living for himself and family without fear or favor, what could a hundred or five hundred millions avail in the way of enabling its possessor to extort or tyrannize ?

The upper millstone alone cannot grind. That it may do so, the nether millstone as well is needed. No amount of force will break an egg-shell if exerted on one side alone. So capital could not squeeze labor as long as labor was free to natural opportunities, and in a world where these natural materials and opportunities were as free to all as is the air to us, there could be no difficulty in finding employment, no willing hands conjoined with hungry stomachs, no tendency of wages toward the minimum on which the worker could barely live. In such a world we would no more think of thanking anybody for furnishing us employment than we here think of thanking anybody for furnishing us with appetites.

That the Creator might have put us in the kind of world I have sought to imagine, as readily as in this kind of a world, I have no doubt. Why he has not done so may, however, I think, be seen. That kind of a world would be best for fools. This is the best for men who will use the intelligence with which they have been gifted. Of this, however, I shall speak hereafter. What I am now trying to do by asking my readers to endeavor to imagine a world in which natural opportunities were "as free as air," is to show that the barrier which prevents labor from freely using land is the nether millstone against which labor is ground, the true cause of the difficulties which are apparent through the whole industrial organization.

But it may be said, as I have often heard it said, "We do not all want land! We cannot all become farmers!"

To this I reply that we *do* all want land, though it may be in different ways and in varying degrees. Without land no human being can live; without land no human occupation can be carried on. Agriculture is not the only use of land. It is only one of many. And just as the uppermost story of the tallest building rests upon land as truly as the lowest, so is the operative as truly a user of land as is the farmer. As all wealth is in the last analysis the resultant of land and labor, so is all production in the last analysis the expenditure of labor upon land.

Nor is it true that we could not all become farmers. That *is* the one thing that we might all become. If all men were merchants, or tailors, or mechanics, all men would soon starve. But there have been, and still exist, societies in which all get their living directly from nature. The occupations that resort directly to nature are the primitive occupations, from which, as society progresses, all others are differentiated. No matter how complex the industrial organization, these must always remain the fundamental occupations, upon which all other occupations rest, just as the upper stories of a building rest upon the foundation. Now, as ever, " the farmer feedeth all." And necessarily, the condition of labor in these first and widest of occupations, determines the general condition of labor, just as the level of the ocean determines the level of all its arms and bays and seas. Where there is a great demand for labor in agriculture, and wages are high, there must soon be a great demand for labor, and high wages, in all occupations. Where it is difficult to get employment in agriculture, and wages are low, there must soon be a difficulty of obtaining employment, and low wages, in all occupations. Now, what determines the demand for labor and the rate of wages in agriculture is manifestly the ability of labor to employ itself—that is to say, the ease with which land can be obtained. This is the reason that in new countries, where land is easily had, wages, not merely in agriculture, but in all occupations, are higher than in older countries, where land is hard to get. And thus it is that, as the value of land increases, wages fall, and the difficulty in finding employment arises.

This whoever will may see by merely looking around him. Clearly the difficulty of finding employment, the fact that in all vocations, as a rule, the supply of labor seems to exceed the demand for labor, springs from difficulties that prevent labor finding employment for itself—from the barriers that fence labor off from land. That there is a surplus of labor in any one occupation arises from the difficulty of finding employment in other occupations, but for which the surplus would be immediately drained off. When there was a great demand for clerks no bookkeeper could suffer for want of employment. And so on, down to the fundamental employments which directly extract wealth from land, the opening in which of opportunities for labor to employ itself would soon drain off any surplus in derivative occupations. Not that every unemployed mechanic, or operative, or clerk, could or would get himself a farm; but that from all the various occupations enough would betake themselves to the land to relieve any pressure for employment.

CHAPTER XIV.

HOW ignorance, neglect or contempt of human rights may turn public benefits into public misfortunes we may clearly see if we trace the effect of labor-saving inventions.

It is not altogether from a blind dislike of innovation that even the more thoughtful and intelligent Chinese set their faces against the introduction into their dense population of the labor-saving machinery of Western civilization. They recognize the superiority which in many things invention has given us, but to their view this superiority must ultimately be paid for with too high a price. The Eastern mind, in fact, regards the greater powers grasped by Western civilization somewhat as the medieval European mind regarded the powers which it believed might be gained by the Black Art, but for which the user must finally pay in destruction of body and damnation of soul. And there is much in the present aspects and tendencies of our civilization to confirm the Chinese in this view.

It is clear that the inventions and discoveries which during this century have so enormously increased the power of producing wealth have not proved an unmixed good. Their benefits are not merely unequally distributed, but they are bringing about absolutely injurious effects. They are concentrating capital, and increasing the power of these concentrations to monopolize and oppress; are rendering the workman more dependent; depriving him of the advantages of skill and of opportunities to acquire it; lessening his control over his own condition and his hope of improving it; cramping his mind, and in many cases distorting and enervating his body.

It seems to me impossible to consider the present tendencies of our industrial development without feeling that if there be no escape from them, the Chinese philosophers are right, and that the powers we have called into our service must ultimately destroy us. We are reducing the cost of production; but in doing so, are stunting children, and unfitting women for the duties of maternity, and degrading men into the position of mere feeders of machines. We are not lessening the fierceness of the struggle for existence. Though we work with an intensity and application that with the great majority of us leaves time and power for little else, we have increased, not decreased, the anxieties of life. Insanity is increasing, suicide is increasing, the disposition to shun marriage is increasing. We are developing, on the one side, enormous fortunes, but on the other side, utter pariahs. These are symptoms of disease for which no gains can compensate.

Yet it is manifestly wrong to attribute either necessary good or necessary evil to the improvements and inventions which are so changing industrial and social relations. They simply increase power—and power may work either good or evil as intelligence controls or fails to control it.

Let us consider the effects of the introduction of laborsaving machinery—or rather, of all discoveries, inventions and improvements, that increase the produce a given amount of labor can obtain.

In that primitive state in which the labor of each family supplies its wants, any invention or discovery which increases the power of supplying one of these wants will increase the power of supplying all, since the labor saved in one direction may be expended in other directions.

When division of labor has taken place, and different parts in production are taken by different individuals, the gain obtained by any labor-saving improvement in one branch of production will, in like manner, be averaged with all. If, for instance, improvements be made in the weaving of cloth and the working of iron, the effect will be that a bushel of grain will exchange for more cloth and more iron, and thus the farmer will be enabled to obtain the same quantity of all the things he wants with less labor, or a somewhat greater quantity with the same labor. And so with all other producers.

Even when the improvement is kept a secret, or the inventor is protected for a time by a patent, it is only in part that the benefit can be retained. It is the general characteristic of labor-saving improvements, after at least a certain stage in the arts is reached, that the production of larger quantities is necessary to secure the economy. And those who have the monopoly are impelled by their desire for the largest profit to produce more at a lower price, rather than to produce the same quantity at the previous price, thus enabling the producers of other things to obtain for less labor the particular things in the production of which the saving has been effected, and thus diffusing part of the benefit, and generally the largest part, over the whole field of industry.

In this way all labor-saving inventions tend to increase the productive power of all labor, and, except in so far as they are monopolized, their whole benefit is thus diffused. For, if in one occupation labor become more profitable than in others, labor is drawn to it until the net average in different occupations is restored. And so, where not artificially prevented, does the same tendency bring to a common level the earnings of capital. The direct effect of improvements and inventions which add to productive power is, it is to be remarked, always to increase the earnings of labor, never to increase the earnings of capital. The advantage, even in such improvements as may seem primarily to be rather capital-saving than labor-saving— as, for instance, an invention which lessens the time required for the tanning of hides—becomes a property and advantage of labor. The reason is, not to go into a more elaborate explanation, that labor is the active factor in production. Capital is merely its tool and instrument. The great gains made by particular capitalists in the utilization of improvements, are not the gains of capital, but generally the gains of monopoly, though sometimes they may be gains of adventure or of management. The rate of interest, which is the measure of the earnings of capital, has not increased with all the enormous labor-saving improvements of our century; on the contrary, its tendency has been to diminish. But the requirement of larger amounts of capital, which is generally characteristic of labor-saving improvements, may increase the facility with which those who have large capitals can establish monopolies that enable them to intercept what would naturally go to labor. This, however, is an effect, rather than a cause, of the failure of labor to get the benefit of improvements in production.

For the cause we must go further. While labor-saving improvements increase the power of labor, no improvement or invention can release labor from its dependence upon land. Labor-saving improvements only increase the power of producing wealth from land. And land being monopolized as the private property of certain persons, who can thus prevent others from using it, all these gains, which accrue primarily to labor, can be demanded from labor by the owners of land, in higher rents and higher prices. Thus, as we see it, the march of improvement and invention has increased neither interest nor wages, but its general effect has everywhere been to increase the value of land. Where increase of wages has been won, it has been by combination, or the concurrence of special causes; but what of the increased productiveness which primarily attaches to labor has been thus secured by labor is comparatively trivial. Some part of it has gone to various other monopolies, but the great bulk has gone to the monopoly of the soil, has increased ground-rents and raised the value of land.

The railroad, for instance, is a great labor-saving invention. It does not increase the quantity of grain which the farmer can raise, nor the quantity of goods which the manufacturer can turn out; but by reducing the cost of transportation it increases the quantity of all the various things which can be obtained in exchange for produce of either kind; which practically amounts to the same thing.

These gains primarily accrue to labor; that is to say, the advantage given by the railroad in the district which it affects, is to save labor; to enable the same labor to procure more wealth. But as we see where railroads are built, it is not labor that secures the gain. The railroad being a monopoly—and in the United States, a practically unrestricted monopoly—as large a portion as possible of these gains, over and above the fair returns on the capital invested, is intercepted by the managers, who by fictitious costs, watered stock, and in various other ways, thinly disguise their levies, and who generally rob the stockholders while they fleece the public. The rest of the gain —the advantage which, after these deductions, accrues to labor—is intercepted by the monopolists of land. As the productiveness of labor is increased, or even as there is a promise of its increase, so does the value of land increase, and labor, having to pay proportionately more for land.

is shorn of all the benefit.   Taught by experience, when a
railroad opens a new district we do not expect wages to
increase ; what we expect to increase is the value of land.

The elevated railroads of New York are great labor-
saving machines, which have greatly reduced the time and
labor necessary to take people from one end of the city to
the other.   They have made accessible to the overcrowded
population of the lower part of the island, the vacant
spaces at the upper.   But they have not added to the
earnings of labor, nor made it easier for the mere laborer
to live.   Some portion of the gain has been intercepted
by Mr. Cyrus Field, Mr. Samuel J. Tilden, Mr. Jay Gould,
and other managers and manipulators.   Over and above
this, the advantage has gone to the owners of land.   The
reduction in the time and cost of transportation has made
much vacant land accessible to an overcrowded population,
but as this land has been made accessible, so has its value
risen, and the tenement-house population is as crowded as
ever.   The managers of the roads have gained some millions; the owners of the land affected, some hundreds of
millions; but the working-classes of New York are no
better off.   What they gain in improved transportation
they must pay in increased rent.

And so would it be with any improvement or material
benefaction.   Supposing the very rich men of New York
were to become suddenly imbued with that public spirit
which shows itself in the Astor Library and the Cooper
Institute, and that it should become among them a passion,
leading them even to beggar themselves in the emulation
to benefit their fellow-citizens.   Supposing such a man as
Mr. Gould were to make the elevated roads free, were to
assume the cost of the Fire Department, and give every
house a free telephone connection ; and Mr. Vanderbilt,
not to be outdone, were to assume the cost of putting
down good pavements, and cleaning the streets, and run-

ning the horse-cars for nothing; while the Astors were to build libraries in every ward. Supposing the fifty, twenty, ten, and still smaller millionaires, seized by the same passion, were singly or together, at their own cost, to bring in plentiful supplies of water; to furnish heat, light and power free of charge; to improve and maintain the schools; to open theaters and concerts to the public; to establish public gardens and baths and markets; to open stores where everything could be bought at retail for the lowest wholesale price;—in short, were to do everything that could be done to make New York a cheap and pleasant place to live in? The result would be that New York being so much more desirable a place to live in, more people would desire to live in it, and the landowners could charge so much the more for the privilege. All these benefactions would increase rent.

And so, whatever be the character of the improvement, its benefit, land being monopolized, must ultimately go to the owners of land. Were labor-saving invention carried so far that the necessity of labor in the production of wealth were done away with, the result would be that the owners of land could command all the wealth that could be produced, and need not share with labor even what is necessary for its maintenance. Were the powers and capacities of land increased, the gain would be that of landowners. Or were the improvement to take place in the powers and capacities of labor, it would still be the owners of land, not laborers, who would reap the advantage.

For land being indispensable to labor, those who monopolize land are able to make their own terms with labor; or rather, the competition with each other of those who cannot employ themselves, yet must find employment or starve, will force wages down to the lowest point at which the habits of the laboring-class permit them to live and reproduce. At this point, in all countries where land is fully monopolized, the wages of common labor must rest, and toward it all other wages tend, being kept up above it only by the special conditions, artificial or otherwise, which give labor in some occupations higher wages than in others. And so no improvement even in the power of labor itself—whether it come from education, from the actual increase of muscular force, or from the ability to do with less sleep and work longer hours—could raise the reward of labor above this point. This we see in countries and in occupations where the labor of women and children is called in to aid the natural breadwinner in the support of the family. While as for any increase in economy and thrift, as soon as it became general it could only lessen, not increase, the reward of labor.

This is the "iron law of wages," as it is styled by the Germans—the law which determines wages to the minimum on which laborers will consent to live and reproduce. It is recognized by all economists, though by most of them attributed to other causes than the true one. It is manifestly an inevitable result of making the land from which all must live the exclusive property of some. The lord of the soil is necessarily lord of the men who live upon it. They are as truly and as fully his slaves as though his ownership in their flesh and blood were acknowledged. Their competition with each other to obtain from him the means of livelihood must compel them to give up to him all their earnings save the necessary wages of slavery—to wit, enough to keep them in working condition and maintain their numbers. And as no possible increase in the power of his labor, or reduction in his expenses of living, can benefit the slave, neither can it, where land is monopolized, benefit those who have nothing but their labor. It can only increase the value of land—the proportion of the produce that goes to the landowner. And this being the

case, the greater employment of machinery, the greater
division of labor, the greater contrasts in the distribution
of wealth, become to the working-masses positive evils
—making their lot harder and more hopeless as material
progress goes on.   Even education adds but to the capacity
for suffering.   If the slave must continue to be a slave, it
is cruelty to educate him.

All this we may not yet fully realize, because the
industrial revolution which began with the introduction
of steam, is as yet in its first stages, while up to this time
the overrunning of a new continent has reduced social
pressure, not merely here, but even in Europe.   But the
new continent is rapidly being fenced in, and the indus
trial revolution goes on faster and faster.

CHAPTER XV.

SLAVERY AND SLAVERY.

I MUST leave it to the reader to carry on in other directions, if he choose, such inquiries as those to which the last three chapters have been devoted.* The more carefully he examines, the more fully will he see that at the root of every social problem lies a social wrong, that "ignorance, neglect or contempt of human rights are the causes of public misfortunes and corruptions of government." Yet, in truth, no elaborate examination is necessary. To understand why material progress does not benefit the masses requires but a recognition of the self-evident truth that man cannot live without land; that it is only on land and from land that human labor can produce.

Robinson Crusoe, as we all know, took Friday as his slave. Suppose, however, that instead of taking Friday as his slave, Robinson Crusoe had welcomed him as a man and a brother; had read him a Declaration of Independence, an Emancipation Proclamation and a Fifteenth Amendment, and informed him that he was a free and independent citizen, entitled to vote and hold office; but had at the same time also informed him that that particular island was his (Robinson Crusoe's) private and exclusive

---

* They are pursued in more regular and scientific form in "Progress and Poverty," a book to which I must refer the reader a more elaborate discussion of economic questions.

property. What would have been the difference? Since
Friday could not fly up into the air nor swim off through
the sea, since if he lived at all he must live on the island,
he would have been in one case as much a slave as in the
other. Crusoe's ownership of the island would be equivalent to his ownership of Friday.

Chattel slavery is, in fact, merely the rude and primitive
mode of property in man. It only grows up where population is sparse; it never, save by virtue of special circumstances, continues where the pressure of population gives
land a high value, for in that case the ownership of land
gives all the power that comes from the ownership of men,
in more convenient form. When in the course of history
we see the conquerors making chattel slaves of the conquered, it is always where population is sparse and land
of little value, or where they want to carry off their human
spoil. In other cases, the conquerors merely appropriate
the lands of the conquered, by which means they just as
effectually, and much more conveniently, compel the conquered to work for them. It was not until the great estates
of the rich patricians began to depopulate Italy that the
importation of slaves began. In Turkey and Egypt, where
chattel slavery is yet legal, it is confined to the inmates
and attendants of harems. English ships carried negro
slaves to America, and not to England or Ireland, because
in America land was cheap and labor was valuable, while
in western Europe land was valuable and labor was cheap.
As soon as the possibility of expansion over new land
ceased, chattel slavery would have died out in our Southern
States. As it is, Southern planters do not regret the abolition of slavery. They get out of the freedmen as tenants
as much as they got out of them as slaves. While as for
predial slavery—the attachment of serfs to the soil—the
form of chattel slavery which existed longest in Europe,
it is only of use to the proprietor where there is little

competition for land. Neither predial slavery nor absolute
chattel slavery could have added to the Irish landlord's
virtual ownership of men—to his power to make them
work for him without return. Their own competition for
the means of livelihood insured him all they possibly could
give. To the English proprietor the ownership of slaves
would be only a burden and a loss, when he can get
laborers for less than it would cost to maintain them as
slaves, and when they are become ill or infirm can turn
them on the parish. Or what would the New England
manufacturer gain by the enslavement of his operatives?
The competition with each other of so-called freemen, who
are denied all right to the soil of what is called *their*
country, brings him labor cheaper and more conveniently
than would chattel slavery.

That a people can be enslaved just as effectually by
making property of their lands as by making property of
their bodies, is a truth that conquerors in all ages have
recognized, and that, as society developed, the strong and
unscrupulous who desired to live off the labor of others,
have been prompt to see. The coarser form of slavery, in
which each particular slave is the property of a particular
owner, is fitted only for a rude state of society, and with
social development entails more and more care, trouble
and expense upon the owner. But by making property
of the land instead of the person, much care, supervision
and expense are saved the proprietors; and though no
particular slave is owned by a particular master, yet the
one class still appropriates the labor of the other class as
before.

That each particular slave should be owned by a particular master would in fact become, as social development
went on, and industrial organization grew complex, a
manifest disadvantage to the masters. They would be
at the trouble of whipping, or otherwise compelling the

slaves to work; at the cost of watching them, and of
keeping them when ill or unproductive; at the trouble of
finding work for them to do, or of hiring them out, as at
different seasons or at different times, the number of
slaves which different owners or different contractors
could advantageously employ would vary.   As social
development went on, these inconveniences might, were
there no other way of obviating them, have led slave-
owners to adopt some such device for the joint ownership
and management of slaves, as the mutual convenience of
capitalists has led to in the management of capital.   In a
rude state of society, the man who wants to have money
ready for use must hoard it, or, if he travels, carry it with
him.   The man who has capital must use it himself or
lend it.   But mutual convenience has, as society developed,
suggested methods of saving this trouble.   The man who
wishes to have his money accessible turns it over to a
bank, which does not agree to keep or hand him back
that particular money, but money to that amount.   And
so by turning over his capital to savings-banks or trust
companies, or by buying the stock or bonds of corporations
he gets rid of all trouble of handling and employing it
Had chattel slavery continued, some similar device for the
ownership and management of slaves would in time have
been adopted.   But by changing the form of slavery—by
freeing men and appropriating land—all the advantages
of chattel slavery can be secured without any of the dis-
advantages which in a complex society attend the owning
of a particular man by a particular master.

Unable to employ themselves, the nominally free laborers are forced by their competition with each other to
pay as rent all their earnings above a bare living, or to
sell their labor for wages which give but a bare living; and
as landowners the ex-slaveholders are enabled as before,
to appropriate to themselves the labor or the produce of

the labor of their former chattels, having in the value which this power of appropriating the proceeds of labor gives to the ownership of land, a capitalized value equivalent, or more than equivalent, to the value of their slaves. They no longer have to drive their slaves to work; want and the fear of want do that more effectually than the lash. They no longer have the trouble of looking out for their employment or hiring out their labor, or the expense of keeping them when they cannot work. That is thrown upon the slaves. The tribute that they still wring from labor seems like voluntary payment. In fact, they take it as their honest share of the rewards of production—since *they* furnish the land! And they find so-called political economists, to say nothing of so-called preachers of Christianity, to tell them it is so.

We of the United States take credit for having abolished slavery. Passing the question of how much credit the majority of us are entitled to for the abolition of negro slavery, it remains true that we have abolished only one form of slavery—and that a primitive form which had been abolished in the greater portion of the country by social development, and that, notwithstanding its race character gave it peculiar tenacity, would in time have been abolished in the same way in other parts of the country. We have not really abolished slavery; we have retained it in its most insidious and wide-spread form—in a form which applies to whites as to blacks. So far from having abolished slavery, it is extending and intensifying, and we make no scruple of selling into it our own children —the citizens of the Republic yet to be. For what else are we doing in selling the land on which future citizens must live, if they are to live at all?

The essence of slavery is the robbery of labor. It consists in compelling men to work, yet taking from them all the produce of their labor except what suffices for a bare living. Of how many of our "free and equal American citizens" is that already the lot? And of how many more is it coming to be the lot?

In all our cities there are, even in good times, thousands and thousands of men who would gladly go to work for wages that would give them merely board and clothes —that is to say, who would gladly accept the wages of slaves. As 1 have previously stated, the Massachusetts Bureau of Labor Statistics and the Illinois Bureau of Labor Statistics both declare that in the majority of cases the earnings of wage-workers will not maintain their families, and must be pieced out by the earnings of women and children. In our richest States are to be found men reduced to a virtual peonage—living in their employers' houses, trading at their stores, and for the most part unable to get out of their debt from one year's end to the other. In New York, shirts are made for thirty-five cents a dozen, and women working from fourteen to sixteen hours a day average three dollars or four dollars a week. There are cities where the prices of such work are lower still. As a matter of dollars and cents, no master could afford to work slaves so hard and keep them so cheaply.

But it may be said that the analogy between our industrial system and chattel slavery is only supported by the consideration of extremes. Between those who get but a bare living and those who can live luxuriously on the earnings of others, are many gradations, and here lies the great middle class. Between all classes, moreover, a constant movement of individuals is going on. The millionaire's grandchildren may be tramps, while even the poor man who has lost hope for himself may cherish it for his son. Moreover, it is not true that all the difference between what labor fairly earns and what labor really gets goes to the owners of land. And with us, in the United States, a great many of the owners of land are small owners—men who own the homesteads in which they live or the soil which they till, and who combine the characters of laborer and landowner.

These objections will be best met by endeavoring to imagine a well-developed society, like our own, in which chattel slavery exists without distinction of race. To do this requires some imagination, for we know of no such case. Chattel slavery had died out in Europe before modern civilization began, and in the New World has existed only as race slavery, and in communities of low industrial development.

But if we do imagine slavery without race distinction in a progressive community, we shall see that society, even if starting from a point where the greater part of the people were made the chattel slaves of the rest, could not long consist of but the two classes, masters and slaves. The indolence, interest and necessity of the masters would soon develop a class of intermediaries between the completely enslaved and themselves. To supervise the labor of the slaves, and to keep them in subjection, it would be necessary to take, from the ranks of the slaves, overseers, policemen, etc.. and to reward them by more of the produce of slave labor than goes to the ordinary slave. So, too, would it be necessary to draw out special skill and talent. And in the course of social development a class of traders would necessarily arise, who, exchanging the products of slave labor, would retain a considerable portion ; and a class of contractors, who, hiring slave labor from the masters, would also retain a portion of its produce. Thus, between the slaves forced to work for a bare living and the masters who lived without work, intermediaries of various grades would be developed, some of whom would doubtless acquire large wealth.

And in the mutations of fortune, some slaveholders would be constantly falling into the class of intermediaries, and finally into the class of slaves, while individual slaves would be rising. The conscience, benevolence or gratitude of masters would lead them occasionally to manumit slaves; their interest would lead them to reward the diligence, inventiveness, fidelity to themselves, or treachery to their fellows, of particular slaves. Thus, as has often occurred in slave countries, we would find slaves who were free to make what they could on condition of paying so much to their masters every month or every quarter; slaves who had partially bought their freedom, for a day or two days or three days in the week, or for certain months in the year, and those who had completely bought themselves, or had been presented with their freedom. And, as has always happened where slavery had not race character, some of these ex-slaves or their children would, in the constant movement, be always working their way to the highest places, so that in such a state of society the apologists of things as they are would triumphantly point to these examples, saying, "See how beautiful a thing is slavery! Any slave can become a slaveholder himself if he is only faithful, industrious and prudent! It is only their own ignorance and dissipation and laziness that prevent all slaves from becoming masters!" And then they would indulge in a moan for human nature. "Alas!" they would say, "the fault is not in slavery; it is in human nature"—meaning, of course, other human nature than their own. And if any one hinted at the abolition of slavery, they would charge him with assailing the sacred rights of property, and of endeavoring to rob poor blind widow women of the slaves that were their sole dependence; call him a crank and a communist; an enemy of man and a defier of God!

Consider, furthermore, the operation of taxation in an advanced society based on chattel slavery; the effect of the establishment of monopolies of manufacture, trade and transportation; of the creation of public debts, etc., and you will see that in reality the social phenomena would be essentially the same if men were made property as they are under the system that makes land property.

It must be remembered, however, that the slavery that results from the appropriation of land does not come suddenly, but insidiously and progressively. Where population is sparse and land of little value, the institution of private property in land may exist without its effects being much felt. As it becomes more and more difficult to get land, so will the virtual enslavement of the laboring-classes go on. As the value of land rises, more and more of the earnings of labor will be demanded for the use of land, until finally nothing is left to laborers but the wages of slavery—a bare living.

But the degree as well as the manner in which individuals are affected by this movement must vary very much. Where the ownership of land has been much diffused, there will remain, for some time after the mere laborer has been reduced to the wages of slavery, a greater body of smaller landowners occupying an intermediate position, and who, according to the land they hold, and the relation which it bears to their labor, may, to make a comparison with chattel slavery, be compared, in their gradations, to the owners of a few slaves; to those who own no slaves but are themselves free; or to partial slaves, compelled to render service for one, two, three, four or five days in the week, but for the rest of the time their own masters. As land becomes more and more valuable this class will gradually pass into the ranks of the completely enslaved. The independent American farmer working with his own hands on his own land is doomed as certainly as two thousand years ago his prototype of Italy was doomed. He must disappear, with the development of the private ownership of land, as the English yeoman has already disappeared.

We have abolished negro slavery in the United States.
But how small is the real benefit to the slave. George M.
Jackson writes me from St. Louis, under date of August
15, 1883 :

> During the war I served in a Kentucky regiment in the Federal
> army. When the war broke out, my father owned sixty slaves. I
> had not been back to my old Kentucky home for years until a short
> time ago, when I was met by one of my father's old negroes, who
> said to me : "Mas George, you say you sot us free; but 'fore God,
> I'm wus off than when I belonged to your father." The planters, on
> the other hand, are contented with the change. They say : "How
> foolish it was in us to go to war for slavery. We get labor cheaper
> now than when we owned the slaves." How do they get it cheaper?
> Why, in the shape of rents they take more of the labor of the negro
> than they could under slavery, for then they were compelled to return
> him sufficient food, clothing and medical attendance to keep him
> well, and were compelled by conscience and public opinion, as well
> as by law, to keep him when he could no longer work. Now their
> interest and responsibility cease when they have got all the work out
> of him they can.

In one of his novels, Capt. Marryat tells of a schoolmaster who announced that he had abandoned the use of
the rod. When tender mothers, tempted by this announce-
ment, brought their boys to his institution, he was eloquent
in his denunciations of the barbarism of the rod ; but no
sooner had the doors closed upon them than the luckless
pupils found that the master had only abandoned the use
of the rod for the use of the cane ! Very much like this
is our abolition of negro slavery.

The only one of our prominent men who had any glim-
mering of what was really necessary to the abolition of
slavery was Thaddeus Stevens, but it was only a glim-
mering. "Forty acres and a mule" would have been a
measure of scant justice to the freedmen, and it would for
a while have given them something of that personal independence which is necessary to freedom. Yet only for a

while. In the course of time, and as the pressure of population increased, the forty acres would, with the majority of them, have been mortgaged and the mule sold, and they would soon have been, as now, competitors for a foothold upon the earth and for the means of making a living from it. Such a measure would have given the freedmen a fairer start, and for many of them would have postponed the evil day; but that is all. Land being private property, that evil day *must* come.

I do not deny that the blacks of the South have in some things gained by the abolition of chattel slavery. I will not even insist that, on the whole, their material condition has not been improved. But it must be remembered that the South is yet but sparsely settled, and is behindhand in industrial development. The continued existence of slavery there was partly the effect and partly the cause of this. As population increases, as industry is developed, the condition of the freedmen must become harder and harder. As yet, land is comparatively cheap in the South, and there is much not only unused but unclaimed. The consequence is, that the freedmen are not yet driven into that fierce competition which must come with denser population; there is no seeming surplus of labor seeking employment on any terms, as in the North. The freedmen merely get a living, as in the days of slavery, and in many cases not so good a living; but still there is little or no difficulty in getting that. To compare fairly the new estate of the freedmen with the old, we must wait until in population and industrial development the South begins to approach the condition of the North.

But not even in the North (nor, for that matter, even in Europe) has that form of slavery which necessarily results from the disinheritance of labor by the monopolization of land, yet reached its culmination. For the vast area of unoccupied land on this continent has prevented the full

effects of modern development from being felt.   As it
becomes more and more difficult to obtain land, so will the
virtual enslavement of the laboring-classes go on.   As the
value of land rises, more and more of the earnings of
labor will be demanded for the use of land—that is to say,
laborers must give a greater and greater portion of their
time up to the service of the landlord, until, finally, no
matter how hard they work, nothing is left them but a
bare living.

Of the two systems of slavery, I think there can be no
doubt that upon the same moral level, that which makes
property of persons is more humane than that which
results from making private property of land.   The cruelties which are perpetrated under the system of chattel
slavery are more striking and arouse more indignation
because they are the conscious acts of individuals.   But
for the suffering of the poor under the more refined system
no one in particular seems responsible.   That one human
being should be deliberately burned by other human beings
excites our imagination and arouses our indignation much
more than the great fire or railroad accident in which a
hundred people are roasted alive.   But this very fact
permits cruelties that would not be tolerated under the
one system to pass almost unnoticed under the other.
Human beings are overworked, are starved, are robbed
of all the light and sweetness of life, are condemned to
ignorance and brutishness, and to the infection of physical
and moral disease ; are driven to crime and suicide, not by
other individuals, but by iron necessities for which it seems
that no one in particular is responsible.

To match from the annals of chattel slavery the horrors
that day after day transpire unnoticed in the heart of
Christian civilization it would be necessary to go back to
ancient slavery, to the chronicles of Spanish conquest in
the New World, or to stories of the Middle Passage.

That chattel slavery is not the worst form of slavery we know from the fact that in countries where it has prevailed irrespective of race distinctions, the ranks of chattel slaves have been recruited from the ranks of the free poor, who, driven by distress, have sold themselves or their children. And I think no one who reads our daily papers can doubt that even already, in the United States, there are many who, did chattel slavery, without race distinction, exist among us, would gladly sell themselves or their children, and who would really make a good exchange for their nominal freedom in doing so.

We have not abolished slavery. We never can abolish slavery, until we honestly accept the fundamental truth asserted by the Declaration of Independence and secure to all the equal and unalienable rights with which they are endowed by their Creator. If we cannot or will not do that, then, as a matter of humanity and social stability, it might be well, would it avail, to consider whether it were not wise to amend our constitution and permit poor whites and blacks alike to sell themselves and their children to good masters. If we must have slavery, it were better in the form in which the slave knows his owner, and the heart and conscience and pride of that owner can be appealed to. Better breed children for the slaves of good, Christian, civilized people, than breed them for the brothel or the penitentiary. But alas! that recourse is denied. Supposing we did legalize chattel slavery again, who would buy men when men can be hired so cheaply?

CHAPTER XVI.

THE more we examine, the more clearly may we see that public misfortunes and corruptions of government *do* spring from neglect or contempt of the natural rights of man.

That, in spite of the progress of civilization, Europe is to-day a vast camp, and the energies of the most advanced portion of mankind are everywhere taxed so heavily to pay for preparations for war or the costs of war, is due to two great inventions, that of indirect taxation and that of public debt.

Both of these devices by which tyrannies are maintained, governments are corrupted, and the common people plundered, spring historically from the monopolization of land, and both directly ignore the natural rights of man. Under the feudal system the greater part of public expenses was defrayed from the rent of land, and the landholders had to do the fighting or bear its cost. Had this system been continued, England, for instance, would to-day have had no public debt. And it is safe to say that her people and the world would have been saved those unnecessary and cruel wars in which in modern times English blood and treasure have been wasted. But by the institution of indirect taxes and public debts the great landholders were enabled to throw off on the people at large the burdens which constituted the condition on which they held their lands, and to throw them off in such a way that those on whom they rested, though they might feel the pressure, could not tell from whence it came. Thus it was that the holding of land was insidiously changed from a trust into an individual possession, and the masses stripped of the first and most important of the rights of man.

The institution of public debts, like the institution of private property in land, rests upon the preposterous assumption that one generation may bind another generation. If a man were to come to me and say, "Here is a promissory note which your great-grandfather gave to my great-grandfather, and which you will oblige me by paying," I would laugh at him, and tell him that if he wanted to collect his note he had better hunt up the man who made it; that I had nothing to do with my great-grandfather's promises. And if he were to insist upon payment and to call my attention to the terms of the bond in which my great-grandfather expressly stipulated with his great-grandfather that I should pay him, I would only laugh the more, and be the more certain that he was a lunatic. To such a demand any one of us would reply in effect, "My great-grandfather was evidently a knave or a joker, and your great-grandfather was certainly a fool, which quality you surely have inherited if you expect me to pay you money because my great-grandfather promised that I should do so. He might as well have given your great-grandfather a draft upon Adam or a check upon the First National Bank of the Moon."

Yet upon this assumption that ascendants may bind descendants, that one generation may legislate for another generation, rests the assumed validity of our land titles and public debts.

If it were possible for the present to borrow of the future, for those now living to draw upon wealth to be created by those who are yet to come, there could be no

more dangerous power, none more certain to be abused;
and none that would involve in its exercise a more flagrant
contempt for the natural and unalienable rights of man.
But we have no such power, and there is no possible
invention by which we can obtain it. When we talk
about calling upon future generations to bear their part
in the costs and burdens of the present, about imposing
upon them a share in expenditures we take the liberty of
assuming they will consider to have been made for their
benefit as well as for ours, we are carrying metaphor into
absurdity. Public debts are not a device for borrowing
from the future, for compelling those yet to be to bear a
share in expenses which a present generation may choose
to incur. That is, of course, a physical impossibility.
They are merely a device for obtaining control of wealth in
the present by promising that a certain distribution of
wealth in the future shall be made—a device by which the
owners of existing wealth are induced to give it up under
promise, not merely that other people shall be taxed to
pay them, but that other people's children shall be taxed
for the benefit of their children or the children of their
assigns. Those who get control of governments are thus
enabled to get sums which they could not get by immediate taxation without arousing the indignation and resistance of those who could make the most effective resistance.
Thus tyrants are enabled to maintain themselves, and
extravagance and corruption are fostered. If any cases
can be pointed to in which the power to incur public debts
has been in any way a benefit, they are as nothing compared with the cases in which the effects have been purely
injurious.

The public debts for which most can be said are those
contracted for the purpose of making public improvements,
yet what extravagance and corruption the power of contracting such debts has engendered in the United States is

too well known to require illustration, and has led, in a number of the States, to constitutional restrictions. Even the quasi-public debts of railroad and other such corporations have similarly led to extravagance and corruption that have far outweighed any good results accomplished through them. While as for the great national debts of the world, incurred as they have been for purposes of tyranny and war, it is impossible to see in them anything but evil. Of all these great national debts that of the United States will best bear examination; but it is no exception.

As I have before said, the wealth expended in carrying on the war did not come from abroad or from the future, but from the existing wealth in the States under the national flag, and if, when we called on men to die for their country, we had not shrunk from taking, if necessary, nine hundred and ninety-nine thousand dollars from every millionaire, we need not have created any debt. But instead of that, what taxation we did impose was so levied as to fall on the poor more heavily than on the rich, and incidentally to establish monopolies by which the rich could profit at the expense of the poor. And then, when more wealth still was needed, instead of taking it from those who had it, we told the rich that if they would voluntarily let the nation use some of their wealth we would make it profitable to them by guaranteeing the use of the taxing power to pay them back, principal and interest. And we did make it profitable with a vengeance. Not only did we, by the institution of the national banking system, give them back nine-tenths of much of the money thus borrowed while continuing to pay interest on the whole amount, but even where it was required neither by the letter of the bond nor the equity of the circumstances we made debt incurred in depreciated greenbacks payable on its face in gold. The consequence of this method of

carrying on the war was to make the rich richer instead
of poorer. The era of monstrous fortunes in the United
States dates from the war.

But if this can be said of the debt of the United States,
what shall be said of other national debts !

In paying interest upon their enormous national debt,
what is it that the people of England are paying ? They
are paying interest upon sums thrown or given away by
profligate tyrants and corrupt oligarchies in generations
past—upon grants made to courtezans, and panders, and
sycophants, and traitors to the liberties of their country ;
upon sums borrowed to corrupt their own legislatures and
wage wars against both their own liberties and the liberties
of other peoples. For the Hessians hired and the Indians
armed and the fleets and armies sent to crush the American
colonies into submission, with the effect of splitting into
two what might but for that have perhaps yet been one
great confederated nation ; for the cost of treading down
the Irish people and inflicting wounds that yet rankle ; for
the enormous sums spent in the endeavor to maintain on
the continent of Europe the blasphemy of divine right ;
for expenditures made to carry rapine among unoffending
peoples in the four quarters of the globe, Englishmen of
to-day are taxed. It is not the case of asking a man to
pay a debt contracted by his great-grandfather ; it is asking
him to pay for the rope with which his great-grandfather
was hanged, or the fagots with which he was burned.

The so-called Egyptian debt which the power of England
has recently been used to enforce is a still more flagrant
instance of spoliation. The late Khedive was no more
than an Arab robber, living at free quarters in the country
and plundering its people. All he could get by stripping
them to starvation and nakedness not satisfying his insen-
sate and barbarian profligacy, European money-lenders,
relying upon the assumed sanctity of national debts,

offered him money on the most usurious terms. The money was spent with the wildest recklessness, upon harems, palaces, yachts, diamonds, presents and entertainments; yet to extort interest upon it from poverty-stricken fellahs, Christian England sends fleets and armies to murder and burn, and with her power maintains the tyranny and luxury of a khedival puppet at the expense of the Egyptian people.

Thus the device of public debts enables tyrants to intrench themselves, and adventurers who seize upon government to defy the people. It permits the making of great and wasteful expenditures, by silencing, and even converting into support, the opposition of those who would otherwise resist these expenditures with most energy and force. But for the ability of rulers to contract public debts, nine-tenths of the wars of Christendom for the past two centuries could never have been waged. The destruction of wealth and the shedding of blood, the agony of wives and mothers and children thus caused, cannot be computed, but to these items must be added the waste and loss and demoralization caused by constant preparation for war.

Nor do the public misfortunes and corruptions of government which arise from the ignorance and contempt of human rights involved in the recognition of public debts, end with the costs of war and warlike preparation, and the corruptions which such vast public expenditures foster. The passions aroused by war, the national hatreds, the worship of military glory, the thirst for victory or revenge, dull public conscience; pervert the best social instincts into that low, unreasoning extension of selfishness miscalled patriotism; deaden the love of liberty; lead men to submit to tyranny and usurpation from the savage thirst for cutting the throats of other people, or the fear of having their own throats cut. They so pervert religious perceptions that professed followers of Christ bless in his name the standards of murder and rapine, and thanks are given to the Prince of Peace for victories that pile the earth with mangled corpses and make hearthstones desolate!

Nor yet does the evil end here. William H. Vanderbilt, with his forty millions of registered bonds, declares that the national debt ought not to be paid off; that, on the contrary, it ought to be increased, because it gives stability to the government, "every man who gets a bond becoming a loyal and loving citizen." * Mr. Vanderbilt expresses the universal feeling of his kind. It was not loyal and loving citizens with bonds in their pockets who rushed to the front in our civil war, or who rush to the front in any war; but the possession of a bond does tend to make a man loyal and loving to whoever may grasp the machinery of government, and will continue to cash coupons. A great public debt creates a great moneyed interest that wants "strong government" and fears change, and thus forms a powerful element on which corrupt and tyrannous government can always rely as against the people. We may see already in the United States the demoralization of this influence; while in Europe, where it has had more striking manifestations, it is the mainstay of tyranny, and the strongest obstacle to political reform.

Thomas Jefferson was right when, as a deduction from 'the self-evident truth that the land belongs in usufruct to the living," he declared that one generation should not hold itself bound by the laws or the debts of its predecessors, and as this widest-minded of American patriots and greatest of American statesmen said, measures which would give practical effect to this principle will appear the more salutary the more they are considered.

Indirect taxation, the other device by which the people are bled without feeling it, and those who could make the most effective resistance to extravagance and corruption

---

* Interview in *New York Times.*

are bribed into acquiescence, is an invention whereby taxes are so levied that those who directly pay are enabled to collect them again from others, and generally to collect them with a profit, in higher prices. Those who directly pay the taxes and, still more important, those who desire high prices, are thus interested in the imposition and maintenance of taxation, while those on whom the burden ultimately falls do not realize it.

The corrupting effects of indirect taxation are obvious wherever it has been resorted to, but nowhere more obvious than in the United States. Ever since the war the great effort of our National Government has not been to reduce taxation, but to find excuses for maintaining war taxation. The most corrupting extravagance in every department of administration has thus been fostered, and every endeavor used to increase expense. We have deliberately substituted a costly currency for a cheap currency; we have deliberately added to the cost of paying off the public debt; we maintain a costly navy for which we have no sort of use, and which, in case of war, would be of no sort of use to us; and an army twelve times as large and fifteen times as expensive as we need. We are digging silver out of certain holes in the ground in Nevada and Colorado and poking it down other holes in the ground in Washington, New York and San Francisco. We are spending great sums in useless "public improvements," and are paying pensions under a law which seems framed but to put a premium upon fraud and get away with public money. And yet the great question before Congress is what to do with the surplus. Any proposition to reduce taxation arouses the most bitter opposition from those who profit or who imagine they profit from the imposition of this taxation, and a clamorous lobby surrounds Congress, begging, bullying, bribing, log-rolling *against* the reduction of taxation, each interest protesting and insisting that whatever tax is reduced, its own pet tax must be left intact. This clamor of special interests for the continuance of indirect taxation may give us some idea of how much greater are the sums these taxes take from the people than those they put in the treasury.   But it is only a faint idea, for besides what goes to the government and what is intercepted by private interests, there are the loss and waste caused by the artificial restrictions and difficulties which this system of indirect taxation places in the way of production and exchange, and which unquestionably amount to far more than the other two items.

The cost of this system that can be measured in money is, however, of little moment as compared with its effect in corrupting government, in debasing public morals and befogging the thought of the people.   The first thing every man is called upon to do when he reaches this "land of liberty" is to take a false oath; the next thing he is called upon to do is to bribe a Custom-House officer.   And so on, through every artery of the body politic and every fiber of the public mind, runs the poisonous virus.   Law is brought into contempt by the making of actions that are not crimes in morals crimes in law; the unscrupulous are given an advantage over the scrupulous; voters are bought, officials are corrupted, the press is debauched; and the persistent advocacy of these selfish interests has so far beclouded popular thought that a very large number —I am inclined to think a very large majority—of the American people actually believe that they are benefited by being thus taxed!

To recount in detail the public misfortunes and corruptions of government which arise from this vicious system of taxation would take more space than I can here devote to the subject.   But what I wish specially to point out is, that, like the evils arising from public debts, they are in the last analysis due to "ignorance, neglect or con-

tempt of human rights." While every citizen may properly
be called upon to bear his fair share in all proper expenses
of government, it is manifestly an infringement of natural
rights to use the taxing power so as to give one citizen
an advantage over another, to take from some the proceeds
of their labor in order to swell the profit of others, and to
punish as crimes actions which in themselves are not
injurious.

CHAPTER XVII.

THE FUNCTIONS OF GOVERNMENT.

TO prevent government from becoming corrupt and tyrannous, its organization and methods should be as simple as possible, its functions be restricted to those necessary to the common welfare, and in all its parts it should be kept as close to the people and as directly within their control as may be.

We have ignored these principles in many ways, and the result has been corruption and demoralization, the loss of control by the people, and the wresting of government to the advantage of the few and the spoliation of the many. The line of reform, on one side at least, lies in simplification.

The first and main purpose of government is admirably stated in that grand document which we Americans so honor and so ignore—the Declaration of Independence. It is to secure to men those equal and unalienable rights with which the Creator has endowed them. I shall hereafter show how the adoption of the only means by which, in civilized and progressive society, the first of these unalienable rights—the equal right to land—can be secured, will at the same time greatly simplify government and do away with corrupting influences. And beyond this, much simplification is possible, and should be sought wherever it can be attained. As political corruption makes it easier to resist the demand for reform, whatever may be done to purify politics and bring government within the intelligent supervision and control of the people is in itself not merely an end to be sought, but a means to larger ends.

The American Republic has no more need for its burlesque of a navy than a peaceable giant would have for a stuffed club or a tin sword. It is maintained only for the sake of the officers and the naval rings. In peace it is a source of expense and corruption; in war it would be useless. We are too strong for any foreign power wantonly to attack, we ought to be too great wantonly to attack others. If war should ever be forced upon us, we could safely rely upon science and invention, which are already superseding navies faster than they can be built.

So with our army. All we need, if we even now need that, is a small force of frontier police, such as is maintained in Australia and Canada. Standing navies and standing armies are inimical to the genius of democracy, and it ought to be our pride, as it is our duty, to show the world that a great republic can dispense with both. And in organization, as in principle, both our navy and our army are repugnant to the democratic idea. In both we maintain that distinction between commissioned officers and common soldiers and sailors which arose in Europe when the nobility who furnished the one were considered a superior race to the serfs and peasants who supplied the other. The whole system is an insult to democracy, and ought to be swept away.

Our diplomatic system, too, is servilely copied from the usages of kings who plotted with each other against the liberties of the people, before the ocean steamship and the telegraph were invented. It serves no purpose save to reward unscrupulous politicians and corruptionists, and occasionally to demoralize a poet. To abolish it would save expense, corruption and national dignity.

In legal administration there is a large field for radical reform. Here, too, we have servilely copied English pre-cedents, and have allowed lawyers to make law in the interests of their class until justice is a costly gamble for which a poor man cannot afford to sue. The best use that could be made of our great law libraries, to which the reports of thirty-eight States, of the Federal courts, and of the English, Scotch and Irish courts are each year being added, would be to send them to the paper-mills, and to adopt such principles and methods of procedure as would reduce our great army of lawyers at least to the French standard. At the same time our statute-books are full of enactments which could, with advantage, be swept away. It is not the business of government to make men virtuous or religious, or to preserve the fool from the consequences of his own folly. Government should be repressive no further than is necessary to secure liberty by protecting the equal rights of each from aggression on the part of others, and the moment governmental prohibitions extend beyond this line they are in danger of defeating the very ends they are intended to serve. For while the tendency of laws which prohibit or command what the moral sense does not, is to bring law into contempt and produce hypocrisy and evasion, so the attempt to bring law to the aid of morals as to those acts and relations which do not plainly involve violation of the liberty of others, is to weaken rather than to strengthen moral influences; to make the standard of wrong and right a legal one, and to enable him who can dexterously escape the punishment of the law to escape all punishment. Thus, for instance, there can be no doubt that the standard of commercial honesty would be much higher in the absence of laws for the collection of debts. As to all such matters, the cun-ning rogue keeps within the law or evades the law, while the existence of a legal standard lowers the moral standard and weakens the sanction of public opinion.

Restrictions, prohibitions, interferences with the liberty of action in itself harmless, are evil in their nature, and, though they may sometimes be necessary, may for the most part be likened to medicines which suppress or modify some symptom without lessening the disease; and, generally, where restrictive or prohibitive laws are called for, the evils they are designed to meet may be traced to previous restriction—to some curtailment of natural rights.

All the tendencies of the time are to the absorption of smaller communities, to the enlargement of the area within which uniformity of law and administration is necessary or desirable. But for this very reason we ought with the more tenacity to hold, wherever possible, to the principle of local self-government—the principle that, in things which concern only themselves, the people of each political sub-division—township, ward, city or State, as may be— shall act for themselves. We have neglected this principle within our States even more than in the relations between the State and National Governments, and in attempting to govern great cities by State commissions, and in making what properly belongs to County Supervisors and Township Trustees the business of legislatures, we have divided responsibility and promoted corruption.

Much, too, may be done to restrict the abuse of party machinery, and make the ballot the true expression of the will of the voter, by simplifying our elective methods. And a principle should always be kept in mind which we have largely ignored, that the people cannot manage details, nor intelligently choose more than a few officials. To call upon the average citizen to vote at each election for a long string of candidates, as to the majority of whom he can know nothing unless he makes a business of politics, is to relegate choice to nominating conventions and political rings. And to divide power is often to destroy responsibility, and to provoke, not to prevent, usurpation.

I can but briefly allude to these matters, though in themselves they deserve much attention. It is the more necessary to simplify government as much as possible and to improve, as much as may be, what may be called the mechanics of government, because, with the progress of society, the functions which government must assume steadily increase. It is only in the infancy of society that the functions of government can be properly confined to providing for the common defense and protecting the weak against the physical power of the strong. As society develops in obedience to that law of integration and increasing complexity of which I spoke in the first of these chapters, it becomes necessary in order to secure equality that other regulations should be made and enforced ; and upon the primary and restrictive functions of government are superimposed what may be called coöperative functions, the refusal to assume which leads in many cases, to the disregard of individual rights as surely as does the assumption of directive and restrictive functions not properly belonging to government.

In the division of labor and the specialization of vocation that begin in an early stage of social development, and increase with it, the assumption by individuals of certain parts in the business of society necessarily operates to the exclusion of other individuals. Thus when one opens a store or an inn, or establishes a regular carriage of passengers or goods, or devotes himself to a special trade or profession of which all may have need, his doing of these things operates to prevent others from doing them, and leads to the establishment of habits and customs which make resort to him a necessity to others, and which would put those who were denied this resort at a great disadvantage as compared with other individuals. Thus to secure quality it becomes necessary so to limit liberty of action as to oblige those who thus take upon themselves quasi-public functions to serve without discrimination those who may apply to them upon customary conditions. This principle is recognized by all nations that have made any progress in civilization, in their laws relating to common carriers, innkeepers, etc.

As civilization progresses and industrial development goes on, the concentration which results from the utilization of larger powers and improved processes operates more and more to the restriction and exclusion of competition, and to the establishment of complete monopolies. This we may see very clearly in the railroad. It is but a sheer waste of capital and labor to build one railroad alongside of another; and even where this is done, an irresistible tendency leads either to consolidation or to combination; and even at what are called competing points, competition is only transitional. The consolidation of companies, which in a few years bids fair to concentrate the whole railway business of the United States in the hands of half a dozen managements, the pooling of receipts, and agreements as to business and charges, which even at competing points prevent competition, are due to a tendency inherent in the development of the railroad system, and of which it is idle to complain.

The primary purpose and end of government being to secure the natural rights and equal liberty of each, all businesses that involve monopoly are within the necessary province of governmental regulation, and businesses that are in their nature complete monopolies become properly functions of the state. As society develops, the state must assume these functions, in their nature coöperative, in order to secure the equal rights and liberty of all. That is to say, as, in the process of integration, the individual becomes more and more dependent upon and subordinate to the all, it becomes necessary for government, which is properly that social organ by which alone the whole body of individuals can act, to take upon itself, in the interest of all, certain functions which cannot safely be left to individuals. Thus out of the principle that it is the proper end and purpose of government to secure the natural rights and equal liberty of the individual, grows the principle that it is the business of government to do for the mass of individuals those things which cannot be done, or cannot be so well done, by individual action. As in the development of species, the power of conscious, coördinated action of the whole being must assume greater and greater relative importance to the automatic action of parts, so is it in the development of society. This is the truth in socialism, which, although it is being forced upon us by industrial progress and social development, we are so slow to recognize.

In the physical organism, weakness and disease result alike from the overstraining of functions and from the non-use of functions. In like manner governments may be corrupted and public misfortunes induced by the failure to assume, as governmental, functions that properly belong to government as the controlling organ in the management of common interests, as well as from interferences by government in the proper sphere of individual action. This we may see in our own case. In what we attempt to do by government and what we leave undone we are like a man who should leave the provision of his dinner to the promptings of his stomach while attempting to govern his digestion by the action of his will; or like one who, in walking through a crowded street or over a bad road, should concentrate all his conscious faculties upon the movement of his legs without paying any attention to where he was going.

To illustrate : It is not the business of government to interfere with the views which any one may hold of the Creator or with the worship he may choose to pay him, so long as the exercise of these individual rights does not conflict with the equal liberty of others; and the result of governmental interference in this domain has been hypocrisy, corruption, persecution and religious war. It is not the business of government to direct the employment of labor and capital, and to foster certain industries at the expense of other industries; and the attempt to do so leads to all the waste, loss and corruption due to protective tariffs.

On the other hand, it is the business of government to issue money. This is perceived as soon as the great labor-saving invention of money supplants barter. To leave it to every one who chose to do so to issue money would be to entail general inconvenience and loss, to offer many temptations to roguery, and to put the poorer classes of society at a great disadvantage. These obvious considerations have everywhere, as society became well organized, led to the recognition of the coinage of money as an exclusive function of government. When, in the progress of society, a further labor-saving improvement becomes possible by the substitution of paper for the precious metals as the material for money, the reasons why the issuance of this money should be made a government function become still stronger. The evils entailed by wildcat banking in the United States are too well remembered to need reference. The loss and inconvenience, the swindling and corruption that flowed from the assumption by each State of the Union of the power to license banks of issue ended with the war, and no one would now go back to them. Yet instead of doing what every public consideration impels us to, and assuming wholly and fully as the exclusive function of the General Government the power to issue paper money, the private interests of bankers have, up to this, compelled us to the use of a hybrid currency, of which a large part, though guaranteed by the

General Government, is issued and made profitable to corporations. The legitimate business of banking—the safekeeping and loaning of money, and the making and exchange of credits, is properly left to individuals and associations; but by leaving to them, even in part and under restrictions and guaranties, the issuance of money, the people of the United States suffer an annual loss of millions of dollars, and sensibly increase the influences which exert a corrupting effect upon their government.

The principle evident here may be seen in even stronger light in another department of social life.

The great "railroad question," with its dangers and perplexities, is a most striking instance of the evil consequences which result from the failure of the state to assume functions that properly belong to it.

In rude stages of social development, and where government, neglectful of its proper functions, has been occupied in making needless wars and imposing harmful restrictions, the making and improvement of highways have been left to individuals, who, to recompense themselves, have been permitted to exact tolls. It has, however, from the first, been recognized that these tolls are properly subject to governmental control and regulation. But the great inconveniences of this system, and the heavy taxes which, in spite of attempted regulation, are under it levied upon production, have led, as social advance went on, to the assumption of the making and maintenance of highroads as a governmental duty. In the course of social development came the invention of the railroad, which merged the business of making and maintaining roads with the business of carrying freight and passengers upon them. It is probably due to this that it was not at first recognized that the same reasons which render it necessary for the state to make and maintain common roads apply with even greater force to the building and operating of railroads. In Great Britain and the United States, and, with partial exceptions, in other countries, railroads have been left to private enterprise to build and private greed to manage. In the United States, where railroads are of more importance than in any other country in the world, our only recognition of their public character has been in the donation of lands and the granting of subsidies, which have been the cause of much corruption, and in some feeble attempts to regulate fares and freights.

But the fact that the railroad system as far as yet developed (and perhaps necessarily) combines transportation with the maintenance of roadways, renders competition all the more impossible, and brings it still more clearly within the province of the state. That it makes the assumption of the railroad business by the state a most serious matter is not to be denied. Even if it were possible, which may well be doubted, as has been sometimes proposed, to have the roadway maintained by the state, leaving the furnishing of trains to private enterprise, it would be still a most serious matter. But look at it which way we may, it is so serious a matter that it must be faced. As the individual grows from childhood to maturity, he must meet difficulties and accept responsibilities from which he well might shrink. So is it with society. New powers bring new duties and new responsibilities. Imprudence in going forward involves danger, but it is fatal to stand still. And however great be the difficulties involved in the assumption of the railroad business by the state, much greater difficulties are involved in the refusal to assume it.

It is not necessary to go into any elaborate argument to show that the ownership and management of railroads are functions of the state. That is proved beyond dispute by the logic of events and of existing facts. Nothing is more obvious—at least in the United States, where the tendencies of modern development may be seen much more clearly than in Europe—than that a union of railroading with the other functions of government is inevitable. We may not like it, but we cannot avoid it. Either government must manage the railroads, or the railroads must manage the government. There is no escape. To refuse one horn of the dilemma is to be impaled on the other.

As for any satisfactory state regulation of railroads, the experience of our States shows it to be impossible. A strong-willed despot, clothed with arbitrary power, might curb such leviathans; but popular governments cannot. The power of the whole people is, of course, greater than the power of the railroads, but it cannot be exerted steadily and in details. Even a small special interest is, by reason of its intelligence, compactness and flexibility, more than a match for large and vague general interests; it has the advantage which belongs to a well-armed and disciplined force in dealing with a mob. But in the number of its employees, the amount of its revenues, and the extent of the interests which it controls, the railroad power is gigantic. And, growing faster than the growth of the country, it is tending still faster to concentration. It may be that the man is already born who will control the whole railroad system of the United States, as Vanderbilt, Gould and Huntington now control great sections of it.

Practical politicians all over the United States recognize the utter hopelessness of contending with the railroad power. In many if not in most of the States, no prudent man will run for office if he believes the railroad power is against him. Yet in the direct appeal to the people a power of this kind is weakest, and railroad kings rule States where, on any issues that came fairly before the people, they would be voted down. It is by throwing their weight into primaries, and managing conventions, by controlling the press, manipulating legislatures, and filling the bench with their creatures, that the railroads best exert political power. The people of California, for instance, have voted against the railroad time and again, or rather imagined they did, and even adopted a very bad new constitution because they supposed the railroad was against it. The result is, that the great railroad company, of whose domain California, with an area greater than twice that of Great Britain, is but one of the provinces, absolutely dominates the State. The men who really fought it are taken into its service or crushed, and powers are exerted in the interests of the corporation managers which no government would dare attempt. This company, heavily subsidized, in the first place, as a great public convenience, levies on commerce, not tolls, but tariffs. If a man goes into business requiring transportation he must exhibit his profits and take it into partnership for the lion's share. Importers are bound by an "iron-clad agreement" to give its agents access to their books, and if they do anything the company deems against its interests they are fined or ruined by being placed at a disadvantage to their rivals in business. Three continental railroads heavily subsidized by the nation under the impression that the competition would keep down rates, have now reached the Pacific. Instead of competing they have pooled their receipts. The line of steamers from San Francisco to New York *via* the Isthmus receives $100,000 a month to keep up fares and freights to a level with those exacted by the railroad, and if you would send goods from New York to San Francisco by way of the Isthmus, the cheapest way is first to ship them to England. Shippers to interior points are charged as much as though their goods were carried to the end of the road and then shipped back again ; and even, by means of the agreements mentioned, an embargo is laid upon ocean commerce by sailing-vessels, wherever it might interfere with the monopoly.

I speak of California only as an instance. The power of the railroads is apparent in State after State, as it is in the National Government. Nothing can be clearer than that, if present conditions must continue, the American people might as well content themselves to surrender political power to these great corporations and their affiliated interests. There is no escape from this. The railroad managers cannot keep out of politics, even if they wished to. The difficulties of the railroad question do not arise from the fact that peculiarly bad men have got control of the railroads; they arise from the nature of the railroad business and its intimate relations to other interests and industries.

But it will be said: " If the railroads are even now a corrupting element in our politics, what would they be if the government were to own and to attempt to run them? Is not governmental management notoriously corrupt and inefficient? Would not the effect of adding such a vast army to the already great number of government employees, of increasing so enormously the revenues and expenditures of government, be to enable those who got control of government to defy opposition and perpetuate their power indefinitely; and would it not be, finally, to sink the whole political organization in a hopeless slough of corruption?"

My reply is, that great as these dangers may be, they must be faced, lest worse befall us. When a gale sets him on a lee shore, the seaman must make sail, even at the risk of having his canvas fly from the bolt-ropes and his masts go by the board. The dangers of wind and sea urge him to make everything snug as may be, alow and aloft; to get rid of anything that might diminish the weatherly qualities of his ship, and to send his best helmsman to the wheel,—not supinely to accept the certain destruction of the rocks.

Instead of belittling the dangers of adding to the functions of government as it is at present, what I am endeavoring to point out is the urgent necessity of simplifying and improving government, that it may safely assume the additional functions that social development forces upon it. It is not merely necessary to prevent government from getting more corrupt and more inefficient, though we can no more do that by a negative policy than the seaman can lay to in a gale without drifting; it is necessary to make government much more efficient and much less corrupt. The dangers that menace us are not accidental. They spring from a universal law which we cannot escape. That law is the one I pointed out in the first chapter of this book —that every advance brings new dangers and requires higher and more alert intelligence. As the more highly organized animal cannot live unless it have a more fully developed brain than those of lower animal organizations, so the more highly organized society must perish unless it bring to the management of social affairs greater intelligence and higher moral sense. The great material advances which modern invention has enabled us to make, necessitate corresponding social and political advances. Nature knows no "Baby Act." We must live up to her conditions or not live at all.

My purpose here is to show how important it is that we simplify government, purify politics and improve social conditions, as a preliminary to showing how much in all these directions may be accomplished by one single great reform. But although I shall be obliged to do so briefly, it may be worth while, even if briefly, to call attention to some principles that should not be forgotten in thinking of the assumption by the state of such functions as the running of railroads.

In the first place, I think it may be accepted as a principle proved by experience, that any considerable interest having necessary relations with government is more corruptive of government when acting upon government from without than when assumed by government. Let a ship in mid-ocean drop her anchor and pay out her cable, and though she would be relieved of some weight, since part of the weight of anchor and cable would be supported by the water, not only would her progress be retarded, but she would refuse to answer her helm, and become utterly unmanageable. Yet, assumed as part of the ship, and properly stowed on board, anchor and cable no longer perceptibly interfere with her movements.

A standing army is a corrupting influence, and a danger to popular liberties; but who would maintain that on this ground it were wiser, if a standing army must be kept, that it should be enlisted and paid by private parties, and hired of them by the state? Such an army would be far more corrupting and far more dangerous than one maintained directly by the state, and would soon make its leaders masters of the state.

I do not think the postal department of the government, with its extensive ramifications and its numerous employees, begins to be as important a factor in our politics, or exerts so corrupting an influence, as would a private corporation carrying on this business, and which would be constantly tempted or forced into politics to procure favorable or prevent unfavorable legislation. Where individual States and the General Government have substituted public printing-offices for Public Printers, who themselves furnished material and hired labor, I think the result has been to lessen, not to increase, corruptive influences; and speaking generally, I think experience shows that in all departments of government the system of contracting for work and supplies has, on the whole, led to

more corruption than the system of direct employment
The reason I take to be, that there is in one case a much
greater concentration of corruptive interests and power
than in the other.

The inefficiency, extravagance and corruption which we
commonly attribute to governmental management are
mostly in those departments which do not come under
the public eye, and little concern, if they concern at all,
public convenience. Whether the six new steel cruisers
which the persistent lobbying of contractors has induced
Congress to order, are well or ill built the American people
will never know, except as they learn through the newspapers, and the fact will no more affect their comfort and
convenience than does the fitting of the Sultan's new
breeches, or the latest changes in officers' uniforms which
it has pleased the Secretary of the Navy to order. But
let the mails go astray or the postman fail in his rounds,
and there is at once an outcry. The post-office department
is managed with greater efficiency than any other department of the National Government, because it comes close
to the people. To say the very least, it is managed as
efficiently as any private company could manage such a vast
business, and I think, on the whole, as economically. And
the scandals and abuses that have arisen in it have been,
for the most part, as to out-of-the-way places, and things
of which there was little or no public consciousness. So in
England, the telegraph and parcel-carrying and savings-
bank businesses are managed by government more efficiently
and economically than before by private corporations.

Like these businesses—perhaps even more so—the railroad business comes directly under the notice of the people.
It so immediately concerns the interests, the convenience
and the safety of the great body, that under public management it would compel that clos_ and quick attention that
secures efficiency.

It seems to me that in regard to public affairs we too
easily accept the dictum that faithful and efficient work
can be secured only by the hopes of pecuniary profit, or
the fear of pecuniary loss. We get faithful and efficient
work in our colleges and similar institutions without this,
not to speak of the army and navy, or of the postal and
educational departments of government; and be this as
it may, our railroads are really run by men who, from
switch-tender to general superintendent, have no pecu
niary interest in the business other than to get their pay
—in most cases paltry and insufficient—and hold their
positions. Under governmental ownership they would
have, at the very least, all the incentives to faithfulness
and efficiency that they have now, for that governmental
management of railroads must involve the principles of
civil service reform goes without the saying. The most
determined supporter of the spoils system would not care
to resign the safety of limb and life to engineers and
brakemen appointed for political services.

Look, moreover, at the railroad system as it exists now.
That it is not managed in the interests of the public is
clear; but is it managed in the interests of its owners?
Is it managed with that economy, efficiency and intelligence that are presumed to be the results of private
ownership and control? On the contrary, while the
public interests are utterly disregarded, the interests of
the stockholders are in most cases little better considered.
Our railroads are really managed in the interests of
unscrupulous adventurers, whose purpose is to bull and
bear the stock-market; by men who make the interests of
the property they manage subservient to their personal
interests in other railroads or in other businesses; who
speculate in lands and town sites, who give themselves or
their friends contracts for supplies and special rates for
transportation, and who often deliberately wreck the cor-

poration they control and rob stockholders to the last
cent. From one end to the other, the management of our
railroad system, as it now exists, reeks with jobbery and
fraud.

That ordinary roads, bridges, etc., should not be maintained for profit, either public or private, is an accepted
principle, and the State of New York has recently gone so
far as to abolish all tolls on the Erie Canal. Our postal
service we merely aim to make self-sustaining, and no one
would now think of proposing that the rates of postage
should be increased in order to furnish public revenues ;
still less would any one think of proposing to abandon
the government postal service, and turn the business over
to individuals or corporations. In the beginning the postal
service was carried on by individuals with a view to profits.
Had that system been continued to the present day, it is
certain that we should not begin to have such extensive
and regular postal facilities as we have now, nor such
cheap rates ; and all the objections that are now urged
against the government assumption of the railroad business
would be urged against government carriage of letters.
We never can enjoy the full benefits of the invention of
the railroad until we make the railroads public property,
managed by public servants in the public interests. And
thus will a great cause of the corruption of government,
and a great cause of monstrous fortunes, be destroyed.

All I have said of the railroad applies, of course, to the
telegraph, the telephone, the supplying of cities with gas,
water, heat and electricity,—in short to all businesses
which are in their nature monopolies. I speak of the
railroad only because the magnitude of the business makes
its assumption by the state the most formidable of such
undertakings.

Businesses that are in their nature monopolies are properly functions of the state. The state must control or

assume them, in self-defense, and for the protection of the equal rights of citizens. But beyond this, the field in which the state may operate beneficially as the executive of the great coöperative association, into which it is the tendency of true civilization to blend society, will widen with the improvement of government and the growth of public spirit.

We have already made an important step in this direction in our public-school system. Our public schools are not maintained for the poor, as are the English board schools—where, moreover, payment is required from all who can pay; nor yet is their main motive the protection of the state against ignorance. These are subsidiary motives. But the main motive for the maintenance of our public schools is, that by far the greater part of our people find them the best and most economical means of educating their children. American society is, in fact, organized by the operation of government into coöperative educational associations, and with such happy results that in no State where the public-school system has obtained would any proposition to abolish it get respectful consideration. In spite of the corruption of our politics, our public schools are, on the whole, much better than private schools; while by their association of the children of rich and poor, of Jew and Gentile, of Protestant and Catholic, of Republican and Democrat, they are of inestimable value in breaking down prejudice and checking the growth of class feeling. It is likewise to be remarked as to our public-school system, that corruptive influences seem to spring rather from our not having gone far enough than from our having gone too far in the direction of state action. In some of our States the books used by the children are supplied at public expense, being considered school property, which the pupil receives on entering the school or class, and returns when leaving. In most of them, however, the pupils, unless their parents cannot afford the outlay, are required to furnish their own books. Experience has shown the former system to be much the better, not only because, when books are furnished to all, there is no temptation of those who can afford to purchase books falsely to plead indigence, and no humiliation on the part of those who cannot; but because the number of books required is much less, and they can be purchased at cheaper rates. This not only effects a large economy in the aggregate expenditure, but lessens an important corruptive influence. For the strife of the great school-book publishers to get their books adopted in the public schools, in which most of them make no scruple of resorting to bribery wherever they can, has done much to degrade the character of school boards. This corruptive influence can only be fully done away with by manufacturing school-books at public expense, as has been in a number of the States proposed.

The public-library system, which, beginning in the public-spirited city of Boston, is steadily making its way over the country, and under which both reading and lending libraries are maintained at public expense for the free use of the public, is another instance of the successful extension of the coöperative functions of government. So are the public parks and recreation grounds which we are beginning to establish.

Not only is it possible to go much further in the direction of thus providing, at public expense, for the public health, education and recreation, and for public encouragement of science and invention, but if we can simplify and purify government it will become possible for society in its various sub-divisions to obtain in many other ways, but in much larger degree, those advantages for its members that voluntary coöperative societies seek to obtain. Not only could the most enormous economies thus be obtained, but the growing tendency to adulteration and dishonesty, as fatal to morals as to health, would be checked,* and at least such an organization of industry be reached as would very greatly reduce the appropriative power of aggregated capital, and prevent those strifes that may be likened to wars. The natural progress of social development is unmistakably toward coöperation, or, if the word be preferred, toward socialism, though I dislike to use a word to which such various and vague meanings are attached. Civilization is the art of living together in closer relations. That mankind should dwell together in unity is the evident intent of the Divine mind, —of that Will expressed in the immutable laws of the physical and moral universe which reward obedience and punish disobedience. The dangers which menace modern society are but the reverse of blessings which modern society may grasp. The concentration that is going on in all branches of industry is a necessary tendency of our advance in the material arts. It is not in itself an evil. If in anything its results are evil, it is simply because of our bad social adjustments. The construction of this world in which we find ourselves is such that a thousand men working together can produce many times more than the same thousand men working singly. But this does

---

* There are many manufactured articles for which the producer now receives only a third of the price paid by the consumer, while adulteration has gone far beyond detection by the individual purchaser. Not to speak of the compounding of liquors, of oleomargarine and glucose, a single instance will show how far adulteration is carried. The adulterations in ground coffee have driven many people to purchase their coffee in the bean and grind it themselves. To meet this, at least one firm of large coffee-roasters, and I presume most of them, have adopted an invention by means of which imitation coffee-beans, exactly resembling in appearance the genuine article, are stamped out of a paste. These they mix in large quantities with real coffee.

not make it necessary·that the nine hundred and ninety·
nine must be the virtual slaves of the one.

Let me repeat it, though again and again, for it is, it
seems to me, the great lesson which existing social facts
impress upon him who studies them, and that it is all
important that we should heed: The natural laws which
permit of social advance, require that advance to be
intellectual and moral as well as material. The natural
laws which give us the steamship, the locomotive, the
telegraph, the printing-press, and all the thousand inventions by which our mastery over matter and material
conditions is increased, *require* greater social intelligence
and a higher standard of social morals. Especially do
they make more and more imperative that justice between
man and man which demands the recognition of the
equality of natural rights.

"Seek first the kingdom of God and his righteousness
[right or just doing] and all these things shall be added
unto you." The first step toward a natural and healthy
organization of society is to secure to all men their natu·
ral, equal and unalienable rights in the material universe.
To do this is not to do everything that may be necessary;
but it is to make all else easier. And unless we do this
nothing else will avail.

I have in this chapter touched briefly upon subjects
that for thorough treatment would require much more
space. My purpose has been to show that the simplification and purification of government are rendered the more
necessary, on account of functions which industrial development is forcing upon government, and the further functions which it is becoming more and more evident that it
would be advantageous for government to assume. In
succeeding chapters I propose to show how, by recognizing
in practicable method the equal and unalienable rights
of men to the soil of their country, government may be

greatly simplified, and corrupting influences destroyed. For it is indeed true, as the French Assembly declared, that public misfortunes and corruptions of government spring from ignorance, neglect or contempt of human rights.

Of course in this chapter and elsewhere in speaking of government, the state, the community, etc., I use these terms in a general sense, without reference to existing political divisions. What should properly belong to the township or ward, what to the county or State, what to the nation, and what to such federations of nations as it is in the manifest line of civilization to evolve, is a matter into which I have not entered. As to the proper organization of government, and the distribution of powers, there is much need for thought.

CHAPTER XVIII.

AT the risk of repetition let me recapitulate:
The main source of the difficulties that menace us
is the growing inequality in the distribution of wealth.
To this all modern inventions seem to contribute, and the
movement is hastened by political corruption, and by
special monopolies established by abuse of legislative
power. But the primary cause lies evidently in fundamental social adjustments—in the relations which we have
established between labor and the natural material and
means of labor—between man and the planet which is his
dwelling-place, workshop and storehouse. As the earth
must be the foundation of every material structure, so
institutions which regulate the use of land constitute the
foundation of every social organization, and must affect
the whole character and development of that organization.
In a society where the equality of natural rights is recognized, it is manifest that there can be no great disparity
in fortunes. None except the physically incapacitated will
be dependent on others; none will be forced to sell their
labor to others. There will be differences in wealth, for
there are differences among men as to energy, skill, prudence, foresight and industry; but there can be no very
rich class, and no very poor class; and, as each generation
becomes possessed of equal natural opportunities, whatever
differences in fortune grow up in one generation will not

tend to perpetuate themselves. In such a community, whatever may be its form, the political organization must be essentially democratic.

But, in a community where the soil is treated as the property of but a portion of the people, some of these people from the very day of their birth must be at a disadvantage, and some will have an enormous advantage. Those who have no rights in the land will be forced to sell their labor to the landholders for what they can get; and, in fact, cannot live without the landlords' permission. Such a community must inevitably develop a class of masters and a class of serfs—a class possessing great wealth, and a class having nothing; and its political organization, no matter what its form, must become a virtual despotism.

Our fundamental mistake is in treating land as private property. On this false basis modern civilization everywhere rests, and hence, as material progress goes on, is everywhere developing such monstrous inequalities in condition as must ultimately destroy it. As without land man cannot exist; as his very physical substance, and all that he can acquire or make, must be drawn from the land, the ownership of the land of a country is necessarily the ownership of the people of that country—involving their industrial, social and political subjection. Here is the great reason why the labor-saving inventions, of which our century has been so strikingly prolific, have signally failed to improve the condition of laborers. Labor-saving inventions primarily increase the power of labor, and should, therefore, increase wages and improve the condition of the laboring-classes. But this only where land is free to labor; for labor cannot exert itself without land. No labor-saving inventions can enable us to make something out of nothing, or in any wise lessen our dependence upon land. They can merely add to the efficiency of labor in

working up the raw materials drawn from land. Therefore, wherever land has been subjected to private ownership, the ultimate effect of labor-saving inventions, and of
all improved processes and discoveries, is to enable landowners to demand, and labor to pay, more for the use of
land. Land becomes more valuable, but the wages of
labor do not increase; on the contrary, if there is any
margin for possible reductions, they may be absolutely
reduced.

This we already see, and that in spite of the fact that a
very important part of the effect of modern invention has
been, by the improvement of transportation, to open up
new land. What will be the effect of continued improvement in industrial processes when the land of this continent
is all "fenced in," as in a few more years it will be, we
may imagine if we consider what would have been the
effect of labor-saving inventions upon Europe had no New
World been opened.

But it may be said that, in asserting that where land is
private property the benefit of industrial improvements
goes ultimately to landowners, I ignore facts, and attribute
to one principle more importance than is its due, since it
is clear that a great deal of the increased wealth arising
from modern improvements has not gone to the owners
of land, but to capitalists, manufacturers, speculators,
railroad-owners, and the holders of other monopolies than
that of land. It may be pointed out that the richest
family in Europe are the Rothschilds, who are more loan-
jobbers and bankers than landowners; that the richest in
America are the Vanderbilts, and not the Astors; that Jay
Gould got his money, not by securing land, but by bulling
and bearing the stock-market, by robbing people with
hired lawyers and purchased judges and corrupted legislatures. I may be asked if I attach no importance to the
jobbery and robbery of the tariff, under pretense of

"protecting American labor;" to the jugglery with the monetary system, from the wildcat State banks and national banking system down to the trade-dollar swindle?

In previous chapters I have given answers to all such objections; but to repeat in concise form, my reply is, that I do not ignore any of these things, but that they in no wise invalidate the self-evident principle that land being private property, the ultimate benefit of all improvements in production must go to the landowners. To say that if a man continues to play at rondo the table will ultimately get his money, is not to say that in the meantime he may not have his pocket picked. Let me illustrate:

Suppose an island, the soil of which is conceded to be the property of a few of the inhabitants. The rest of the inhabitants of this island must either hire land of these landowners, paying rent for it, or sell their labor to them, receiving wages. As population increases, the competition between the non-landowners for employment or the means of employment must increase rent and decrease wages until the non-landowners get merely a bare living, and the landholders get all the rest of the produce of the island. Now, suppose any improvement or invention made which will increase the efficiency of labor, it is manifest that, as soon as it becomes general, the competition between the non-landholders must give to the landholders all the benefit. No matter how great the improvement be, it can have but this ultimate result. If the improvements are so great that all the wealth the island can produce or that the landowners care for can be obtained with one-half the labor, they can let the other half of the laborers starve or evict them into the sea; or if they are pious people of the conventional sort, who believe that God Almighty intended these laborers to live, though he did not provide any land for them to live on, they may support them as paupers or ship them off to some other country as the English government is shipping the "surplus" Irishmen. But whether they let them die or keep them alive, they would have no use for them, and, if improvement still went on, they would have use for less and less of them.

This is the general principle.

But in addition to this population of landowners and their tenants and laborers, let us suppose there are on the island a storekeeper, an inventor, a gambler and a pirate. To make our supposition conform to modern fashions, we will suppose a highly respectable gambler—one of the kind who endows colleges and subscribes to the conversion of the heathen—and a very gentlemanly pirate, who flies on his swift cruiser the ensign of a yacht club instead of the old rawhead and bloody-bones, but who, even more regularly and efficiently than the old-fashioned pirate, levies his toll.

Let us suppose the storekeeper, the gambler and the pirate well established in business and making money. Along comes the inventor, and says: "I have an invention which will greatly add to the efficiency of labor and enable you greatly to increase the produce of this island, so that there will be very much more to divide among you all; but, as a condition for telling you of it, I want you to agree that I shall have a royalty upon its use." This is agreed to, the invention is adopted, and does greatly increase the production of wealth. But it does not benefit the laborers. The competition between them still forces them to pay such high rent or take such low wages that they are no better off than before. They still barely live. But the whole benefit of the invention does not in this case go to the landowners. The inventor's royalty gives him a great income, while the storekeeper, the gambler and the pirate all find their incomes much increased. The incomes of each one of these four, we may readily suppose, are larger than any single one of the landowners and

their gains offer the most striking contrast to the poverty
of the laborers, who are bitterly disappointed at not getting any share of the increased wealth that followed the
improvement. Something they feel is wrong, and some
among them even begin to murmur that the Creator of
the island surely did not make it for the benefit of only a
few of its inhabitants, and that, as the common creatures
of the Creator, they, too, have some rights to the use of
the soil of the island.

Suppose then some one to arise and say : " What is the
use of discussing such abstractions as the land question,
that cannot come into practical politics for many a day,
and that can only excite dissension and general unpleas-
antness, and that, moreover, savor of communism, which
as you laborers, who have nothing but your few rags, very
well know is a highly wicked and dangerous thing, meaning the robbery of widow women and orphans, and being
opposed to religion ? Let us be practical. You laborers
are poor and can scarcely get a living, because you are
swindled by the storekeeper, taxed by the inventor, gouged
by the gambler and robbed by the pirate. Landholders
and non-landholders, our interests are in common as
against these vampires. Let us unite to stop their exac-
tions. The storekeeper makes a profit of from ten to fifty
per cent. on all that he sells. Let us form a coöperative
society, which will sell everything at cost and enable
laborers to get rich by saving the storekeeper's profit on
all that they use. As for the inventor, he has been already
well enough paid. Let us stop his royalty, and there will
be so much more to divide between the landowners and
the non-landowners. As for the gambler and the pirate,
let us put a summary end to their proceedings and drive
them off the island ! "

Let us imagine a roar of applause, and these propositions carried out. What then ? Then the landowners

would become so much the richer.   The laborers would
gain nothing, unless it might be in a clearer apprehension
of the ultimate cause of their poverty.   For although, by
getting rid of the storekeeper, the laborers might be able
to live cheaper, the competition between them would soon
force them to give up this advantage to the landowners
by taking lower wages or giving higher rents.   And so
the elimination of the inventor's royalty, and of the pick-
ings and stealings of the gambler and pirate, would only
make land more valuable and increase the incomes of the
landholders.   The saving made by getting rid of the
storekeeper, inventor, gambler and pirate would accrue
to their benefit, as did the increase in production from the
application of the invention.

That all this is true we may see, as I have shown.   The
growth of the railroad system has, for instance, resulted
in putting almost the whole transportation business of the
country in the hands of giant monopolies, who, for the
most part, charge "what the traffic will bear," and who
frequently discriminate in the most outrageous way against
localities.   The effect where this is done, as is alleged in
the complaints that are made, is to reduce the price of
land.   And all this might be remedied, without raising
wages or improving the condition of labor.   It would only
make land more valuable—that is to say, in consideration
of the saving effected in transportation, labor would have
to pay a higher premium for land.

So with all monopolies, and their name is legion.   If
all monopolies, save the monopoly of land, were abolished;
if, even, by means of coöperative societies, or other devices,
the profits of exchange were saved, and goods passed from
producer to consumer at the minimum of cost; if government were reformed to the point of absolute purity and
economy, nothing whatever would be done toward equalization in the distribution of wealth.   The competition

between laborers, who, having no rights in the land, cannot work without some one else's permission, would increase the value of land, and force wages to the point of bare subsistence.

Let me not be misunderstood. I do not say that in the recognition of the equal and unalienable right of each human being to the natural elements from which life must be supported and wants satisfied, lies the solution of all social problems. I fully recognize the fact that even after we do this, much will remain to do. We might recognize the equal right to land, and yet tyranny and spoliation be continued. But whatever else we do, so long as we fail to recognize the equal right to the elements of nature, nothing will avail to remedy that unnatural inequality in the distribution of wealth which is fraught with so much evil and danger. Reform as we may, until we make this fundamental reform our material progress can but tend to differentiate our people into the monstrously rich and the frightfully poor. Whatever be the increase of wealth, the masses will still be ground toward the point of bare subsistence—we must still have our great criminal classes, our paupers and our tramps, men and women driven to degradation and desperation from inability to make an honest living.

CHAPTER XIX.

THE FIRST GREAT REFORM.

DO what we may, we can accomplish nothing real and lasting until we secure to all the first of those equal and unalienable rights with which, as our Declaration of Independence has it, man is endowed by his Creator—the equal and unalienable right to the use and benefit of natural opportunities.

There are people who are always trying to find some mean between right and wrong—people who, if they were to see a man about to be unjustly beheaded, might insist that the proper thing to do would be to chop off his feet. These are the people who, beginning to recognize the importance of the land question, propose in Ireland and England such measures as judicial valuations of rents and peasant proprietary, and in the United States, the reservation to actual settlers of what is left of the public lands, and the limitation of estates.

Nothing whatever can be accomplished by such timid, illogical measures. If we would cure social disease we must go to the root.

There is no use in talking of reserving what there may be left of our public domain to actual settlers. That would be merely a locking of the stable door after the horse had been stolen, and even if it were not, would avail nothing.

There is no use in talking about restricting the amount of land any one man may hold. That, even if it were practicable, were idle, and would not meet the difficulty. The ownership of an acre in a city may give more command of the labor of others than the ownership of a hundred thousand acres in a sparsely settled district, and it is utterly impossible by any legal device to prevent the concentration of property so long as the general causes which irresistibly tend to the concentration of property remain untouched. So long as the wages tend to the point of a bare living for the laborer we cannot stop the tendency of property of all kinds to concentration, and this must be the tendency of wages until equal rights in the soil of their country are secured to all. We can no more abolish industrial slavery by limiting the size of estates than we could abolish chattel slavery by putting a limit on the number of slaves a single slaveholder might own. In the one case as in the other, so far as such restrictions could be made operative they would only increase the difficulties of abolition by enlarging the class who would resist it.

There is no escape from it. If we would save the Republic before social inequality and political demoralization have reached the point when no salvation is possible, we must assert the principle of the Declaration of Independence, acknowledge the equal and unalienable rights which inhere in man by endowment of the Creator, and make land common property.

If there seems anything strange in the idea that all men have equal and unalienable rights to the use of the earth, it is merely that habit can blind us to the most obvious truths. Slavery, polygamy, cannibalism, the flattening of children's heads, or the squeezing of their feet, seem perfectly natural to those brought up where such institutions or customs exist. But, as a matter of fact, nothing is more repugnant to the natural perceptions of men than that land should be treated as subject to individual ownership, like things produced by labor. It is only among an insignificant fraction of the people who have lived on the earth that the idea that the earth itself could be made private property has ever obtained; nor has it ever obtained save as the result of a long course of usurpation, tyranny and fraud. This idea reached development among the Romans, whom it corrupted and destroyed. It took many generations for it to make its way among our ancestors; and it did not, in fact, reach full recognition until two centuries ago, when, in the time of Charles II., the feudal dues were shaken off by a landholders' parliament. We accepted it as we have accepted the aristocratic organization of our army and navy, and many other things, in which we have servilely followed European custom. Land being plenty and population sparse, we did not realize what it would mean when in two or three cities we should have the population of the thirteen colonies. But it is time that we should begin to think of it now, when we see ourselves confronted, in spite of our free political institutions, with all the problems that menace Europe—when, though our virgin soil is not yet quite fenced in, we have a "working-class," a "criminal class" and a "pauper class;" when there are already thousands of so-called *free* citizens of the Republic who cannot by the hardest toil make a living for their families, and when we are, on the other hand, developing such monstrous fortunes as the world has not seen since great estates were eating out the heart of Rome.

What more preposterous than the treatment of land as individual property? In every essential land differs from those things which being the product of human labor are rightfully property. It is the creation of God; they are produced by man. It is fixed in quantity; they may be increased illimitably. It exists, though generations come and go; they in a little while decay and pass again into the elements. What more preposterous than that one

tenant for a day of this rolling sphere should collect rent
for it from his co-tenants, or sell to them for a price what
was here ages before him and will be here ages after him?
What more preposterous than that we, living in New York
city in this year, 1883, should be working for a lot of
landlords who get the authority to live on our labor from
some English king, dead and gone these centuries? What
more preposterous than that we, the present population of
the United States, should presume to grant to our own
people or to foreign capitalists the right to strip of their
earnings American citizens of the next generation? What
more utterly preposterous than these titles to land?
Although the whole people of the earth in one generation
were to unite, they could no more sell title to land against
the next generation than they could sell that generation.
It is a self-evident truth, as Thomas Jefferson said, that
the earth belongs in usufruct to the living.

Nor can any defense of private property in land be made
on the ground of expediency. On the contrary, look
where you will, and it is evident that the private ownership of land keeps land out of use; that the speculation
it engenders crowds population where it ought to be more
diffused, diffuses it where it ought to be closer together;
compels those who wish to improve to pay away a large
part of their capital, or mortgage their labor for years
before they are permitted to improve; prevents men from
going to work for themselves who would gladly do so,
crowding them into deadly competition with each other
for the wages of employers; and enormously restricts the
production of wealth while causing the grossest inequality
in its distribution.

No assumption can be more gratuitous than that constantly made that absolute ownership of land is necessary
to the improvement and proper use of land. What is
necessary to the best use of land is the security of improve-

ments—the assurance that the labor and capital expended upon it shall enjoy their reward. This is a very different thing from the absolute ownership of land. Some of the finest buildings in New York are erected upon leased ground. Nearly the whole of London and other English cities, and great parts of Philadelphia and Baltimore, are so built. All sorts of mines are opened and operated on leases. In California and Nevada the most costly mining operations, involving the expenditure of immense amounts of capital, were undertaken upon no better security than the mining regulations, which gave no ownership of the land, but only guaranteed possession as long as the mines were worked.

If shafts can be sunk and tunnels can be run, and the most costly machinery can be put up on public land on mere security of possession, why could not improvements of all kinds be made on that security? If individuals will use and improve land belonging to other individuals, why would they not use and improve land belonging to the whole people? What is to prevent land owned by Trinity Church, by the Sailors' Snug Harbor, by the Astors or Rhinelanders, or any other corporate or individual owners, from being as well improved and used as now, if the ground-rents, instead of going to corporations or individuals, went into the public treasury?

In point of fact, if land were treated as the common property of the whole people, it would be far more readily improved than now, for then the improver would get the whole benefit of his improvements. Under the present system, the price that must be paid for land operates as a powerful deterrent to improvement. And when the improver has secured land either by purchase or by lease, he is taxed upon his improvements, and heavily taxed in various ways upon all that he uses. Were land treated as the property of the whole people, the ground-rent

accruing to the community would suffice for public purposes, and all other taxation might be dispensed with.
The improver could more easily get land to improve, and
would retain for himself the full benefit of his improvements exempt from taxation.

To secure to all citizens their equal right to the land on
which they live, does not mean, as some of the ignorant
seem to suppose, that every one must be given a farm,
and city land be cut up into little pieces. It would be
impossible to secure the equal rights of all in that way,
even if such division were not in itself impossible. In
a small and primitive community of simple industries
and habits, such as that Moses legislated for, substantial
equality may be secured by allotting to each family an
equal share of the land and making it unalienable. Or, as
among our rude ancestors in western Europe, or in such
primitive society as the village communities of Russia and
India, substantial equality may be secured by periodical
allotment or cultivation in common. Or in sparse populations, such as the early New England colonies, substantial
equality may be secured by giving to each family its town-
lot and its seed-lot, holding the rest of the land as town
land or common. But among a highly civilized and rapidly
growing population, with changing centers, with great
cities and minute division of industry, and a complex
system of production and exchange, such rude devices
become ineffective and impossible.

Must we therefore consent to inequality—must we
therefore consent that some shall monopolize what is the
common heritage of all? Not at all. If two men find a
diamond, they do not march to a lapidary to have it cut
in two. If three sons inherit a ship, they do not proceed
to saw her into three pieces; nor yet do they agree that if
this cannot be done equal division is impossible. Nor yet
is there no other way to secure the rights of the owners of

a railroad than by breaking up track, engines, cars and depots into as many separate bits as there are stockholders. And so it is not necessary, in order to secure equal rights to land, to make an equal division of land. All that it is necessary to do is to collect the ground-rents for the common benefit.

Nor, to take ground-rents for the common benefit, is it necessary that the state should actually take possession of the land and rent it out from year to year, or from term to term, as some ignorant people suppose. It can be done in a much more simple and easy manner by means of the existing machinery of taxation. All it is necessary to do is to abolish all other forms of taxation until the weight of taxation rests upon the value of land irrespective of improvements, and take the ground-rent for the public benefit.

In this simple way, without increasing governmental machinery, but, on the contrary, greatly simplifying it, we could make land common property. And in doing this we could abolish all other taxation, and still have a great and steadily increasing surplus—a growing common fund, in the benefits of which all might share, and in the management of which there would be such a direct and general interest as to afford the strongest guaranties against misappropriation or waste. Under this system no one could afford to hold land he was not using, and land not in use would be thrown open to those who wished to use it, at once relieving the labor market and giving an enormous stimulus to production and improvement, while land in use would be paid for according to its value, irrespective of the improvements the user might make. On these he would not be taxed. All that his labor could add to the common wealth, all that his prudence could save, would be his own, instead of, as now, subjecting him to fine. Thus would the sacred right of property be acknowledged by securing to each the reward of his exertion

Practically, then, the greatest, the most fundamental of all reforms, the reform which will make all other reforms easier, and without which no other reform will avail, is to be reached by concentrating all taxation into a tax upon the value of land, and making that heavy enough to take as near as may be the whole ground-rent for common purposes.

To those who have never studied the subject, it will seem ridiculous to propose as the greatest and most far-reaching of all reforms a mere fiscal change. But whoever has followed the train of thought through which in preceding chapters I have endeavored to lead, will see that in this simple proposition is involved the greatest of social revolutions—a revolution compared with which that which destroyed ancient monarchy in France, or that which destroyed chattel slavery in our Southern States, were as nothing.

In a book such as this, intended for the casual reader, who lacks inclination to follow the close reasoning necessary to show the full relation of this seemingly simple reform to economic laws, I cannot exhibit its full force, but I may point to some of the more obvious of its effects.

To appropriate ground-rent * to public uses by means of taxation would permit the abolition of all the taxation which now presses so heavily upon labor and capital. This would enormously increase the production of wealth by the removal of restrictions and by adding to the incentives to production.

It would at the same time enormously increase the production of wealth by throwing open natural opportunities. It would utterly destroy land monopoly by making the holding of land unprofitable to any but the user. There

---

* I use the term ground-rent because the proper economic term, rent, might not be understood by those who are in the habit of using it in its common sense, which applies to the income from buildings and improvements. as well as land.

would be no temptation to any one to hold land in expectation of future increase in its value when that increase was certain to be demanded in taxes. No one could afford to hold valuable land idle when the taxes upon it would be as heavy as they would be were it put to the fullest use. Thus speculation in land would be utterly destroyed, and land not in use would become free to those who wished to use it.

The enormous increase in production which would result from thus throwing open the natural means and opportunities of production, while at the same time removing the taxation which now hampers, restricts and fines production, would enormously augment the annual fund from which all incomes are drawn. It would at the same time make the distribution of wealth much more equal. That great part of this fund which is now taken by the owners of land, not as a return for anything by which they add to production, but because they have appropriated as their own the natural means and opportunities of production, and which as material progress goes on, and the value of land rises, is constantly becoming larger and larger, would be virtually divided among all, by being utilized for common purposes. The removal of restrictions upon labor, and the opening of natural opportunities to labor, would make labor free to employ itself. Labor, the producer of all wealth, could never become "a drug in the market" while desire for any form of wealth was unsatisfied. With the natural opportunities of employment thrown open to all, the spectacle of willing men seeking vainly for employment could not be witnessed; there could be no surplus of unemployed labor to beget that cutthroat competition of laborers for employment which crowds wages down to the cost of merely living. Instead of the one-sided competition of workmen to find employment, employers would compete with each other to obtain workmen.

There would be no need of combinations to raise or maintain wages; for wages, instead of tending to the lowest point at which laborers can live, would tend to the highest point which employers could pay, and thus, instead of getting but a mere fraction of his earnings, the workman would get the full return of his labor, leaving to the skill, foresight and capital of the employer those additional earnings that are justly their due.

The equalization in the distribution of wealth that would thus result would effect immense economies and greatly add to productive power. The cost of the idleness, pauperism and crime that spring from poverty would be saved to the community; the increased mobility of labor, the increased intelligence of the masses, that would result from this equalized distribution of wealth, the greater incentive to invention and to the use of improved processes that would result from the increase in wages, would enormously increase production.

To abolish all taxes save a tax upon the value of land would at the same time greatly simplify the machinery and expenses of government, and greatly reduce government expenses. An army of Custom-House officers, and internal revenue officials, and license collectors and assessors, clerks, accountants, spies, detectives, and government employees of every description, could be dispensed with. The corrupting effect of indirect taxation would be taken out of our politics. The rings and combinations now interested in keeping up taxation would cease to contribute money for the debauching of voters and to beset the lawmaking power with their lobbyists. We should get rid of the fraud and false swearing, of the bribery and subornation which now attend the collection of so much of our public revenues. We should get rid of the demoralization that proceeds from laws which prohibit actions in themselves harmless, punish men for crimes which the moral sense does not condemn, and offer a constant premium to evasion. "Land lies out of doors." It cannot be hid or carried off. Its value can be ascertained with greater ease and exactness than the value of anything else, and taxes upon that value can be collected with absolute certainty and at the minimum of expense. To rely upon land values for the whole public revenue would so simplify government, would so eliminate incentives to corruption, that we could safely assume as governmental functions the management of telegraphs and railroads, and safely apply the increasing surplus to securing such common benefits and providing such public conveniences as ad. vancing civilization may call for.

And in thinking of what is possible in the way of the management of common concerns for the common benefit, not only is the great simplification of government which would result from the reform I have suggested to be con. sidered, but the higher moral tone that would be given to social life by the equalization of conditions and the abolition of poverty. The greed of wealth, which makes it a business motto that every man is to be treated as though he were a rascal, and induces despair of getting in places of public trust men who will not abuse them for selfish ends, is but the reflection of the fear of want. Men trample over each other from the frantic dread of being trampled upon, and the admiration with which even the unscrupulous money-getter is regarded springs from habits of thought engendered by the fierce struggle for existence to which the most of us are obliged to give up our best energies. But when no one feared want, when every one felt assured of his ability to make an easy and independent living for himself and his family, that popular admiration which now spurs even the rich man still to add to his wealth would be given to other things than the getting of money. We should learn to regard the man who strove to get more than he could use, as a fool—as indeed he is.

He must have eyes only for the mean and vile, who has mixed with men without realizing that selfishness and greed and vice and crime are largely the result of social conditions which bring out the bad qualities of human nature and stunt the good; without realizing that there is even now among men patriotism and virtue enough to secure us the best possible management of public affairs if our social and political adjustments enabled us to utilize those qualities. Who has not known poor men who might safely be trusted with untold millions? Who has not met with rich men who retained the most ardent sympathy with their fellows, the warmest devotion to all that would benefit their kind? Look to-day at our charities, hopeless of permanent good though they may be! They at least show the existence of unselfish sympathies, capable, if rightly directed, of the largest results.

It is no mere fiscal reform that I propose; it is a conforming of the most important social adjustments to natural laws. To those who have never given thought to the matter, it may seem irreverently presumptuous to say that it is the evident intent of the Creator that land values should be the subject of taxation; that rent should be utilized for the benefit of the entire community. Yet to whoever does think of it, to say this will appear no more presumptuous than to say that the Creator has intended men to walk on their feet, and not on their hands. Man in his social relations is as much included in the creative scheme as man in his physical relations. Just as certainly as the fish was intended to swim in the water, and the bird to fly through the air, and monkeys to live in trees, and moles to burrow underground, was man intended to live with his fellows. He is by nature a social animal. And the creative scheme must embrace

the life and development of society, as truly as it embraces
the life and development of the individual. Our civilization cannot carry us beyond the domain of law. Railroads, telegraphs and labor-saving machinery are no more
accidents than are flowers and trees.

Man is driven by his instincts and needs to form society.
Society, thus formed, has certain needs and functions for
which revenue is required. These needs and functions
increase with social development, requiring a larger and
larger revenue. Now, experience and analogy, if not the
instinctive perceptions of the human mind, teach us that
there is a natural way of satisfying every natural want.
And if human society is included in nature, as it surely
is, this must apply to social wants as well as to the wants
of the individual, and there must be a natural or right
method of taxation, as there is a natural or right method
of walking.

We know, beyond peradventure, that the natural or
right way for a man to walk is on his feet, and not on his
hands. We know this of a surety—because the feet are
adapted to walking, while the hands are not; because in
walking on the feet all the other organs of the body are
free to perform their proper functions, while in walking
on the hands they are not; because a man can walk on
his feet with ease, convenience and celerity, while no
amount of training will enable him to walk on his hands
save awkwardly, slowly and painfully. In the same way
we may know that the natural or right way of raising the
revenues which are required by the needs of society is by
the taxation of land values. The value of land is in its
nature and relations adapted to purposes of taxation, just
as the feet in their nature and relations are adapted to
the purposes of walking. The value of land * only arises

---

* Value, it must always be remembered, is a totally different thing
from utility. From the confounding of these two different ideas

as in the integration of society the need for some public or common revenue begins to be felt. It increases as the development of society goes on, and as larger and larger revenues are therefore required. Taxation upon land values does not lessen the individual incentive to production and accumulation, as do other methods of taxation; on the contrary, it leaves perfect freedom to productive forces, and prevents restrictions upon production from arising. It does not foster monopolies, and cause unjust inequalities in the distribution of wealth, as do other taxes; on the contrary, it has the effect of breaking down monopoly and equalizing the distribution of wealth. It can be collected with greater certainty and economy than any other tax; it does not beget the evasion, corruption and dishonesty that flow from other taxes. In short, it conforms to every economic and moral requirement. What can be more in accordance with justice than that the value of land, which is not created by individual effort, but arises from the existence and growth of society, should be taken by society for social needs?

In trying, in a previous chapter, to imagine a world in which natural material and opportunities were free as air, I said that such a world as we find ourselves in is best for men who will use the intelligence with which man has been gifted. So, evidently, it is. The very laws which cause social injustice to result in inequality, suffering and degradation are in their nature beneficent. All this evil is the wrong side of good that might be.

Man is more than an animal. And the more we consider the constitution of this world in which we find ourselves, the more clearly we see that its constitution is such as to develop more than animal life. If the purpose for which

---

much error and confusion arise. No matter how useful it may be, nothing has a value until some one is willing to give labor or the produce of labor for it.

this world existed were merely to enable animal man to
eat, drink and comfortably clothe and house himself for
his little day, some such world as I have previously endeavored to imagine would be best. But the purpose of this
world, so far at least as man is concerned, is evidently the
development of moral and intellectual, even more than of
animal, powers. Whether we consider man himself or
his relations to nature external to him, the substantial
truth of that bold declaration of the Hebrew scriptures,
that man has been created in the image of God, forces
itself upon the mind.

If all the material things needed by man could be produced equally well at all points on the earth's surface, it
might seem more convenient for man the animal, but how
would he have risen above the animal level? As we see
in the history of social development, commerce has been
and is the great civilizer and educator. The seemingly
infinite diversities in the capacity of different parts of the
earth's surface lead to that exchange of productions which
is the most powerful agent in preventing isolation, in
breaking down prejudice, in increasing knowledge and
widening thought. These diversities of nature, which
seemingly increase with our knowledge of nature's powers,
like the diversities in the aptitudes of individuals and
communities, which similarly increase with social development, call forth powers and give rise to pleasures which
could never arise had man been placed, like an ox, in a
boundless field of clover. The "international law of God"
which we fight with our tariffs—so short-sighted are the
selfish prejudices of men—is the law which stimulates
mental and moral progress; the law to which civilization
is due.

And so, when we consider the phenomenon of rent, it
reveals to us one of those beautiful and beneficent adapta-
tions, in which more than in anything else the human

mind recognizes evidences of Mind infinitely greater, and catches glimpses of the Master Workman.

This is the law of rent: As individuals come together in communities, and society grows, integrating more and more its individual members, and making general interests and general conditions of more and more relative importance, there arises, over and above the value which individuals can create for themselves, a value which is created by the community as a whole, and which, attaching to land, becomes tangible, definite and capable of computation and appropriation. As society grows, so grows this value, which springs from and represents in tangible form what society as a whole contributes to production, as distinguished from what is contributed by individual exertion. By virtue of natural law in those aspects which it is the purpose of the science we call political economy to discover—as it is the purpose of the sciences which we call chemistry and astronomy to discover other aspects of natural law—all social advance necessarily contributes to the increase of this common value; to the growth of this common fund.

Here is a provision made by natural law for the increasing needs of social growth; here is an adaptation of nature by virtue of which the natural progress of society is a progress toward equality, not toward inequality; a centripetal force tending to unity, growing out of and ever balancing a centrifugal force tending to diversity. Here is a fund belonging to society as a whole from which, without the degradation of alms, private or public, provision can be made for the weak, the helpless, the aged; from which provision can be made for the common wants of all as a matter of common right to each, and by the utilization of which society, as it advances, may pass, by natural methods and easy stages, from a rude association for purposes of defense and police, into a coöperative association, in which combined power guided by combined intelligence can give to each more than his own exertions multiplied manyfold could produce.

By making land private property, by permitting individuals to appropriate this fund which nature plainly intended for the use of all, we throw the children's bread to the dogs of Greed and Lust; we produce a primary inequality which gives rise in every direction to other tendencies to inequality; and from this perversion of the good gifts of the Creator, from this ignoring and defying of his social laws, there arise in the very heart of our civilization those horrible and monstrous things that betoken social putrefaction.

CHAPTER XX.

IT is frequently asserted that no proposition for the recognition of common rights to land can become a practical question in the United States because of the opposition of the farmers who own their own farms, and who constitute the great body of our population, wielding when they choose to exert it a dominating political power.

That new ideas make their way more slowly among an agricultural population than among the population of cities and towns is true—though, I think, in less degree true of the United States than of any other country. But beyond this, it seems to me that those who look upon the small farmers of the United States as forming an impregnable bulwark to private property in land very much miscalculate.

Even admitting, which I do not, that farmers could be relied upon to oppose measures fraught with great general benefits if seemingly opposed to their smaller personal interests, it is not true that such measures as I have suggested are opposed to the interests of the great body of farmers. On the contrary, these measures would be as clearly to their advantage as to the advantage of wage-workers. The average farmer may at first start at the idea of virtually making land common property, but given time for discussion and reflection, and those who are already trying to persuade him that to put all taxation

upon the value of land would be to put all taxation upon
him, have as little chance of success as the slaveholders
had of persuading their negroes that the Northern armies
were bent on kidnapping and selling them in Cuba.   The
average farmer can read, write and cipher—and on matters
connected with his own interests ciphers pretty closely.
He is not out of the great currents of thought, though they
may affect him more slowly, and he is anything but a
contented peasant, ignorantly satisfied with things as they
are, and impervious to ideas of change.   Already dissatisfied, he is becoming more so.   His hard and barren life
seems harder and more barren as contrasted with the
excitement and luxury of cities, of which he constantly
reads even if he does not frequently see, and the great
fortunes accumulated by men who do nothing to add to
the stock of wealth arouse his sense of injustice.   He is
at least beginning to feel that he bears more than his fair
share of the burdens of society, and gets less than his fair
share of its benefits; and though the time for his awakening has not yet come, his thought, with the decadence of
old political issues, is more and more turning to economic
and social questions.

It is clear that the change in taxation which I propose
as the means whereby equal rights to the soil may be
asserted and maintained, would be to the advantage of
farmers who are working land belonging to others, of
those whose farms are virtually owned by mortgagees, and
of those who are seeking farms.   And not only do the
farmers whose opposition is relied upon—those who own
their own farms—form, as I shall hereafter show, but a
decreasing minority of the agricultural vote, and a small
and even more rapidly decreasing minority of the aggregate vote; but the change would be so manifestly to the
advantage of the smaller farmers who constitute the great
body, that when they come to understand it they will

favor instead of opposing it. The farmer who cultivates
his own small farm with his own hands is a landowner,
it is true, but he is in greater degree a laborer, and in his
ownership of stock, improvements, tools, etc., a capitalist.
It is from his labor, aided by this capital, rather than from
any advantage represented by the value of his land, that
he derives his living. His main interest is that of a producer, not that of a landowner.

There lived in Dublin, some years ago, a gentleman
named Murphy—"Cozy" Murphy, they called him, for
short, and because he was a very comfortable sort of a
Murphy. Cozy Murphy owned land in Tipperary; but as
he had an agent in Tipperary to collect his rents and evict
his tenants when they did not pay, he himself lived in
Dublin, as being the more comfortable place. And he
concluded, at length, that the most comfortable place in
Dublin, in fact the most comfortable place in the whole
world, was—in bed. So he went to bed and stayed there
for nearly eight years; not because he was at all ill, but
because he liked it. He ate his dinners, and drank his
wine, and smoked his cigars, and read, and played cards,
and received visitors, and verified his agent's accounts,
and drew checks—all in bed. After eight years' lying in
bed, he grew tired of it, got up, dressed himself, and for
some years went around like other people, and then died.
But his family were just as well off as though he had never
gone to bed—in fact, they were better off; for while his
income was not a whit diminished by his going to bed, his
expenses were.

This was a typical landowner—a landowner pure and
simple. Now let the working farmer consider what would
become of himself and family if he and his boys were to
go to bed and stay there, and he will realize how much
his interests as a laborer exceed his interests as a landowner.

It requires no grasp of abstractions for the working farmer to see that to abolish all taxation, save upon the value of land, would be really to his interest, no matter how it might affect larger landholders. Let the working farmer consider how the weight of indirect taxation falls upon him without his having power to shift it off upon any one else; how it adds to the price of nearly everything he has to buy, without adding to the price of what he has to sell; how it compels him to contribute to the support of government in far greater proportion to what he possesses than it does those who are much richer, and he will see that by the substitution of direct for indirect taxation, he would be largely the gainer. Let him consider further, and he will see that he would be still more largely the gainer if direct taxation were confined to the value of land. The land of the working farmer is improved land, and usually the value of the improvements and of the stock used in cultivating it bears a very high proportion to the value of the bare land. Now, as all valuable land is not improved as is that of ·the working farmer, as there is much more of valuable land than of improved land, to substitute for the taxation now levied upon improvements and stock, a tax upon the naked value of land, irrespective of improvements, would be manifestly to the advantage of the owners of improved land, and especially of small owners, the value of whose improvements bears a much greater ratio to the value of their land than is the case with larger owners; and who, as one of the effects of treating improvements as a proper subject of taxation, are taxed far more heavily, even upon the value of their land, than are larger owners.

The working farmer has only to look about him to realize this. Near by his farm of eighty or one hundred and sixty acres he will find tracts of five hundred or a thousand, or, in some places, tens of thousands of acres, of equally valuable land, on which the improvements, stock, tools and household effects are much less in proportion than on his own small farm, or which may be totally unimproved and unused. In the villages he will find acre, half-acre and quarter-acre lots, unimproved or slightly improved, which are more valuable than his whole farm. If he looks further, he will see tracts of mineral land, or land with other superior natural advantages, having immense value, yet on which the taxable improvements amount to little or nothing; while, when he looks to the great cities, he will find vacant lots, twenty-five by one hundred feet, worth more than a whole section of agricultural land such as his; and as he goes toward their centers he will find most magnificent buildings less valuable than the ground on which they stand, and block after block where the land would sell for more per front foot than his whole farm. Manifestly to put all taxes on the value of land would be to lessen relatively and absolutely the taxes the working farmer has to pay.

So far from the effect of placing all taxes upon the value of land being to the advantage of the towns at the expense of the agricultural districts, the very reverse of this is obviously true. The great increase of land values is in the cities, and with the present tendencies of growth this must continue to be the case. To place all taxes on the value of land would be to reduce the taxation of agricultural districts relatively to the taxation of towns and cities. And this would be only just; for it is not alone the presence of their own populations which gives value to the land of towns and cities, but the presence of the more scattered agricultural population, for whom they constitute industrial, commercial and financial centers.

While at first blush it may seem to the farmer that to abolish all taxes upon other things than the value of land would be to exempt the richer inhabitants of cities from taxation, and unduly to tax him, discussion and reflection will certainly show him that the reverse is the case. Per sonal property is not, never has been, and never can be, fairly taxed. The rich man always escapes more easily than the man who has but little; the city, more easily than the country. Taxes which add to prices bear upon the inhabitants of sparsely settled districts with as much weight, and in many cases with much more weight, than upon the inhabitants of great cities. Taxes upon improve. ments manifestly fall more heavily upon the working farmer, a great part of the value of whose farm consists of the value of improvements, than upon the owners of valuable unimproved land, or upon those whose land, as that of cities, bears a higher relation in value to the improvements.

The truth is, that the working farmer would be an immense gainer by the change. Where he would have to pay more taxes on the value of his land, he would be released from the taxes now levied on his stock and improvements, and from all the indirect taxes that now weigh so heavily upon him. And as the effect of taxing unimproved land as heavily as though it were improved would be to compel mere holders to sell, and to destroy mere speculative values, the farmer in sparsely settled districts would have little or no taxes to pay. It would not be until equally good land all about him was in use, and he had all the advantages of a well-settled neighbor-hood, that his taxes would be more than nominal.

What the farmer who owns his own farm would lose would be the selling value of his land, but its usefulness to him would be as great as before—greater than before, in fact, as he would get larger returns from his labor upon it; and as the selling value of other land would be similarly affected, this loss would not make it harder for him to get another farm if he wished to move, while it would be easier for him to settle his children or to get more land if he could advantageously cultivate more. The loss would be nominal; the gain would be real. It is better for the small farmer, and especially for the small farmer with a growing family, that labor should be high than that land should be high. Paradoxical as it may appear, small landowners do not profit by the rise in the value of land. On the contrary they are extinguished. But before speaking of this let me show how much misapprehension there is in the assumption that the small independent farmers constitute, and will continue to constitute, the majority of the American people.

Agriculture is the primitive occupation; the farmer is the American pioneer; and even in those cases, comparatively unimportant, where settlement is begun in the search for the precious metals, it does not become permanent until agriculture in some of its branches takes root. But as population increases and industrial development goes on, the relative importance of agriculture diminishes. That the non-agricultural population of the United States is steadily and rapidly gaining on the agricultural population is of course obvious. According to the census report the urban population of the United States was in 1790 but 3.3 per cent. of the whole population, while in 1880 it had risen to 22.5 per cent.* Agriculture is yet the largest occupation, but in the aggregate other occupations much exceed it. According to the census, which, unsatisfactory as it is, is yet the only authority we have, the number of

---

* It is an illustration of the carelessness with which the census reports have been shoveled together, that although the Compendium (Table V) gives the urban population, no information is given as to what is meant by urban population. The only clue given the inquirer is that the urban population is stated to be contained in 286 cities. Following up this clue through other tables, I infer that the population of towns and cities of over 8000 people is meant.

persons engaged in agriculture in 1880 was 7,670,493 out of 17,392,099 returned as engaged in gainful occupations of all kinds. Or, if we take the number of adult males as a better comparison of political power, we may find, with a little figuring, that the returns show 6,491,116 males of sixteen years and over engaged in agriculture, against 7,422,639 engaged in other occupations. According to these figures the agricultural vote is already in a clear minority in the United States, while the preponderance of the non-agricultural vote, already great, is steadily and rapidly increasing.*

But while the agricultural population of the United States is thus already in a minority, the men who own their own farms are already in a minority in the agricultural population. According to the census the number of farms and plantations in the United States in 1880 was 4,008,907. The number of tenant farmers, paying money rents or share rents, is given by one of the census bulletins at 1,024,601. This would leave but 2,984,306 nominal owners of farms, out of the 7,679,493 persons employed in agriculture. The real owners of their farms must be greatly less even than this. The most common form of agricultural tendency in the United States is not that of money or share rent, but of mortgage. What proportion of American farms occupied by their nominal owners are under mortgage we can only guess. But there can be little doubt that the number of mortgaged farms must largely exceed the number of rented farms, and it may not be too high an estimate to put the number of mort-

---

* Comparing the returns as to occupations for 1870 with 1880, it will be seen that while during the last decade the increase of persons engaged in agriculture has been only 29.5 per cent., in personal and professional services the increase has been 51.7 per cent., in trade and transportation, 51.9 per cent., and in manufacturing, mechanical and mining industries, 41.7 per cent.

gaged farms at one-half the number of unrented ones.* However this may be, it is certain that the farmers who really own their farms are but a minority of farmers, and a small minority of those engaged in agriculture.

Further than this, all the tendencies of the time are to the extinction of the typical American farmer—the man who cultivates his own acres with his own hands. This movement has only recently begun, but it is going on, and must go on, under present conditions, with increasing rapidity. The remarkable increase in the large farms and diminution in the small ones, shown by the analysis of the census figures which will be found in the Appendix, is but evidence of the fact—too notorious to need the proof of figures—that the tendency to concentration, which in so many other branches of industry has substituted the factory for self-employing workmen, has reached agriculture. One invention after another has already given the

---

* Could the facts be definitely ascertained, I have not the least doubt that they would show that at least fifty per cent. of the small farm-ownerships in the older States are merely nominal. That that number, at least, of the small farmers in those States are so deeply in debt, so covered by mortgages, that their supreme effort is to pay the constantly accruing interest, that a roof may be kept over the heads of the family—an effort that can have but the one ending.

In the newer States is found a similar condition of things. The only difference is, that there the small farmer is usually compelled to commence with what, to him, is a mountain of debt. He must obtain his land upon deferred payments, drawing interest, and can obtain no title until those deferred payments, with the interest, are paid in full. He must also obtain his farm implements on part credit, with interest, for which he mortgages his crops. Credit must help him to his farm stock, his hovel, his seed, his food, his clothing. With this load of debt must the small farmer in the newer States commence, if he is not a capitalist, or he cannot even make a beginning. With such a commencement the common ending is not long in being found.

In traveling through those sections, one of the most notable things that meets the attention of the observer is the great number of pub-

large farmer a crushing advantage over the small farmer, and invention is still going on.* And it is not merely in the making of his crops, but in their transportation and marketing, and in the purchase of his supplies, that the large producer in agriculture gains an advantage over the small one. To talk, as some do, about the bonanza farms breaking up in a little while into small homesteads, is as foolish as to talk of the great shoe-factory giving way again to journeymen shoemakers with their lap-stones and awls. The bonanza farm and the great wire-fenced stock-ranch have come to stay while present conditions last. If they show themselves first on new land, it is because there is on new land the greatest freedom of development, but the tendency exists wherever modern industrial influences are felt, and is showing itself in the British Isles as well as in our older States.†

---

lications, everywhere met with, devoted exclusively to the advertising of small farm holdings, more or less improved, that are for sale. One is almost forced to the conclusion that the entire class of small farmers are compelled, from some cause, to find the best and quickest market that can be obtained for all that they possess.

The entire agricultural regions of our country are crowded with loan agents, representing capital from all the great money centers of the world, who are making loans and taking mortgages upon the farms to an amount that, in aggregate, appears to be almost beyond calculation. In this movement the local capitalists, lawyers and traders appear as active co-workers.—*Land and Labor in the United States*, by William Godwin Moody, New York, 1883, p. 85.

* One of the most important agricultural inventions yet made is just announced in the long-sought cotton-picker. If this machine will do what is said to have been already demonstrated, it must revolutionize the industry of the cotton States, and produce as far-reaching social and political effects as the invention of the cotton-gin. which revived and extended negro slavery in the United States, and made it an aggressive political power.

† The persistence of small properties in some parts of the continent of Europe is due, I take it, to the prevalence of habits differing from those of the people of English speech, and to the fact that modern tendencies are not yet felt there as strongly.

This tendency means the extirpation of the typical American farmer, who with his own hands and the aid of his boys cultivates his own small farm.   When a Brooklyn lawyer or Boston banker can take a run in a palace-car out to the New Northwest; buy some sections of land; contract for having it broken up, seeded, reaped and threshed; leave on it a superintendent, and make a profit on his first year's crop of from six to ten thousand dollars a section, what chance has the emigrant farmer of the old type who comes toiling along in the wagon which contains his wife and children, and the few traps that with his team constitute his entire capital?   When English and American capitalists can run miles of barbed-wire fence, and stock the great inclosure with large herds of cattle, which can be tended, carried to market, and sold, at the minimum of expense and maximum of profit, what chance has the man who would start stock-raising with a few cows?

From the typical American farmer of the era now beginning to pass away, two types are differentiating—the capitalist farmer and the farm-laborer.   The former does not work with his own hands, but with the hands of other men.   He passes but a portion of his time, in some cases hardly any of it, upon the land he cultivates.   His home is in a large town or great city, and he is, perhaps, a banker and speculator as well as a farmer.   The latter is a proletarian, a nomad—part of the year a laborer and part of the year a tramp, migrating from farm to farm and from place to place, without family or home or any of the influences and responsibilities that develop manly character.   If our treatment of land continues as now, some of our small independent farmers will tend toward one of these extremes, and many more will tend toward the other.   But besides the tendency to production on a large scale, which is operating to extirpate the small independent farmer, there is, in the rise of land values, another powerful tendency operating in the same direction.

At the looting of the Summer Palace at Pekin by the allied forces in 1860, some valuable jewels were obtained by private soldiers. How long did they remain in such possession? If a Duke of Brunswick were to distribute his hoard of diamonds among the poor, how long would the poor continue to hold them? The peasants of Ireland and the costermongers of London have their donkeys, which are worth only a few shillings. But if by any combination of circumstances the donkey became as valuable as a blooded horse, no peasant or costermonger would be found driving a donkey. Where chickens are cheap, the common people eat them; where they are dear, they are to be found only on the tables of the rich. So it is with land. As it becomes valuable it must gravitate from the hands of those who work for a living into the possession of the rich.

What has caused the extreme concentration of land-ownership in England is not so much the conversion of the feudal tenures into fee simple, the spoliation of the religious houses and the inclosure of the commons, as this effect of the rise in the value of land. The small estates, of which there were many in England two centuries and even a century ago,* have become parts of large estates mainly by purchase. They gravitated to the possession of the rich, just as diamonds, or valuable paintings, or fine horses, gravitate to the possession of the rich.

So long as the masses are fools enough to permit private property in land, it is rightly esteemed the most secure possession. It cannot be burned, or destroyed by any accident; it cannot be carried off; it tends constantly to increase in value with the growth of population and improvement in the arts. Its possession being a visible

---

* According to Macaulay. at the accession of James II., in 1685, the majority of English farmers were owners of the land they culti-vated.

sign of secure wealth, and putting its owner, as competition becomes sharp, in the position of a lord or god to the
human creatures who have no legal rights to this planet,
carries with it social consideration and deference.   For
these reasons land commands a higher price in proportion
to the income it yields than anything else, and the man
to whom immediate income is of more importance than
a secure investment finds it cheaper to rent land than to
buy it.

Thus, as land grew in value in England, the small
owners were not merely tempted or compelled by the
vicissitudes of life to sell their land, but it became more
profitable to them to sell it than to hold it, as they could
hire land cheaper than they could hire capital.   By selling
and then renting, the English farmer, thus converted from
a landowner into a tenant, acquired, for a time at least,
the use of more land and more capital, and the ownership
of land thus gravitated from the hands of those whose
prime object is to get a living into the hands of those
whose prime object is a secure investment.

This process must go on in the United States as land
rises in value.   We may observe it now.   It is in the newer
parts of our growing cities that we find people of moderate
means living in their own houses.   Where land is more
valuable, we find such people living in rented houses.   In
such cities, block after block is built and sold, generally
under mortgage, to families who thus endeavor to secure
a home of their own.   But I think it is the general experience, that as years pass by, and land acquires a greater
value, these houses and lots pass from the nominal ownership of dwellers into the possession of landlords, and are
occupied by tenants.   So, in the agricultural districts, it
is where land has increased little if anything in value
that we find homesteads which have been long in the
possession of the same family of working farmers.   A

general officer of one of the great trunk railroad lines told me that his attention had been called to the supreme importance of the land question by the great westward emigration of farmers, which, as the result of extensive inquiries, he found due to the rise of land values. As land rises in value the working farmer finds it more and more difficult for his boys to get farms of their own, while the price for which he can sell will give him a considerably larger tract of land where land is cheaper; or he is tempted or forced to mortgage, and the mortgage eats and eats until it eats him out, or until he concludes that the wisest thing he can do is to realize the difference between the mortgage and the selling value of his farm and emigrate west. And in many cases he commences again under the load of a mortgage; for as settlement is now going, very much of the land sold to settlers by railroad companies and speculators is sold upon mortgage. And what is the usual result may be inferred from such announcements as those placarded in the union depot at Council Bluffs, offering thousands of improved farms for sale on liberal terms as to payment. One man buys upon mortgage, fails in his payments, or gets disgusted, and moves on, and the farm he has improved is sold to another man upon mortgage. Generally speaking, the ultimate result is, that the mortgagee, not the mortgageor, becomes the full owner. Cultivation under mortgage is, in truth, the transitional form between cultivation by the small owner and cultivation by the large owner or by tenant.

The fact is, that the typical American farmer, the cultivator of a small farm of which he is the owner, is the product of conditions under which labor is dear and land is cheap. As these conditions change, labor becoming cheap and land becoming dear, he must pass away as he has passed away in England.

It has already become impossible in our older States for a man starting with nothing to become by his labor the owner of a farm. As the public domain disappears this will become impossible all over the United States. And as in the accidents and mutations of life the small owners are shaken from their holdings, or find it impossible to compete with the grand culture of capitalistic farming, they will not be able to recover, and must swell the mass of tenants and laborers. Thus the concentration of land-ownership is proceeding, and must proceed, if private property in land be continued. So far from it being to the interest of the working farmer to defend private property in land, its continued recognition means that his children, if not himself, shall lose all right whatever in their native soil; shall sink from the condition of free-men to that of serfs.

CHAPTER XXI.

CITY AND COUNTRY.

COBBETT compared London, even in his day, to a great wen growing upon the fair face of England. There is truth in such comparison. Nothing more clearly shows the unhealthiness of present social tendencies than the steadily increasing concentration of population in great cities. There are about 12,000 head of beef cattle killed weekly in the shambles of New York, while, exclusive of what goes through for export, there are about 2100 beef carcasses per week brought in refrigerator-cars from Chicago. Consider what this single item in the food-supply of a great city suggests as to the elements of fertility, which, instead of being returned to the soil from which they come, are swept out through the sewers of our great cities. The reverse of this is the destructive character of our agriculture, which is year by year decreasing the productiveness of our soil, and virtually lessening the area of land available for the support of our increasing millions.

In all the aspects of human life similar effects are being produced. The vast populations of these great cities are utterly divorced from all the genial influences of nature. The great mass of them never, from year's end to year's end, press foot upon mother earth, or pluck a wild flower, or hear the tinkle of brooks, the rustle of grain, or the murmur of leaves as the light breeze comes through the woods. All the sweet and joyous influences of nature are shut out from them. Her sounds are drowned by the roar of the streets and the clatter of the people in the next room, or the next tenement; her sights are hidden from their eyes by rows of high buildings. Sun and moon rise and set, and in solemn procession the constellations move across the sky, but these imprisoned multitudes behold them only as might a man in a deep quarry. The white snow falls in winter only to become dirty slush on the pavements, and as the sun sinks in summer a worse than noonday heat is refracted from masses of brick and stone. Wisely have the authorities of Philadelphia labeled with its name every tree in their squares; for how else shall the children growing up in such cities know one tree from another? how shall they even know grass from clover?

This life of great cities is not the natural life of man. He must, under such conditions, deteriorate, physically, mentally, morally. Yet the evil does not end here. This is only one side of it. This unnatural life of the great cities means an equally unnatural life in the country. Just as the wen or tumor, drawing the wholesome juices of the body into its poisonous vortex, impoverishes all other parts of the frame, so does the crowding of human beings into great cities impoverish human life in the country.

Man is a gregarious animal. He cannot live by bread alone. If he suffers in body, mind and soul from being crowded into too close contact with his fellows, so also does he suffer from being separated too far from them. The beauty and the grandeur of nature pall upon man where other men are not to be met; her infinite diversity becomes monotonous where there is not human companionship; his physical comforts are poor and scant, his nobler powers languish; all that makes him higher than the animal suffers for want of the stimulus that comes from

the contact of man with man. Consider the barrenness
of the isolated farmer's life—the dull round of work and
sleep, in which so much of it passes. Consider, what is
still worse, the monotonous existence to which his wife is
condemned; its lack of recreation and excitement, and of
gratifications of taste, and of the sense of harmony and
beauty; its steady drag of cares and toils that make
women worn and wrinkled when they should be in their
bloom. Even the discomforts and evils of the crowded
tenement-house are not worse than the discomforts and
evils of such a life. Yet as the cities grow, unwholesomely
crowding people together till they are packed in tiers,
family above family, so are they unwholesomely separated
in the country. The tendency everywhere that this process of urban concentration is going on, is to make the life
of the country poor and hard, and to rob it of the social
stimulus and social gratifications that are so necessary to
human beings. The old healthy social life of village and
townland is everywhere disappearing. In England, Scotland and Ireland, the thinning out of population in the
agricultural districts is as marked as is its concentration
in cities and large towns. In Ireland, as you ride along
the roads, your car-driver, if he be an old man, will point
out to you spot after spot, which, when he was a boy,
were the sites of populous hamlets, echoing in the summer
evenings with the laughter of children and the joyous
sports of young people, but now utterly desolate, showing,
as the only evidences of human occupation, the isolated
cabins of miserable herds. In Scotland, where in such
cities as Glasgow, human beings are so crowded together
that two-thirds of the families live in a single room, where
if you go through the streets of a Saturday night, you
will think, if you have ever seen the Tierra del Fuegans,
that these poor creatures might envy them, there are wide

tracts once populous, now given up to cattle, to grouse and to deer—glens that once sent out their thousand fighting men, now tenanted by a couple of gamekeepers. So across the Tweed, while London, Liverpool, Leeds, Manchester and Nottingham have grown, the village life of "merrie England" is all but extinct. Two-thirds of the entire population is crowded into cities. Clustering hamlets, such as those through which, according to tradi tion, Shakespeare and his comrades rollicked, have disappeared; village greens where stood the May-pole, and the cloth-yard arrow flew from the longbow to the bull's-eye of the butt, are plowed under or inclosed by the walls of some lordly demesne, while here and there stand mementos alike of a bygone faith and a departed population, in great churches or their remains—churches such as now could never be filled unless the congregations were brought from town by railroad excursion trains.

So in the agricultural districts of our older States the same tendency may be beheld; but it is in the newer States that its fullest expression is to be found—in ranches measured by square miles, where live half-savage cowboys, whose social life is confined to the excitement of the "round-up" or a periodical "drunk" in a railroad town; and in bonanza farms, where in the spring the eye wearies of seas of waving grain before resting on a single home —farms where the cultivators are lodged in barracks, and only the superintendent enjoys the luxury of a wife.

That present tendencies are hurrying modern society toward inevitable catastrophe, is apparent from the constantly increasing concentration of population in great cities, if in nothing else. A century ago New York and its suburbs contained about 25,000 souls; now they contain over 2,000,000. The same growth for another century would put here a population of 160,000,000. Such a city is impossible. But what shall we say of the cities of ten and twenty millions, that, if present tendencies continue, children now born shall see?

On this, however, I will not dwell. I merely wish to call attention to the fact that this concentration of population impoverishes social life at the extremities, as well as poisons it at the center; that it is as injurious to the farmer as it is to the inhabitant of the city.

This unnatural distribution of population, like that unnatural distribution of wealth which gives one man hundreds of millions and makes other men tramps, is the result of the action of the new industrial forces in social conditions not adapted to them. It springs primarily from our treatment of land as private property, and secondarily from our neglect to assume social functions which material progress forces upon us. Its causes removed, there would ensue a natural distribution of population, which would give every one breathing-space and neighborhood.

It is in this that would be the great gain of the farmer in the measures I have proposed. With the resumption of common rights to the soil, the overcrowded population of the cities would spread, the scattered population of the country would grow denser. When no individual could profit by advance in the value of land, when no one need fear that his children could be jostled out of their natural rights, no one would want more land than he could profitably use. Instead of scraggy, half-cultivated farms, separated by great tracts lying idle, homesteads would come close to each other. Emigrants would not toil through unused acres, nor grain be hauled for thousands of miles past half-tilled land. The use of machinery would not be abandoned: where culture on a large scale secured economies it would still go on; but with the breaking up of monopolies, the rise in wages and the better distribution

of wealth, industry of this kind would assume the coöper.
ative form.   Agriculture would cease to be destructive,
and would become more intense, obtaining more from the
soil and returning what it borrowed.   Closer settlement
would give rise to economies of all kinds ; labor would be
far more productive, and rural life would partake of the
conveniences, recreations and stimulations now to be
obtained only by the favored classes in large towns.   The
monopoly of land broken up, it seems to me that rural life
would tend to revert to the primitive type of the village
surrounded by cultivated fields, with its common pasturage
and woodlands.   But however this may be, the working
farmer would participate fully in all the enormous economies and all the immense gains which society can secure
by the substitution of orderly coöperation for the anarchy
of reckless, greedy scrambling.

  That the masses now festering in the tenement-houses
of our cities, under conditions which breed disease and
death, and vice and crime, should each family have its
healthful home, set in its garden ; that the working farmer
should be able to make a living with a daily average of
two or three hours' work, which more resembled healthy
recreation than toil ; that his home should be replete with
all the conveniences yet esteemed luxuries ; that it should
be supplied with light and heat, and power if needed, and
connected with those of his neighbors by the telephone ;
that his family should be free to libraries, and lectures,
and scientific apparatus, and instruction ; that they should
be able to visit the theater, or concert, or opera, as often
as they cared to, and occasionally to make trips to other
parts of the country or to Europe ; that, in short, not
merely the successful man, the one in a thousand, but the
man of ordinary parts and ordinary foresight and prudence, should enjoy all that advancing civilization can
bring to elevate and expand human life, seems, in the

light of existing facts, as wild a dream as ever entered the brain of hashish-eater. Yet the powers already within the grasp of man make it easily possible.

In our mad scramble to get on top of one another, how little do we take of the good things that bountiful nature offers us! Consider this fact: To the majority of people in such countries as England, and even largely in the United States, fruit is a luxury. Yet mother earth is not niggard of her fruit. If we chose to have it so, every road might be lined with fruit-trees.

CHAPTER XXII.

CONCLUSION.

HERE, it seems to me, is the gist and meaning of the great social problems of our time: More is given to us than to any people at any time before; and, *therefore*, more is required of us. We have made, and still are making, enormous advances on material lines. It is necessary that we commensurately advance on moral lines. Civilization, as it progresses, *requires* a higher conscience, a keener sense of justice, a warmer brotherhood, a wider, loftier, truer public spirit. Failing these, civilization must pass into destruction. It cannot be maintained on the ethics of savagery. For civilization knits men more and more closely together, and constantly tends to subordinate the individual to the whole, and to make more and more important social conditions.

The social and political problems that confront us are darker than they realize who have not given thought to them; yet their solution is a mere matter of the proper adjustment of social forces. Man masters material nature by studying her laws, and in conditions and powers that seemed most forbidding, has already found his richest storehouses and most powerful servants. Although we have but begun to systematize our knowledge of physical nature, it is evident she will refuse us no desire if we but seek its gratification in accordance with her laws.

And that faculty of adapting means to ends which has enabled man to convert the once impassable ocean into his highway, to transport himself with a speed which leaves the swallow behind, to annihilate space in the communication of his thoughts, to convert the rocks into warmth and light and power and material for a thousand uses, to weigh the stars and analyze the sun, to make ice under the equator, and bid flowers bloom in Northern winters, will also, if he will use it, enable him to overcome social difficulties and avoid social dangers. The domain of law is not confined to physical nature. It just as certainly embraces the mental and moral universe, and social growth and social life have their laws as fixed as those of matter and of motion. Would we make social life healthy and happy, we must discover those laws, and seek our ends in accordance with them.

I ask no one who may read this book to accept my views. I ask him to think for himself.

Whoever, laying aside prejudice and self-interest, will honestly and carefully make up his own mind as to the causes and the cure of the social evils that are so apparent, does, in that, the most important thing in his power toward their removal. This primary obligation devolves upon us individually, as citizens and as men. Whatever else we may be able to do, this must come first. For "if the blind lead the blind, they both shall fall into the ditch."

Social reform is not to be secured by noise and shouting; by complaints and denunciation; by the formation of parties, or the making of revolutions; but by the awakening of thought and the progress of ideas. Until there be correct thought, there cannot be right action; and when there is correct thought, right action *will* follow. Power is always in the hands of the masses of men. What oppresses the masses is their own ignorance, their own short-sighted selfishness.

The great work of the present for every man, and every organization of men, who would improve social conditions, is the work of education—the propagation of ideas. It is only as it aids this that anything else can avail. And in this work every one who can think may aid—first by forming clear ideas himself, and then by endeavoring to arouse the thought of those with whom he comes in contact.

Many there are, too depressed, too embruted with hard toil and the struggle for animal existence, to think for themselves. Therefore the obligation devolves with all the more force on those who can. If thinking men are few, they are for that reason all the more powerful. Let no man imagine that he has no influence. Whoever he may be, and wherever he may be placed, the man who thinks becomes a light and a power. That for every idle word men may speak they shall give an account at the day of judgment, seems a hard saying. But what more clear than that the theory of the persistence of force, which teaches us that every movement continues to act and react, must apply as well to the universe of mind as to that of matter? Whoever becomes imbued with a noble idea kindles a flame from which other torches are lit, and influences those with whom he comes in contact, be they few or many. How far that influence, thus perpetuated, may extend, it is not given to him here to see. But it may be that the Lord of the Vineyard will know.

As I said in the first of these chapters, the progress of civilization necessitates the giving of greater and greater attention and intelligence to public affairs. And for this reason I am convinced that we make a great mistake in depriving one sex of voice in public matters, and that we could in no way so increase the attention, the intelligence and the devotion which may be brought to the solution of social problems as by enfranchising our women. Even

if in a ruder state of society the intelligence of one sex
suffices for the management of common interests, the
vastly more intricate, more delicate and more important
questions which the progress of civilization makes of public
moment, require the intelligence of women as of men, and
that we never can obtain until we interest them in public
affairs.   And I have come to believe that very much of
the inattention, the flippancy, the want of conscience,
which we see manifested in regard to public matters of
the greatest moment, arises from the fact that we debar
our women from taking their proper part in these matters.
Nothing will fully interest men unless it also interests
women.   There are those who say that women are less
intelligent than men; but who will say that they are less
influential?

And I am firmly convinced, as I have already said, that
to effect any great social improvement, it is sympathy
rather than self-interest, the sense of duty rather than
the desire for self-advancement, that must be appealed to.
Envy is akin to admiration, and it is the admiration that
the rich and powerful excite which secures the perpetuation of aristocracies.   Where tenpenny Jack looks with
contempt upon ninepenny Joe, the social injustice which
makes the masses of the people hewers of wood and
drawers of water for a privileged few, has the strongest
bulwarks.   It is told of a certain Florentine agitator that
when he had received a new pair of boots, he concluded
that all popular grievances were satisfied.   How often do
we see this story illustrated anew in working-men's movements and trade-union struggles?   This is the weakness
of all movements that appeal only to self-interest.

And as man is so constituted that it is utterly impossible
for him to attain happiness save by seeking the happiness
of others, so does it seem to be of the nature of things
that individuals and classes can obtain their own just

rights only by struggling for the rights of others. To illustrate : When workmen in any trade form a trades-union, they gain, by subordinating the individual interests of each to the common interests of all, the power of making better terms with employers. But this power goes only a little way when the combination of the trades-union is met and checked by the pressure for employment of those outside its limits. No combination of workmen can raise their own wages much above the level of ordinary wages. The attempt to do so is like the attempt to bail out a boat without stopping up the seams. For this reason, it is necessary, if workmen would accomplish anything real and permanent for themselves, not merely that each trade should seek the common interests of all trades, but that skilled workmen should address themselves to those general measures which will improve the condition of unskilled workmen. Those who are most to be considered, those for whose help the struggle must be made, if labor is to be enfranchised, and social justice won, are those least able to help or struggle for themselves, those who have no advantage of property or skill or intelligence, —the men and women who are at the very bottom of the social scale. In securing the equal rights of these we shall secure the equal rights of all.

Hence it is, as Mazzini said, that it is around the standard of duty rather than around the standard of self-interest that men must rally to win the rights of man. And herein may we see the deep philosophy of Him who bade men love their neighbors as themselves.

In that spirit, and in no other, is the power to solve social problems and carry civilization onward.

APPENDICES.

I.

THE UNITED STATES CENSUS REPORT ON THE SIZE OF FARMS.

THE reference on page 41 to the evident incorrectness of the statement of the Census Report as to the decrease in the average size of farms in the United States, led, when originally published in *Frank Leslie's Illustrated Newspaper*, to the following controversy, which is given as there printed:

SUPERINTENDENT WALKER'S EXPLANATION.

BOSTON, May 10, 1883.
To the Editor of Frank Leslie's Illustrated Newspaper.

SIR: In Mr. Henry George's fifth paper on the "Problems of the Time" he declares that the statement of the Census Bureau to the effect that the average size of farms is decreasing in the United States, is inconsistent not only with "facts obvious all over the United States," but with "the returns furnished by the Census Bureau itself;" and at a later point, after citing the Census Statistics of the number of farms of certain classes, as to size, in 1870, and again in 1880, he says: "How, in the face of these figures, the Census Bureau can report a decline in the average size of farms in the United States from 153 acres in 1870 to 134 acres in 1880, I cannot understand."

Perhaps I can offer an explanation which may assist Mr. George toward an understanding of what seems to him incomprehensible.

The average size of farms in 1870 having been 153 acres, any increase during the intervening decade in the number of farms below this limit would tend to lower the average size of farms in 1880; any increase in the number of farms above that limit would tend to raise the average for 1880.

Now, in fact, there has been a greater increase, on the whole, in the number of farms below 153 acres than in the number above 153 acres, and, consequently, the average size has been reduced.

If I have not made the reason of the case plain, I shall be happy to resort to a more elementary statement, illustrated with diagrams, if desired.

Respectfully yours,
FRANCIS A. WALKER.

THE CENSUS REPORT AND SUPERINTENDENT WALKER'S EXPLANATION.

[From Frank Leslie's Illustrated Newspaper, June 9, 1883.]

I must ask the patience of the readers of these articles if in this I make a digression, having reference to the letter from General Francis A. Walker, Superintendent of the Ninth and Tenth Censuses, which appeared in the last issue of this journal.

To my comprehension, General Walker has "not made the reason of the case plain," nor has he explained the discrepancies I pointed out. I shall be happy to have his more elementary statement, and, if he will be so kind, to have it illustrated with diagrams. But, in the meantime, as his reassertion of the statement of the Census Report carries the weight of official authority and professional reputation, I propose in this paper to show in more detail my reasons for disputing its accuracy.

It is specifically asserted in the reports of the Tenth Census that the average size of farms in the United States decreased during the decade ending in 1880 from 153 acres to 134 acres, and this assertion has been quoted all over the country as a conclusive reason why the people of the United States should not trouble themselves about the reckless manner in which what is now left of their once great public domain is being disposed of, and the rapid rate at which it is passing in enormous tracts into the private estates of non-resident speculators, English lords and foreign syndicates. All over the country the press has pointed to this declaration of the Census Bureau as conclusive proof, which no one could question (and which, up to the publication of the fifth paper of this series, no one seems to have thought of questioning), that these things need excite no uneasiness, since the steady tendency is to the sub-division of large landholdings. The inference would not be valid even if the alleged fact were true. But that I will not now discuss. I dispute the fact.

General Walker states that, during the last decade, "there has been a greater increase, on the whole, in the number of farms below 153 acres than in the number above 153 acres." This I shall show from General Walker's own official report is not true—is, in fact, the very reverse of the truth. But such a misstatement of fact, astonishing as it is, is not so astonishing as the misstatement of principle which precedes and follows it—viz., to quote the remainder of the sentence, "and, *consequently*, the average size has been reduced."

I have occasionally met thoughtless people who talked of discounts of 150 and 200 per cent.; I once knew a man who insisted that another man was twice as old as he was, because on a certain birthday, years before, he had been twice as old; but I never yet met anybody, except very little children, to whom all coins were pennies, who would say that when a shopkeeper received one piece of money and handed out two pieces, he had *consequently* reduced the amount of money in his drawer! Yet this is just such a statement as that made by General Walker. In asserting that the general increase in the number of farms under a certain size than in the number above that size must reduce the average size, General Walker ignores area, just as any one who would say that an amount of money had been reduced by adding one coin and taking away two would ignore value. Take, for instance, a farm of 100 acres. Add to it two farms of 50 acres each and one farm of 400 acres. Here there has been a greater increase in the number of farms below 100 acres than the number above 100 acres, but so far from the average having consequently been reduced, it has been increased from 100 to 150 acres!

The truth is, of course, that number is only one of the factors of average, which is in itself an expression of proportion between number and some other property of things, such as size, weight, length, value, etc. An average does not, as General Walker says, increase or diminish according to the numerical preponderance, on one side or the other, of the items added, but according to the preponderance in number and quality. Thus, though the addition of any farm of less than 153 acres would tend to reduce an average of 153 acres, the addition of one farm of three acres would tend much more strongly to reduce the average than the addition of one of 152 acres, and the addition of one farm of 1000 acres would do much more to increase the average than the addition of several farms of 154 acres. Just as weights upon the arms of a lever tend more strongly to counterbalance each other the further they are placed from the fulcrum, so increase in the number of farms will tend more strongly to raise or reduce the average the further in point of area the new farms are from the previous average. And it may be worth while to remark that while the possibilities on the side of decrease are limited, the possibilities on the side of increase are unlimited. A farm less than 153 acres can only be less by something within 153 acres; but a farm greater than 153 acres may be greater by 10,000 or 100,000, or any larger number of acres.

I speak of this simple and obvious principle not merely to show the curious confusion of thought which General Walker exhibits, but for the purpose of pointing out the significance of the facts I have previously cited—a significance which General Walker does not appear, even yet, to realize.

Let me refer those who may wish to verify the accuracy of the figures I am about to quote to Table LXIII., pp. 650–657, Compendium of the Tenth Census, Part I. This table gives the total number of farms for 1880, 1870, 1860 and 1850, the number of farms in eight specified classes for 1880, 1870 and 1860; the farm acreage and the average size of farms for four censuses. We are told in a note that "it will be noticed" that the number of farms given in the specified classes for 1860 fail to agree with the total number given, and that "these discrepancies appear without explanation in the Census of 1860." This is well calculated to impress one who casually turns over the pages of the Compendium with the vigilant care that has been exercised, but it becomes rather amusing when read in the light of the far more striking discrepancies which appear without explanation in the Census of 1880.

What first struck me in glancing over this table, and what is so obvious that I cannot understand how, from Census Superintendent to lowest clerk, any one could have transcribed, or even glanced over—not to say examined —these figures without being struck by it, is that in the face of the fact that we are told that between 1870 and 1880 the average size of farms has been reduced, the same table shows in its very first lines that the great increase in the number of farms between 1870 and 1880 has all been in the four classes of largest areas, and that the larger the area the greater the increase; while the number of farms in the four classes of smaller area have actually diminished, and the smaller the class area the greater the diminution! To recur to our simile, it is not only that more weights have been placed on one end of the lever, but they have been pushed out further from the center. On the other arm the weights have not only been diminished, but they have been drawn in closer to the center. Yet we are told that the lever has tipped toward the end that has been lightened!

This is the fact to which I called attention in the fifth paper of this series as showing the inaccuracy of the assertion that the average size of farms had decreased in the United States during the last decade. So conclusive is it, and so obvious is it, that I am forced to suppose that the Superintendent of the Tenth Census has never even glanced over the totals of his own report. For, although the number of farms in 1880 and 1870 are merely placed in parallel columns in the Census Report, without subtraction, yet such differences as 4352 farms under three acres in 1880, and 6875 in 1870, and of 28,578 farms over 1000 acres in 1880 against 3720 in 1870, are glaring enough to strike the eye of any one who has been told that the average size of farms has diminished, and to put him upon inquiry.

In order to show the striking results of a comparison of the number of farms in the eight specified classes, in 1880 and 1870, as reported by the Census Bureau, I have taken the trouble to do what the Census Bureau has not done, and figure out the differences.

CHANGES DURING DECADE ENDING 1880 IN THE NUMBER OF FARMS IN THE EIGHT SPECIFIED CLASSES, AS REPORTED BY CENSUS BUREAU.

Class.	Decrease in number.	Ratio of decrease.
I.—Under 3 acres	2,523	37 per cent.
II.— 3 to 10 "	37,132	21 " "
III.—10 to 20 "	39,858	14 " "
IV.—20 to 50 "	66,140	8 " "

	Increase in number.	Ratio of increase.
V.— 50 to 100 acres	278,689	37 per cent.
VI.—100 to 500 " 1	1,130,929	200 " "
VII.—500 to 1,000 "	60,099	379 " "
VIII.—Over 1,000 "	24,858	668 " "

This steady progression from a decrease of 37 per cent. in farms under three acres up to an increase of 668 per cent. in farms over 1000 acres is conclusive proof that the average size of farms could not have decreased from 153 to 134 acres. And the figures of numerical decrease and increase are at the same time a disproof of General Walker upon the ground he has chosen. "Now, in fact," he says, "there has been a greater increase, on the whole, in the number of farms below 153 acres than in the number above 153 acres, and, consequently, the average size has been reduced."

The pivotal point, of 153 acres, falls in Class VI., which includes farms between 100 and 500 acres. There is no way of deciding with certainty how many of these farms are between 100 and 153 acres, and how many between 153 and 500 acres; but inasmuch as, in the absence of special reasons to the contrary, there can be no doubt that the average of the class must largely exceed 153 acres (which is very much nearer the class minimum than the class maximum), and therefore that, taken as a whole, the entire class must count on the side of increase, we should reach substantial accuracy in setting down the whole increase in this class as over 153 acres. This would give :

Increase in number of farms above 153 acres.... 1,215,886
Net increase in farms below 153 acres 133,036

Excess in increase of number of farms above 153 acres. 1,082,850

This would be substantially accurate ; but if a greater formal exactness is required, let us try to decide, as best we may, what part of the farms of between 100 and 500 acres should be counted as under 153 acres.

Whoever knows anything of the United States land system, and the parceling of land in our newer States and Territories where the greater part of this increase in the number of farms has taken place, knows that the farms between 100 and 160 acres must be comparatively few. The reason of this is, that the government surveys divide the land into sections and fractions of a section, the practical unit being the quarter-section of 160 acres, which is the amount open to preëmption and homestead entry. The land-grant railroad companies sell their land in the same way by the government surveys ; and, in fact, nearly all the transfers of farms in our new States, long after the land has passed into private hands, is by fractions of a section, the quarter-section of 160 acres being almost universally regarded as the unit. When the quarter-section is divided, it is generally divided into the eighth, or as it is commonly called, the half quarter section, which falls into the class below the one we are considering. There can be no doubt whatever that the great majority of the newer farms of the class between 100 and 500 acres consist of quarter-sections, two-quarter sections, and three-quarter sections. Considering all this, it is certain that we shall be making a most liberal allowance for the farms between 100 and 153 acres if we estimate the farms above 153 acres at 1,000,000 and those below at the odd number of 130,929. This would give:

Increase in farms above 153 acres 1,084,957
Net increase in farms below 153 acres 263,965

Excess in increase of farms above 153 acres... 820,992

I have disposed of General Walker's principle and of his fact, and have sustained my own allegation of the inaccuracy of the Census Report. I will now go further, and prove in another way the glaring discrepancies of the Census Report, and the grossness of the assumption that it shows a reduction in the average size of farms. Subtracting the totals given for 1870 from those given for 1880, we find the increase in acreage and number of farms as follows:

	Total number of farms.	Total acreage.
1880	4,008,907	536,081,835
1870	2,659,985	407,735,041
Increase in decade............	1,348,922	128,346,794

The average size of farms in 1880, given at 134 acres, has been obtained by dividing the total acreage by the given total number of farms. The division is correct, but examination shows that there is an error either in the dividend or in the divisor, which makes the quotient less than it ought to be. Either the number of farms is too high, or the acreage too low. Let me prove this beyond question.

The net increase in the number of farms in the eight specified classes, as I have given it, corresponds with the total increase obtained by subtracting from the total number of farms given for 1880 the total given for 1870. But no estimate can make the increase in area correspond.

To show that it is impossible on any supposition to make the increased acreage of the specified classes as low as the increased acreage according to the census totals, we will, where there has been decrease in the number of farms, consider these farms to have been of the very largest size embraced in the class. Where the number of farms has increased we will consider these farms as having been of the very smallest size embraced in the class.

Thus we have—

Class.   Decrease.

I.—Under 3 acres,	2,523, at	3 acres	....			7,569
II.— 3 to 10 "	37,132, at 10	"	....			371,320
III.—10 to 20 "	39,858, at 20	"	....			797,160
IV.—20 to 50 "	66,140, at 50	"	....			3,307,000

Total decrease in area 4,483,049

Class.   Increase.

V.— 50 to 100 acres,	278,689, at	50 acres,	13,934,450
VI.—100 to 500 "	1,130,929, at	100 "	113,092,900
VII.—500 to 1,000 "	60,099, at	500 "	30,049,500
VIII.— Over 1,000 "	24,858, at 1,000	"	24,858,000

Total increase in area 181,934,850
Subtract decrease 4,483,049
Net increase in farm acreage 177,451,801

Thus this lowest possible estimate of increased farm area exceeds the increase of 128,346,794, according to the census totals, by no less than 49,105,007 acres. According to the census totals the average area of the 1,348,922 new farms was only 95.1 acres. According to this lowest possible estimate of the areas assigned to these new farms in the table of specified classes, the average is 131.6. And adding this very lowest possible estimate of increased average to that given for 1870, the total farm acreage of the United States in 1880 was 585,186,842 acres, instead of 536,081,835 acres, as represented by the Census Bureau, giving an average of 145.9 acres, instead of 134 acres, as reported.

Of course, such an estimate is preposterous, but it shows indisputably the glaring incorrectness of the Census Report.

To obtain from the table of specified classes an estimate of the true increase of farm acreage in the United States during the last decade, our only way is to ascertain from the census of 1870, also made under General Walker's superintendence, the average of class areas which would give the total for that year, and take them for our calculation.

To make the acreage of the specified classes for 1870 agree with the total acreage given, we must make some such estimate as the following :

ACREAGE BY SPECIFIED CLASSES FOR 1870.

Class.		Average acreage.	Number of farms.	Total acres.
I.—Under 3 acres...		2½	6,875	17,187
II.— 3 to 10 " ...		8¼	172,020	1,505,183
III.— 10 to 20 " ...		18	294,607	5,302,926
IV.— 20 to 50 " ...		44	847,014	37,295,016
V.— 50 to 100 " ...		90	754,221	67,879,890
VI.—100 to 500 " ...		400	565,054	226,021,600
VII.—500 to 1,000 " ...		900	15,873	14,285,700
VIII.— Over 1,000 " ...		14,900	3,720	55,428,000
Totals			2,659,985	407,735,502

This is about as close as I can figure with any regard to proportion, and it comes so close to 407,735,041, the acreage given for 1870, that the difference would not perceptibly affect any average.

Now, taking these averages of 1870 as a basis for calculating the true farm acreage in 1880, we have:

ACREAGE BY SPECIFIED CLASSES FOR 1880.

Class.	Acres.	Number of farms.	Acreage.
I.—Under 3 acres...	2½	4,352	10,880
II.— 3 to 10 " ...	8¾	134,889	1,180,278
III.— 10 to 20 " ...	18	254,749	4,585,482
IV.— 20 to 50 " ...	44	781,474	34,384,856
V.— 50 to 100 " ...	90	1,032,910	92,961,900
VI.—100 to 500 " ...	400	1,695,983	678,393,200
VII.—500 to 1,000 " ...	900	75,972	68,374,800
VIII.— Over 1,000 " ...	14,900	28,578	425,812,200
Totals	4,008,907		1,305,703,596

This would make the average size of farms in the United States 325½ acres, instead of 134 acres as reported by the Census Bureau, an increase of 172½ acres, instead of a decrease of 19 acres as reported.

I do not, of course, say that this estimate is correct. I can only say that it is the best that can be made from the Census Reports. These reports show such a lack of intelligent superintendence and editing, that I doubt their reliability for any purpose. The only thing absolutely certain is, that the conclusions of the Census Bureau are not correct.

And further than the gross discrepancies I have shown, these returns of farms and farm areas give no idea of the manner in which the ownership of land is concentrating in the United States. It is not merely that in many cases the same person is the owner of separate farms, but it is evident from the returns that stock farms, cattle ranches, and the large tracts held by absentees, have not been included. This may be seen by the fact that the returns of farms of over 1000 acres number only 14 for Wyoming,

43 for New Mexico, 20 for Montana, 8 for Idaho, 74 for Dakota, and so on.

I have gone into this subject at such length because the authority of the census has been so generally invoked as conclusive proof that the ownership of land is not concentrating in the United States. The truth is, that it is concentrating so rapidly that, should present tendencies continue, it will not be many decades before we shall be a nation of landlords and tenants.

SUPERINTENDENT WALKER'S FURTHER EXPLANATION.

[*From Frank Leslie's Illustrated Newspaper, June 16, 1883.*]

To the Editor of Frank Leslie's Illustrated Newspaper:

Mr. George's attack upon the Census Statistics of the number and size of farms, in your issue of June 9th, affords a capital example of that writer's cleverness in imposing upon the careless reader. Indeed, although somewhat familiar with the subject-matter, I wasn't sure myself, until I had gone through the article more than once, that there might not be something in it, so portentous was the marshaling of figures, so loud and strenuous the assertion that the census was wrong in this and inconsistent in that; so artfully were all the resources of controversy used to produce the impression Mr. George desired. And yet there is absolutely nothing in it which cannot be readily and completely disproved. It is, from beginning to end, an utter sham.

Suppose a township of 25 square miles to have been divided, in 1870, into 64 farms of 250 acres each. These would have been reported, according to the classification in use at each census from 1850 to the present time, as farms of over 100 and under 500 acres; aggregate land in farms, 16,000 acres. Now, suppose precisely the same territory to have been divided in 1880 into farms of 125 acres each. The official record would then read, 128 farms of over 100 and under 500 acres; aggregate land in farms, 16,000 acres. Ah, exclaims the critic, observe this monstrous blunder! Here is an increase of 64 farms in this class, and yet no increase whatever of acreage! Let us, he continues, concede, in the extreme spirit of fairness, that these farms were all of the very smallest size contained in this class, viz.: 100 acres each, we still ought to have, at the least, an increase of 6400 acres over the official return, which is thus shown on the face of it to be false.

This is Mr. George's reasoning, precisely. To omit minor classes, let us take the greatest class of all, that of farms between 100 and 500 acres, the increase in the number of farms of this class being no less than 1,130,929, against 217,993 only of all the other classes combined. Mr. George assumes that these 1,130,929 farms represent a pure net addition to the acreage of inclosed land. Having made such an utterly gratuitous, utterly unfounded, utterly dishonest assumption, Mr. George, with that inimitable show of candor which always characterizes him after a logical larceny of this sort, very graciously gives the Census Office the benefit of his concession that he will only exact 100 acres for each of these 1,130,929 farms; and having proceeded to deal this way with all the other classes, he brings the Census Office out a debtor in the sum of 49,105,007 acres. Perhaps, with that same remarkable candor, he would consent to strike off 105,007 acres and call it only 49,000,000.

Such is the wretched stuff which Mr. George imposes on his readers as a serious statistical argument. That the land of all the older States is in process of sub-division, every one above the grade of a plantation hand, who has lived three years east of the Rocky Mountains, knows perfectly well. In the main, the increase of farms in these

States is by the partition of land previously inclosed. Thus, Connecticut showed 2,364,416 acres in 25,508 farms in 1870, and 2,453,541 acres in 30,598 farms in 1880— an increase of nearly 20 per cent. in farms, and of but 5 per cent. in acreage. New York showed 22,190,810 acres in 216,253 farms in 1870, and 23,780,754 acres in 241,058 farms in 1880. Georgia, to take a State from another section, showed 23,647,941 acres in 69,956 farms in 1870, and 26,043,282 acres in 138,626 farms in 1880— a gain of about 10 per cent. in acreage, and of almost 100 per cent. in farms. This tremendous increase of farms in Georgia is due to the continuous sub-division of the old plantations in order to furnish small farms for the late slaves and the "poor whites" of that region. The same cause is operating, with great force, all over the South, and this it is which has brought about that reduction of the average size of farms in the United States from 153 acres in 1870 to 134 acres in 1880, which arouses such prodigious wrath on the part of Mr. George, who, having started out on a crusade against landed property with the cry that the country is going to the dogs through the aggregation of great estates—*latifundia,* as he magnificently calls it, to the confusion, there is reason to fear, of most of his disciples—is brought violently and injuriously up against hard facts, such as those just cited. The following table shows the increase of the number of farms in the chief cotton-planting States:

	1880.	1870.
Alabama	135,864	67,382
Arkansas	94,433	49,424
Georgia	138,626	69,956
Louisiana	48,292	28,481
Mississippi	101,772	68,023
North Carolina	157,609	93,565
South Carolina	93,864	51,889
Tennessee	165,650	118,141
Texas	174,184	61,125

Such, then, is Mr. George's main argument against the census figures. "Let me," he says, "prove this beyond question." We may, therefore, understand this to be Mr. George's idea of proving a proposition beyond question. And, in truth, it is very much the way he has taken to prove all the propositions I have read from his pen. To make any assumption whatever that suits his purpose, to reason therefrom most logically and felicitously, and to apply thereto, when required, arithmetical computations of the most minute accuracy, is the favorite method of this apostle of a new political economy and a regenerated humanity.

In the case under consideration, he assumes that new farms always represent new lands, a most gratuitous assumption, contrary to the known facts of the situation, and then proceeds, by a faultless series of additions and multiplications, to bring the Census Office in as debtor in the amount of 49,000,000 acres lost to the nation through its carelessness.

Again, Mr. George's assumption that the farms between 100 and 500 acres must be preponderatingly above 153 acres, inasmuch as the government sells land in 160-acre lots, "quarter-sections," as they are called, may be met by the assertion that five-sixths of the present farms of the United States were either not granted originally on the quarter-section plan (as in the Eastern States), or else have been long enough in private hands to allow, as Americans buy and sell, abundant scope for changes of area, in the way of partition, consolidation, etc.

The question at issue between Mr. George and the Census Office really turns upon the average size of the farms between 100 and 500 acres. Mr. George estimates that average at 400 acres! The reasonableness or unreasonableness of this will best be made to appear by presenting the number of farms in the classes above and below :

20 to	50	acres	781,474
50 to	100	"	1,032,910
100 to	500	"	1,695,983
500 to	1,000	"	75,972

Any one who can look at these figures and not see, at a glance, that the probabilities are overwhelmingly in favor of the supposition that the great body of the farms of the third class, in the above table, are nearer, much nearer, very much nearer, to the lower than to the upper limit, is to be pitied for his defective eyesight and his defective mind-sight. If Mr. George cannot see that, there is reason to fear that a diagram would not help him. Who can believe it possible that, while the farms of Class IV. are only 1 in 22 of the farms in Class III., the farms of the latter class lie so close up to the limit of the fourth class as to average 400 acres each, or for that matter, 300 acres, or even 250 acres?

It is certainly to be regretted, since this controversy has arisen, that a new class, 100 to 150, or 100 to 200 acres, was not introduced. But the classification taken for this purpose is that which has always heretofore been employed, alike in 1850, in 1860, and 1870; while, so far as I am aware, no one has ever before complained of its inefficiency or suggested to the Census Office the subdivision of this class.

Mr. George is undoubtedly right in his captious correction of my phraseology in speaking of the effect produced by an increase in the number of farms, above or below the line, 153 acres, upon the average size of all farms in comparison of 1870 with 1880. I think no one would have failed to understand me who desired to do so, and what I had in mind was perfectly just; yet, in a controversy with a gentleman so much more particular about phraseology than about facts, I should have done well to state my meaning more explicitly.

Respectfully,

FRANCIS A. WALKER.

BOSTON, June 10, 1883.

FURTHER ANALYSIS OF THE CENSUS REPORT.

[From Frank Leslie's Illustrated Newspaper, June 30, 1883.]

In his reply to my exhibition of the utter inconsistency between the census figures and census conclusions as to the size of farms, Professor Walker, instead of furnishing the diagrams with which he, in the first place, proposed to enlighten my ignorance, resorts to something more resembling diatribes. To such controversy I cannot descend.

Professor Walker complains that I estimate the average size of farms in the class between 100 and 500 acres at 400 acres, and devotes much space to showing that this estimate is too great. But this estimate is not mine. Had I been making a guess, without reference to the Census Report, I should certainly not have put the average of this class at above 250 acres. But at any such average it is impossible to make the aggregate acreage of the specified classes for 1870 correspond with the total acreage given. As I showed in detail, to make the acreage of these classes agree with the total acreage given, such averages as 90 acres for the class between 50 and 100 acres, 400 acres for the class between 100 and 500, 900 acres for the class between 500 and 1000 acres, and 14,900 for farms over 1000 acres must be assumed. These averages seem to me preposterous; but I am not responsible

for them. Professor Francis A. Walker, Superintendent
of the Tenth Census, must settle this matter with Professor Francis A. Walker, Superintendent of the Ninth
Census.

And to clench what I have already said as to the size of
farms in Class IV., I challenge Professor Walker to give
to the public any computation of acreage by specified
classes by which, putting the average of Class IV. at 153
acres, and having any regard whatever for proportion in
the other classes, he can make the total acreage correspond
with that given in the Census Report.

As for Professor Walker's effort to prove that increase
in the number of farms does not necessarily involve increase
in total area, it would be as pertinent for him to attempt
to prove that in changing a dollar into ten dimes one gets
no more money, or that a big piece of cloth may be cut
into small pieces without increase in the amount of cloth.
This I have never heard denied, unless by Professor Walker
himself, who, in his previous letter, asserted that a greater
increase in the number of farms below than above a certain
point necessarily showed a decrease of average area. The
absurdity of this—a principle which he offered to illustrate with diagrams—I previously pointed out, and he now
admits, but in a style which reminds me of a dispute I
once heard between two colored citizens. One, who gloried
in the title of Professor Johnson, was boasting that he
could polish twelve dozen pairs of boots in half an hour.
A fellow boot-black disputed this, and pressed him with a
bet. Driven into a corner. Professor Johnson, with much
indignation, declared that when he said twelve dozen
pairs of boots he meant six pairs of shoes, and any "fool
nigger" ought to know what he meant. So, Professor
Walker, driven to admit the absurdity of his statement
of principle, speaks of my captious correction of his
phraseology, and declares that no one would have failed to

understand him who desired to do so. This is a rather unbecoming descent from the altitude of an offer of diagrams! A frank admission that he had been betrayed by carelessness would have inspired more respect.

But it is to be feared that such carelessness is a habit with Professor Walker. This letter shows as curious confusion of thought as his first, and, with seemingly utter unconsciousness of the fallacy, he essays, with what the logicians call an *ignoratio elenchi,* to break the force of my marshaling of census figures. To prove the absolute inconsistency of the census, I showed that the lowest possible estimate of increased acreage by specified classes gives an aggregate acreage of 49,105,107 acres in excess of the census total. To this conclusive proof of gross inaccuracy Professor Walker replies by supposing a township of twenty-five square miles. [It may be worth while to remark that a United States township is thirty-six, not twenty-five, square miles.] He supposes this township to have been divided in 1870 into 64 farms of 250 acres each, which would be returned by the census in the class between 100 and 500 acres. In 1880 the same township is divided into 128 farms of 125 acres each. But the acreage of 64 additional farms at the lowest class limit of 100 acres, added to the previous total acreage, would give 6400 more acres than the township contains; which proves, according to Professor Walker, that, in assuming that the net increase of acreage of specified classes must represent an addition to that acreage, I have made "an utterly gratuitous, utterly unfounded, utterly dishonest assumption."

In fact, however, Professor Walker's unfortunate example proves nothing in point, unless it be the truth of the old rhyme:

> If *ifs* and *ans* were pots and pans,
> There'd be few blundering tinkers.

What Professor Walker omits in his example—as, of course, he will see when his attention is called to it—is the essence of the matter, the division into classes. By supposing the farms in his township to be all within one class, Professor Walker ignores this essential element. The case he presents is not analogous to the case presented by the census, but analogous to the case which would be presented by the census were no returns by classes given. If the census report merely gave us the total acreage and total number of farms, we could go no further in verifying what it told us as to increase or decrease of average than by testing the division. But the census gives us more than this. Besides total acreage and total number, it gives us the number of farms in eight specified classes as to area.

To make Professor Walker's supposed township analogous to the case in point, we must suppose its farms to vary in size from under three acres to over 1000 acres, and that we are given for each decade, not merely the total number of farms and total area, but also the number in eight classes of specified areas. This given, in case the average size of the farms in the township had decreased from 250 acres to 125 acres, should we not expect the class returns to show an increase in the number of farms in the classes of smaller acreage, and a decrease in the classes of larger acreage? And if they were to show just the reverse of this—a decrease in the number of smaller farms and an increase in the number of larger farms—should we not say that they were inconsistent with the reduction of average? This inconsistency is just what the Census Report shows.

Professor Walker asserts that I have made a gratuitous assumption, contrary to the known facts of the case, in assuming that additional farms represent additional land. If he will show me, with or without diagrams, any other

basis of computation, I shall be obliged to him. I do not
know what arithmetic they may use in the Boston Tech-
nical School, but I will take an example after the manner
of the old arithmetics :

"A boy's trousers contain two yards of cloth; his
father's, three yards. Last year they had each two pairs
of trousers; this year they have each three pairs. How
much more cloth have they in their trousers this year
than last ?"

Any one—outside, perhaps, the Census Bureau or Tech-
nical School of Boston—would say: "One more pair of
trousers for the boy, two yards; one more for the father,
three yards. Answer—five yards."

Supposing somebody should reply: "You have made
in your calculation an utterly gratuitous, utterly unfounded, utterly dishonest assumption, contrary to all
the known facts of the case. You have assumed the boy's
new trousers to have been made from new cloth, whereas
they were cut down from his father's old ones!"

Any little child would smile, and answer: "That makes
no difference. Whether the father's trousers have been
cut down for the boy, or the boy's trousers have been
pieced out for the father, the boy has one more pair of
trousers with two yards in them, and the father one more
pair of trousers with three yards in them, and together
they have five yards more cloth in their trousers."

And so, though it is true that in many cases farms
of one class are formed from previously existing farms of
another class, the only method of computing increase of
area is by taking the increased number at the given area.
An acre of land may form part of a farm of one class at
one time, and of a farm of another class at another time.
But we cannot suppose it to be in two farms at the same
time.

Without meeting the facts and figures which I gave
from the Census Report in disproof of the assertion that

the average size of farms had been reduced in the last decade, Professor Walker reiterates that assertion. He says:

"That the land of all the older States is in process of sub-division, every one above the grade of a plantation hand, who has lived three years east of the Rocky Mountains, knows perfectly well. In the main, the increase of farms in these States is by the partition of land previously inclosed. Thus, Connecticut showed 2,364,416 acres in 25,508 farms in 1870, and 2,453,541 acres in 30,598 farms in 1880—an increase of nearly 20 per cent. in farms, and of but 5 per cent. in acreage. New York showed 22,190,-810 acres in 216,253 farms in 1870, and 23,780,754 acres in 241,058 farms in 1880. Georgia, to take a State from another section, showed 23,647,941 acres in 69,956 farms in 1870, and 26,043,282 acres in 138,626 farms in 1880—a gain of about 10 per cent. in acreage, and of almost 100 per cent. in farms. This tremendous increase of farms in Georgia is due to the continuous sub-division of the old plantations in order to furnish small farms for the late slaves and the 'poor whites' of that region. The same cause is operating, with great force, all over the South, and this it is which has brought about that reduction of the average size of farms in the United States from 153 acres in 1870 to 134 acres in 1880, which arouses such prodigious wrath on the part of Mr. George."

It is a very pleasant theory that the old plantations in the South are being sub-divided in order to furnish small farms for the late slaves and the "poor whites," and it would be still pleasanter if it involved any presumption that they were getting these small farms as owners and not as rack-rented tenants. But, unfortunately, while it is not borne out by any information from the South that I have been able to get, it is absolutely disproved by the census returns. Professor Walker parades, as though it were proof of this sub-division of plantations, a table giving the total number of farms in nine cotton-growing States in 1870 and 1880, which shows a large increase in the number of farms; but he very prudently neglects to specify the classes in which this increase took place. He could not have done this without showing to the eye of the reader that, instead of a continuous sub-division of the old plantations, the general tendency in those States is to an increase in the size of farms. Whoever will glance over the census returns by specified classes will see that, whereas there was in the decade ending 1870 a striking decrease in the number of large farms, and a striking increase in the number of small farms, yet in the decade ending 1880 the striking increase is in the large farms, and the striking decrease in the small farms. If old plantations are being cut up, then new plantations in greater number are being formed; for in all these States the most striking increase is in the larger classes. The farms having 500 and 1000 acres, and over 1000 acres, are in all these States much more numerous in 1880 than in 1870, and even much more numerous than in 1860.

The following table, drawn from the census reports, shows the number of farms of each class in the nine States referred to by Professor Walker—viz., Alabama, Arkansas, Georgia, Louisiana, Mississippi, North Carolina, South Carolina, Tennessee, Texas—for the last three censuses:

NUMBER OF FARMS IN COTTON STATES BY CLASSES.

Class.				1860.	1870.	1880.
I.—Under	3	acres	.....	No returns	2,053	1,308
II.— 3 to	10	"	.....	11,248	47,088	36,644
III.— 10 to	20	"	.....	37,494	101,272	111,111
IV.— 20 to	50	"	.....	123,977	223,444	277,112
V.— 50 to	100	"	.....	101,576	124,852	229,006
VI.—100 to	500	"	.....	112,193	91,370	410,066
VII.—500 to 1,000		"	.....	11,976	6,407	37,843
VIII.— Over 1,000		"	.....	3,557	1,500	17,394

These figures show that the movement in these nine Southern States was in the last decade the reverse of the movement in the previous decade, and was to the increase, not to the decrease, in the size of farms. This will be even more strikingly shown to the eye of the reader by the following table, which exhibits the percentage of increase or decrease in each class for the decade ending 1870 and the decade ending 1880:

PERCENTAGE OF CHANGE IN NUMBER OF FARMS IN COTTON STATES.

Class.				1870. Per cent.	1880. Per cent.
I.—Under	3 acres	..	No returns for 1860		31 decrease
II.— 3 to	10	"	..	319 increase	22 "
III.— 10 to	20	"	..	170 "	10 increase
IV.— 20 to	50	"	..	80 "	24 "
V.— 50 to	100	"	..	23 "	77 "
VI.—100 to	500	"	..	19 decrease	349 "
VII.—500 to	1,000	"	..	47 "	491 "
VIII.— Over	1,000	"	..	58 "	1,060 "

In the face of this exhibit, what could be more prepos‹ terously false than the census declaration, reiterated by Superintendent Walker, that the average size of farms in these States decreased in the last decade, and decreased almost as much as in the previous decade!—viz., 32 per cent. in the decade ending 1880, and 42 per cent. in the decade ending 1870!

It is a work of supererogation to show in further detail the utter incompatibility of census figures with census conclusions; but inasmuch as Professor Walker calls attention to the three States of Connecticut, New York, and Georgia, let us follow him on the ground he has selected, and look briefly at the returns for these States. We shall see that they too utterly disprove the census conclusions.

For Connecticut the census totals give:

CONNECTICUT.

	Total acreage.	Number of farms.	Average size of farms.
1870—	2,364,416	25,508	93 acres
1880—	2,453,541	30,598	80 "
Increase ...	89,125	5,090	13 acres decrease

Now let us see how this averred reduction in average size of farms from 93 to 80 acres is borne out by the returns of increase by classes. These show:

CHANGE IN NUMBER OF FARMS IN CONNECTICUT,
DECADE ENDING 1880.

Class.		Change in number.	Change per cent.
I.—Under 3 acres	.....	37 decrease	52 decrease
II.— 3 to 10 "	.....	545 increase	32 increase
III.— 10 to 20 "	.....	310 "	10 "
IV.— 20 to 50 "	.....	145 decrease	2 decrease
V.— 50 to 100 "	.....	569 increase	8 increase
VI.—100 to 500 "	.....	3,725 "	64 "
VII.—500 to 1,000 "	.....	107 "	412 "
VIII.— Over 1,000 "	.....	16 "	1,600 "

Net increase in farms under 100 acres 1,242
Increase in farms over 100 acres 3,848

Could anything more conclusively disprove the assertion of reduced average?

Take now New York. The census totals give:

NEW YORK.

	Total acreage.	Number of Farms.	Average size of farms.
1870—	22,190,810	216,253	103 acres
1880—	23,780,754	241,058	99 "
Increase..	1,589,944	24,805	4 acres decrease

Turning to the tables of specified classes, we find the increase has been:

CHANGE IN NUMBER OF FARMS IN NEW YORK,
DECADE ENDING 1880.

Class.				Change in number.		Change per cent.	
I.—Under		3 acres ...		298	increase	414	increase
II.—	3 to	10 "	....	1,537	"	12	"
III.—	10 to	20 "	....	916	decrease	6	decrease
IV.—	20 to	50 "	....	14,495	"	26	"
V.—	50 to	100 "	....	3,295	"	4	"
VI.—100 to		500 "	....	49,325	increase	72	increase
VII.—500 to 1,000		"	....	1,106	"	542	"
VIII.— Over 1,000		"	....	245	"	681	"

Net decrease in farms under 100 acres 16,871
Increase in farms over 100 acres 41,676

In the face of these figures, will Professor Walker assert that the average size of farms in New York has decreased from 103 acres to 99 acres?

Now, let us take the case of Georgia, in which Professor Walker dwells, as the typical Southern State.

The census totals give:

GEORGIA.

	Total acreage.	Number of farms.	Average size of farms.
1870—	23,647,941	69,956	338 acres
1880	26,043,282	138,626	188 "
Increase..	2,395,341	68,670	150 acres decrease

From the table of specified classes we find the increase to have been:

CHANGE IN NUMBER OF FARMS IN GEORGIA,
DECADE ENDING 1880.

Class.				Change in number.		Change per cent.	
I.—Under		3 acres.....		No return for 1870			
II.—	3 to 10	"	.....	147	decrease	4	decrease
III.—	10 to 20	"	.....	1,752	increase	25	increase

Class.	Change in number.	Change per cent.
IV.— 20 to 50 acres...14,553 increase		66 increase
V.— 50 to 100 " ... 7,683 "		41 "
VI.—100 to 500 " ...56,145 "		206 "
VII.—500 to 1,000 " ... 5,511 "		365 "
VIII.— Over 1,000 " ... 3,702 "		733 "

After verifying these figures, will Professor Walker again assert, on the authority of the census, that during the last decade there has been a gain of about 10 per cent. in acreage, and almost 100 per cent. in farms in Georgia, and that the average size of farms has been reduced from 338 acres to 188 acres?

It is, of course, manifest in the case of Georgia as in the cases of Connecticut and New York, and of the United States at large, that the real movement has been in the other direction—to the large increase instead of to the reduction of the average of farms. If we endeavor, from the data which the census gives us, to work out some approximation to the true average, our first step will be to ascertain what averages in the various classes reported for 1870 will give the total acreage for that year. The moment we attempt this we run against an astounding fact. The figures I am about to give I expressly commend to Superintendent Walker, but I request him to remember that it is he, not I, who is responsible for them. What has he to say to the fact that, in order to make the acreage of the farms returned for Georgia by specified classes for 1870 correspond with the total acreage given for that year on which his calculation of average has been based, *it is necessary to assume the very highest limit of each class as the average of that class, and even then to assume the average of the class over* 1000 *acres to be* 24,558 *acres ?*

Here is the tabulation:

FARM ACREAGE OF GEORGIA, 1870.

Total farm acreage of Georgia for 1870, as given by the Census Report...................... 23,647,941

Total number of farms........................ 69,956

ACREAGE BY SPECIFIED CLASSES.

Class.	Average acreage.	Number of farms.	Acres.
II.— 3 to 10 acres	10	3,257	32,570
III.— 10 to 20 "	20	6,942	138,840
IV.— 20 to 50 "	50	21,971	1,098,550
V.— 50 to 100 "	100	18,371	1,837,100
VI.—100 to 500 "	500	17,490	8,745,000
VII.—500 to 1,000 "	1,000	1,506	1,506,000
VIII.— Over 1,000 "	24,558	419	10,289,802
		69,956	23,647,862

After this, it would be wasting space and time to go further. Whoever wants to figure out what, at this rate, has been the increase of farm acreage in Georgia during the decade, or what was the average in 1880, may do so. The Census Report offers opportunities for much amusing arithmetical exercise; but save for this purpose, it is evidently not worth the paper on which it is printed. I have conclusively shown its utter unreliability, both as a whole and in its parts, and with this, must decline further controversy.   HENRY GEORGE.

NEW YORK, June 15, 1883.

CONDITION OF ENGLISH AGRICULTURAL LABORERS.

THE following communication, from Mr. William Saunders, of London, was called forth by a letter signed "A Free-born Englishman," in which some of the statements made in Chapter X. of this book were in general terms denied.

NEW YORK, July 24, 1883.

To the Editor of Frank Leslie's Illustrated Newspaper:

SIR—"A Free-born Englishman," who "emphatically denies" the accuracy of Mr. George's statements, is at a loss to conceive from what source he obtained his information. On this point I may enlighten him, as I can state from experience that Mr. George gained his knowledge by personal investigation in the location to which he refers. I wish that I could sustain the rose-colored view which "A Free-born Englishman" takes of the condition of the agricultural laborer in England. For fifty years I have been intimately acquainted with the state of agriculture in the southern part of the country, and during that time the standard wages have varied from one and a half to three and a half dollars per week. In Wiltshire, at the present time, the wages are from two and a quarter to three dollars per week. It must be noted that these are the wages not of boys but of married men, and that they are the total wages; no food is given, and, as a rule, the laborers pay rent for a cottage, and always a very high rent for garden land, if they have any.   Even the highest rate named is quite inadequate to provide a family with sufficient food of the plainest kind.   It costs four dollars per week to provide food for five persons in the poorhouses of Wiltshire.   Thus, if a man with a wife and three children spend all his wages for food he would still be short of the poorhouse allowance, which is calculated at a very low rate.

The statement of " A Free-born Englishman " that it is a rare thing for the aged of the industrial classes to go to the workhouse is entirely contrary to my experience, and I may ask how is it possible for a man to save for old age when the laborer has to maintain himself and his family upon a sum with which economical poor-law guardians cannot support paupers?

As to commons, they not only have been, but are being inclosed by the owners of land.   This is also the case with spaces on the roadside, so that the working-classes have lost the means they formerly had for maintaining cows, donkeys or geese, and children have been deprived of their ancient playgrounds.   As to foot-paths, these are often closed; but your correspondent is right when he says that interrupting an ancient highway excites the indignation of the people, and sometimes they tear down the obstruction.   They did so recently in a case where Mr. E. P. Bouverie shut up a path near Devizes, in Wiltshire.   Legal proceedings were taken, and, although it was proved that the public had enjoyed the use of the footway for over a century, yet the landlord was enabled to show that during this period the estate had been entailed, so that no owner had the power to give the public a right of way, and thus the path was closed.   By these and similar provisions in laws enacted by landlords, it is possible for a landlord to make constant encroachments upon the public; for, if he maintains a claim for twenty years it is established in his favor, but no length of time can legalize the possession by the public against a claim raised by the owners of a family estate. Thus, all the time family estates are growing and the public are losing.

In referring to a case near London, "A Free-born Englishman" is misleading your readers. The people of London insisted upon exempting an area of fifteen miles around that city from the operation of Commons Inclosure Acts, and, therefore, the instance to which he refers does not apply to England generally.

It must be puzzling to Americans to meet with such different statements respecting English laborers, and as your correspondent does not give the public his name or address, it may be allowable to test his assertions by the internal evidence which his letter affords on the subject of his accuracy. He boldly asserts that "an equal distribution of property is the general principle that underlies" Mr. George's article. I challenge him to refer to a single paragraph in any of the voluminous writings of Mr. George which justifies the idea that he advocates an equal distribution of property. Mr. George's writings are a protest against the confiscation by landlords of property created by industry, and the statement that he advocates an equal distribution of property is entirely unfounded.

Neither is your correspondent more happy in the assertion of his own principles than in his misrepresentation of Mr. George's views. He tells us that "a man obtains in England, as in America and elsewhere, just so much for his labor as his labor is worth, according to the law of supply and demand." One illustration from each side of the Atlantic will disprove this assertion. In Wiltshire, England, thousands of acres of excellent land are uncultivated, while thousands of half-starved but willing workmen demand an opportunity for growing food for themselves and families. The land remains out of cultivation, and the laborers remain without work, solely because a landlord stands upon the land, and says to every farmer who wants to cultivate it, "You shall not do so unless you pay me six dollars an acre per annum, with an increase in future if I choose to demand it at the expiration of any year." If a working-man comes to the landlord and says to him, "Please let me have five acres of that land, upon which I will work and grow food for my own family and others," the landlord replies, "You shall not have that land unless you pay me fifteen dollars an acre per annum;" and when the working-man asks why it is proposed to charge him so much more than is charged the farmer, the landlord tells him, "We do not want working-men to have land, lest the farmers should be unable to obtain laborers." Thus the land remains out of cultivation, and the laborer without work and without food, because the landlord stands between demand and supply.

In New Jersey, not far from where I am writing, thousands of acres of land are producing miasma and mosquitos. Thousands of willing hands would drain this land and cover it with houses and manufactories, but in the meantime a landlord's agent stands upon the marsh and demands, in the name of a man who has done nothing, a payment of one thousand dollars or two thousand dollars an acre before he will allow the mosquitos to be suppressed and houses and factories to be erected.

Under these circumstances your correspondent may well say, "I should be glad to learn where in this country, or in any other country on the globe, does a man who has not capital obtain the 'full fruits of his labor'?" True it is that those who have capital and those who can avail themselves of the unjust privileges which law allows to capital, in connection with the possession of land, are the only persons who can obtain the full fruits of their own or other persons' labor; and if the universality of injustice is a sound reason for upholding it, then undoubtedly Mr. George is in the wrong.

I am willing to admit, as "A Free-born Englishman" contends, that in some respects the agricultural laborer is better off than his brother laborer in the crowded cities of Europe and America; but, gracious heaven! is this a matter for thankfulness? I have had to spend the summer in New York, and with every alleviation that can be provided, my fate has been hard enough; but what must be the condition of families crowded into tenement-houses during the summer heat? No man ought to think of it without a determination to do all in his power to lessen such terrible suffering. And this suffering, in New York and other cities, is the direct and immediate result of landlordism. In London, landlords demand and receive thirty millions of dollars annually from the working-classes, and they are constantly raising their demands. This is the cause of overcrowding. Every month land-lords kill more children than Herod destroyed in his lifetime; and yet, as your correspondent reminds us, they are men of excellent character. That they are all honor-able men, I do not dispute; but the circumstance does not lessen the fearful consequences of the system of which they are the agents. It is not of abuses that we complain, but of the necessary consequences of landlordism, which, like a huge vise, crushes the masses of the people with more horrible effect at every turn of the screw. Industry, intel-ligence and invention hold out promises of improvement which seem to be almost within our reach, but before they are obtained the landlord advances his claims and the result is disappointment and misery. If this state of things continues, it will be the fault, not of the landlords, but of working-men who have the power, and should have the determination, to deliver themselves and their children from a fatal influence. I am,

Yours respectfully,
WILLIAM SAUNDERS.

III.

A PIECE OF LAND.

BY FRANCIS G. SHAW.

SCENE—*A Common.* LABOR *digging the ground with a stick, to plant potatoes.* CAPITAL *passing with a spade on his shoulder.*

LABOR. I say, Capital, shall you use your spade this year?

Capital. No, I'm going a-fishing.

Labor. Lend it to me, then.

Capital. Why should I?

Labor. As a good neighbor. You don't want it, and it would be a great help to me. I could plant more ground, and, perhaps, raise fifty more bushels of potatoes, if I had it.

Capital. That's a very one-sided reason. You'd wear it out by the end of the year. You'd have your fifty bushels extra, and I should have no spade. You'd be so much better off, and I should be so much worse off than I am now. There's not much good-neighborhood in that.

Labor. Oh, I'd give it back to you just as good as it is now; or I'd make a new one for you.

[NOTE.—This is the necessary maintenance or replacement of capital which is consumed by use.]

Capital. That's rather better, but still it's not fair. You'd have your fifty bushels more, which you couldn't have raised without my spade, while I should be no better off than I am now. No, thank you! I'll keep my spade. Go make one for yourself. It took me ten days to make this.

Labor. Yes, but this is the season for planting, and I haven't the time to spare; I want to use it now. I can't see why you shouldn't let me have it as well as leave it to rust, which it will since you're not going to use it.

Capital. It's not going to rust. I'll tell you what I mean to do with it: Farmer wants a spade as well as you, and offers to give a yearling heifer in exchange for this one. I'm on my way now to make the swap, and get her. I shall turn her out on the common, and by the end of the year I shall have a cow with, perhaps, a calf by her side. Don't you think she'll be worth a good deal more than the new spade you offer?

[NOTE.—CAPITAL proposes to take advantage of the active forces of nature which manifest themselves in growth as well as in the productiveness of land, and which can be made available by LABOR, or by CAPITAL, the result of LABOR.]

Labor. Certainly she will. I never thought of that! Yes; if you can swap your spade for the heifer, you've a right to as much return from one as from the other. But how much do you expect to gain if you do make the exchange?

Capital. I suppose quite as much as ten bushels of your potatoes will be worth when you dig them.

Labor. I'll take the spade and give you a new one and ten bushels of potatoes. Will that satisfy you?

Capital. I've rather set my heart on the heifer, and, besides, your crop may fail.

Labor. I hope not; it never has. However, there is

some little risk, I admit, and I'll give you twelve bushels instead of ten. What do you say?

Capital. It's a bargain! Here's the spade, and I'll go and see about my boat.

[NOTE.—Thus LABOR employs the wealth which CAPITAL has accumulated by his past labor, and as both are interested in the crop, LABOR and CAPITAL become partners. The ten bushels which CAPITAL is to receive for the use of the spade may be called interest, to which he is justly entitled, from his ability to exchange the spade for something which will give him an equal profit by its mere growth, and the other two bushels are for insurance against the risk of a failure of the crop.]

Enter LANDOWNER.

Landowner (*leaning over fence*). Hullo, Labor! What are you at work on that moorland for? The soil is much better on this side of the fence. You can raise fifty bushels more potatoes here than you can there, with the same work. You'd much better hire this lot of me; I wouldn't charge you much for the use of it.

Labor. It's true that the soil is better, and I should plant there if you hadn't fenced it in; but you know as well as I do that this common is free, and that everything I can raise on it is mine; while if I should plant on that side of the fence you'd clap me into jail for trespassing, or else you'd let me raise a crop and then take all away from me, unless I came to your terms. The laws seem to be made for you landowners! What right had you to fence in the best land? It was all common once. If you were cultivating it, I wouldn't have a word to say; your right to it is as good as mine, or that of anybody else; but it's no better, and I don't see what right you have to keep me off of it, when you don't want to cultivate it yourself.

Landowner. I did cultivate it for some years, and I

fenced it to keep the cattle away; I hauled off the stone and drained it, and got good crops.

Labor. Did the crops repay you for what you laid out?

Landowner. Pretty well, you may believe; you don't suppose that I was such a fool as to make the improvements if I hadn't been sure of that. But I've got some better land that I mean to till this year, and I should like to let this lot to you at a fair rent.

Labor. Yes; I suppose you have taken the cream out of this. But what do you call a fair rent?

Landowner. Let me see! The land is still a good deal better than the common, and easier to work than when I inclosed it. The drains are there, and there are no stones on the ground; besides, the fence is good for three years, and you'll have to fence your common lot if you want to make a crop. That's something for you to consider. These are real advantages.

Labor. Yes, that's so. Well! I think it will be fair if I agree to give you one-third the value of the fence; say, ten bushels of potatoes, and five bushels more on account of the other improvements.

Landowner. Will you keep the fence in as good repair as it is now?

Labor. No; fifteen bushels is as much as I can afford to give.

Landowner. And how much will you give for the use of the land?

Labor. Nothing whatever. I pay you so much for the use of your improvements, and that's so much gain to you, for you've already been well paid for them by the crops you've taken off, which have diminished the fertility of the soil. I'm willing to pay for the benefit I shall derive from them, and nothing else. If you won't let me have the land for the fifteen bushels, I'll stick to the common; I can do about as well here. But you haven't told me what right you had to fence in the best land, and call it yours?

Landowner. The king gave it to me.

Labor. What right had the king to take away the people's land, and give it to you?

Landowner. No matter whether he had the right or not; he had the might. The land is mine, and you cannot cultivate it without my permission.

Labor. Well! We won't discuss the question of right just now. Will you let me have the lot for the year at the price I offer?

Landowner. Yes; you may have it. It's so much gain to me; but if it wasn't for that confounded common you should pay more.

ANOTHER YEAR.

(*In the meanwhile* Landowner *has succeeded in getting through Parliament an Act authorizing him to inclose the common, and has taken possession. He has accordingly fenced in the whole of it. Not against cattle this time, but against* Labor.)

Labor, going to Landowner. Please, sir, as the common is inclosed, I've now no free land to work upon, and I should be very glad to hire that same lot of you for another year.

Landowner. Humph! You did pretty well on that lot last year, didn't you?

Labor. Yes, sir! I was able to give Capital a new spade, besides paying him for the use of his; and I had enough over to keep my family in comfort after paying you the rent.

Landowner. And you expect to get the land for the same rent this year?

Labor. I hope that you will let me have it on the same terms, sir. If I'm obliged to pay more I shall not be able to give Capital so much for the use of his spade, and my family will suffer for want of the comforts to which they have been accustomed.

Landowner. That's none of my business. Capital must be content with a smaller return, and you must reduce the expenses of your family. There's no common for you to cultivate now, or for him to pasture his heifer on. You must both of you cut your coat according to your cloth, and wear your old clothes when you have no cloth.

Labor. I'm aware of that, sir, and can only hope that you will consider my circumstances.

Landowner. What I shall consider will be my own interest. I shall manage my estate on strictly business principles. You paid me fifteen bushels of potatoes on account of my improvements last year. We agreed upon that as fair, didn't we?

Labor. Yes, sir.

Landowner. Well! I'll be easy with you and charge you no more this year; but you must keep the fence in repair.

Labor. It will be very hard on me, sir, taking so much from the support of my family; but I suppose that I must do as you say; and if I must, I must.

Landowner. Now how much will you agree to give me for the use of my land? Last year you wouldn't give me anything, and I had to come to your terms, because you had the common to fall back upon. This year there's no common, and you've got to come to mine.

Labor. I hope, sir, that they will be such as to enable me to live and keep my family comfortably, which will be hard work enough now, with the additional work I'm obliged to put upon the fence.

Landowner. Comfortably! I don't know and I don't care. You ought to be satisfied with the necessaries of life, and not talk about luxuries. But there's no use in wasting any more talk about the matter. The rent of the lot for this year is fifty bushels in all.

Labor. But, sir,—

Landowner. But me no Buts. That's the rent.

Labor. We shall starve, sir, and then your land will be of no use to you. You must have somebody to cultivate it.

Landowner. There's something in that; but, as I said, fifty bushels is the rent. You know that you must take the land at my price, and I know you'll make the shift to pull through. If you can't, and I find that you really haven't enough to live on, perhaps I'll not exact the whole of the rent, but let a part remain in arrears, for you to make up when you have an extra good year, and I will give you some of the small potatoes in charity, to keep you alive and out of the poorhouse—where (*aside*) I should have to pay for the whole support of you and your family.

INDEX